SKYHOOKS

Also by Kurt R. Stehling
PROJECT VANGUARD

Also by William Beller
SATELLITE (*in collaboration*)

KURT R. STEHLING

and

WILLIAM BELLER

⨯⨯⨯⨯⨯⨯ *SKYHOOKS*

DOUBLEDAY & COMPANY, INC.
Garden City, New York

TABLE OF CONTENTS

INTRODUCTION

From the earliest chronicled times man has experienced his awe of the sky and the firmament above. He envied the birds their freedom to soar and swoop above the earth. In the days of ancient Greece, Rome, and early Christian times many gods and the angels were endowed with wings, a reflection of man's subconscious yearning to fly into the heavens.

Occasionally, some daring individual would try to practice what he dreamed. Several attempts at bird-like flight with crude wings or similar devices were recorded during the Middle Ages and beyond, into the eighteenth century. The almost invariably disastrous endings of such adventures brought man slowly to the realization that he had much to learn about structures, mechanics, and propulsion before he could even crudely imitate birds. It remained for the balloon—using the principle of buoyancy, and a much more passive apparatus than wings—to first lift man from the surface of the earth into free flight.

Almost 180 years have passed since the indomitable French made the first flight on the eve of their revolution. During these years, aeronauts, always courageous, often inventive, and sometimes foolhardy, have flown their balloons in all climes, in war and peace, for science or sport. Some strange adventures resulted, some ending in tragedy, while others added new dimensions to the exploration of the upper atmosphere.

We have tried to relate a few of the more significant flights—and the more colorful ones—that help make up the history and lore of ballooning. An attempt has been made to capture the spirit of the times—one that today had disappeared in the clutch of hyperspecialization, battalion-strength projects, and multi-million-dollar budgets.

We owe many thanks to many people—to Paul Garber, Curator of the National Air Museum, who furnished us with valuable material about Captain Gray and let us read the log of his flight; to Vice-Admiral "Tex" Settle, USN, (Ret.), who gave us data on his Century of Progress Exposition flight; and to Lieutenant General William Kepner, U. S. Army (Ret.), for comments on his "Explorer I" flight.

We cannot forget the help of Elizabeth B. Brown, Historical Librarian of the Institute of Aerospace Science, who was an encyclopedia of source material; and of Henry Lowe Brownback, who let us use the memoirs of his grandfather, T. S. C. Lowe; and of Elizabeth Kieffer, of the Lancaster County Historical Society, who located material for us on John Wise.

Arthur Renstrom of the Library of Congress went far beyond the call of duty and friendship in suggesting sources and gathering data we never thought existed; and we owe thanks to Lieutenant Colonel David Simons, who so kindly gave us documents about his Manhigh flight.

We are grateful also to Melville Payne, Vice-President of the National Geographic Society, for permitting the use of photographs and historical files of some of the many balloon flights that were sponsored or covered by the Society. A word of thanks is also due Commander B. B. Levitt, USN, and J. Gordon Vaeth for Stratolab photographs and contributions to background material and the Chronology.

VIVE LE ROI

They called the thing a "Montgolfier." With it, at 1:54 P.M. on November 21, 1783, man first conquered the air. This was one hundred and twenty years before the Wright brothers achieved their powered flight at Kitty Hawk.

The morning of that historic day broke clear and shining over Paris, and particularly over the gardens of La Muette. For some time an eager and restless crowd had gathered in and around the gardens. Most of the people sensed that something unusual was going to take place, but few realized that this day was going to be historic in man's long struggle to conquer the elements. All were fascinated by the great pear-shaped object about seventy feet high and forty-six feet in diameter which was suspended between two tall poles swaying slightly in the faint cool breeze. The object was gorgeously colored in blue and gold and decorated with fleurs-de-lis and signs of the zodiac around its upper part. The middle bulge was ornamented with the monogram "L," of King Louis XVI, while the lower end was garnished with masks, garlands, and spread eagles. A circular gallery or parapet at its lower extremity was made

of woven cane and festooned with drapes and other ornaments which were attached by a set of cords to the bottom
of the structure. The gallery was three feet wide, protected
by a parapet of three feet in height. The great ovoid object
terminated in a narrow open neck which ended a few feet
above a brick platform raised above the ground.

In the center of this brick platform and directly below the
body was a pit from which billowed tremendous quantities
of black smoke. Two grimy sweating men were stoking a
straw fire and with bellows were blowing smoke into the
object. It expanded lazily as if flexing its muscles and the
many wrinkles in its skin puffed out like a new baby's. About
noontime it was extended almost to its full volume—round
and sleek and fat like a wonderfully colored Easter egg.

A commotion could now be seen in the crowd and
several soldiers and guardsmen shouted "Make way" as two
men in blue velvet suits, white stockings, pumps, and the
cocked hats of the gentlemen of that day came through the
crowd, walking up the stairs without loss of time to the edge
of the brick platform. They anxiously checked the fire and
talked briefly to the stokers and to some of the men who
were holding down the great bag. They bowed deeply
and raised their hats to the honored guests—the Dauphin
and his court—and waved gravely to the rest of the throng.
They then climbed into the circular gallery, signaled to
the men grimly holding onto the straining bag, who at a
shout dropped the ropes that were barely restraining the
puffing giant. The stokers redoubled their efforts, smoke
billowed, choking the spectators and blinding the voyagers momentarily. Then, suddenly, with the restraint gone,
silently as a magic cloud, the unfettered bag rose into the
sky.

This then was man's first balloon journey. This gentle
and charming vehicle ushered in the great age of flight,
starting the mighty epoch of the air age, whose limits are

not the air, but, as we know today, ultimately the boundaries of the universe.

Near the brick platform and among some of the courtiers close by were two men who stood out by their extraordinarily excited wavings, shouts of encouragement, and looks of satisfaction and triumph. These men were Etienne and Joseph Montgolfier, two brothers who were the architects of this balloon and whose experiments had started the air age. The two brothers had toyed with paper balloons in the small city of Annonay, near Lyons, for almost two years before this great event. They had obtained the paper from their father's paper factory, and having noticed that small paper containers could rise in the fireplace of their château, they wondered whether larger bags could not be built. A simple observation, but still of enormous significance. These men did not understand the science of aerostatics at that time and did not realize that it was the hot air rather than the smoke which gave buoyancy to the paper bags. At any rate, they knew that something was doing it and that heated air or smoke must be supplied. They knew also that very thin, light paper must be used and that this paper must be airtight.

After much experimenting they launched increasingly larger free unmanned balloons between November 1782 and October 1783. One of the later flights, on September 19, 1783, carried animals. Although the men encountered vested interests, the enmity of reactionaries, and the suspicion of peasants when the balloons landed in the country, nevertheless they were able to establish the rudiments of ballooning. They learned to make their bags stable and devised fire pots and grates which would hang beneath and hold the combustibles which generated lighter-than-normal air for the balloon.

Just as men's thoughts today are on man's adventures in space with manned spaceships, so did the Montgolfiers and their friends think of manned balloon flights. Everything in their experience pointed to the safety and practicability of a manned balloon undertaking. Had not the animals traveled safely?

The Montgolfiers had a friend named François Pilatre de Rozier who had participated in various adventurous stunts and had greatly interested himself in balloons. He volunteered for a manned flight and the Montgolfiers accepted enthusiastically, for they were more interested in building balloons than in flying them. Several tethered flights were then made, all of them successful, and it needed only the cutting of a rope to begin the historic era of manned air travel.

Pilatre de Rozier's spirits, however, were quickly dampened because of the adamant refusal of Louis XVI to permit any manned free flight to take place. One is not sure whether this was motivated by a kingly impulse of humanity or a fear of arousing the populace, or some other reason best known to himself. Without the King's sanction no such experiment could be undertaken in Paris and it was in Paris that the Montgolfiers and Pilatre de Rozier needed to show the usefulness of the invention and the possibilities of manned flight. Paris was the center of manufacturing and of political and technical activity in France.

Pilatre de Rozier had an influential friend, the Marquis François-Laurent d'Arlandes. D'Arlandes was also greatly interested in balloons and had indeed broached to Pilatre de Rozier the idea that he should accompany him on any such flight with the thought that two men were better than one. At first there was some question of the payload-carrying ability of the balloon, but the Montgolfiers estimated the balloon when fully inflated could carry perhaps three men. Pilatre de Rozier was still hesitant, however, perhaps for the natural and obvious reason that he wished to share the glory with no one. However, as a realist he saw that there would be no sharing of anything, since no flight would occur without Louis XVI's sanction. He prevailed on D'Arlandes to gain an audience with the King and a waiver of the King's refusal.

On the evening of October 21, 1783, a meeting took place at Versailles. One of Louis XVI's favorite courtesans, the Duchesse de Polignac, had been persuaded by D'Arlandes to gain the King's audience. That evening, when D'Arlandes was ushered into a small antechamber in the palace, he realized that a tremendous issue was at stake. If the perverse King refused his permission, manned aerial flight might be held off for months, if not years. The Germans or British, who knew of the Montgolfier inventions and also those of a Professor J. A. C. Charles of Paris, who had substituted light hydrogen in a balloon for the light hot air, might suddenly see the immense import of the balloon as a man-carrying vehicle and deal France a powerful blow for the supremacy of the skies. For many of these early pioneers really felt that balloons would supersede much ground transportation, and even in those early days believed that the nation possessing the greatest aerial balloon fleet would be supreme. This attitude has its counter in these days when the Russian Sputnik anticipated the American satellites.

The Duchesse de Polignac was a skilled debater and a strong-minded woman who, when she believed in a cause, would push it determinedly, using not only the strength of her rhetoric but also the seductiveness of her person. The King was a little weary of the Duchesse's lobbying, but he listened to the earnest entreaties of D'Arlandes, who recounted the many tethered balloon flights that had been made and the safe flights of animals, and the matter of France's prestige and perhaps ultimate supremacy. Louis had his mind on more pressing matters, such as the gradual breakdown in France's financial and social structure and the intrigues of his wife and his mistress. Near the end of the audience he had still not shown any signs of acqui-

escence or sympathy, but when D'Arlandes had finished
pleading that two men be sent up, the King suddenly
exclaimed in exasperation, "Well then, take any two of my
criminals, fetter them to the balloon, and let it go. That
will give you manned flight." D'Arlandes cried out in
shock, "What, let two wild criminals be the first men to
soar into God's great sky? Sire, did you not realize that
the physician Pilatre de Rozier and myself were going
to undertake this journey? Would you deny the gentlemen
of your kingdom the privilege of climbing nearer to God
and thus showing to the world the glory of France?"

While this is nearly all the dialogue that has been recorded of this great interview, it must be said that by this
last outburst Louis XVI's weariness finally prevailed and he
said then with great feeling, "Well, away to the heavens you
go. May God go with you and I give you my royal blessing.
I wish I could escape from my temporal cares that easily."
D'Arlandes and the Duchesse bowed deeply, retreating from
the King, and while we do not know what then took place
in the antechamber, it is known that D'Arlandes dashed
from Versailles as fast as etiquette would permit, and instead of waiting for a carriage, bestrode a horse and gal-
loped to Pilatre de Rozier's quarters in Paris near the Bois de
Boulogne. That night, late, the astonished Pilatre de Rozier
almost had his door torn off its hinges as D'Arlandes ran in
shouting, "His Majesty will let us." Pilatre de Rozier
needed no further explanation. The two went immediately
to the Montgolfiers, who had optimistically built a brick
platform and got the balloon ready for launching. Joseph
Montgolfier was especially excited. He called his workmen
out that night to prepare the great globe.

We find them then on the morning of November 21,
1783, gradually filling the linen-and-paper bag with straw
smoke and readying the vehicle for its two intrepid voyagers. Word spread to the populace quickly. Even though
public handbills and announcements were quickly dis-

tributed saying this was to be a strictly scientific experiment and no public demonstration would be tolerated, a large crowd began to assemble; however, it was somewhat more restrained than usual. The people were impressed not only by the grave announcement of "scientific" import but also by the presence of many members of the nobility, who from the inevitable grapevine had learned the night before that the launching would take place with the King's permission.

As the vehicle rose, the two travelers waved to the crowd, somewhat astonished not only by the silence of the amazed throng, but also by the ease of take-off and the strange sensation of being free of the earth without being restrained by a rope.

D'Arlandes wrote a letter to a friend of his, a Faujas de Saint-Fond. This letter, which has been preserved, describes this voyage, as momentous in its way as the trip of Columbus. D'Arlandes wrote as follows:

"My dear Faujas,

"Because of your questions and that of the public about our aerial voyage I will describe as best as I can this first journey in which man attempted to fly through an element which seemed, prior to the discovery of the MM. Montgolfier, so little fitted to support them.

"We went up on the 21st of November 1783, at near two o'clock, M. Pilatre de Rozier on the west side of the balloon, I on the east. The wind was nearly northwest. The machine, say the public, rose with majesty; but really the position of the balloon altered so that M. Pilatre de Rozier was in the advance of our position, I in the rear.

"I was surprised at the silence and the absence of movement which our departure caused among the spectators, and believed them to be astonished and perhaps awed at the strange spectacle; they might well have reassured themselves. I was still gazing, when M. Pilatre de Rozier cried to me—

"'You are doing nothing, and the balloon is scarcely rising a fathom.'

"'Pardon me,' I answered, as I placed a bundle of straw upon the fire and slightly stirred it. Then I turned quickly, but already we had passed out of sight of La Muette. Astonished, I cast a glance toward the river. I perceived the confluence of the Oise. And naming the principal bends of the river by the places near them, I cried, 'Passy, St.-Germain, St.-Denis, Sèvres!'

"'If you look at the river in that fashion you will be likely to bathe in it soon,' cried Pilatre de Rozier. 'Some fire, my dear friend, some fire!'

"We traveled on; but instead of crossing the river, as our direction seemed to indicate, we bore toward the Invalides, then returned upon the principal bed of the river, and traveled to above the barrier of La Conference, thus dodging about the river, but not crossing it.

"'That river is very difficult to cross,' I remarked to my companion.

"'So it seems,' he answered; 'but you are doing nothing. I suppose it is because you are braver than I, and don't fear a tumble.'

"I stirred the fire, I seized a truss of straw with my fork; I raised it and threw it in the midst of the flames. An instant afterward I felt myself lifted as it were into the heavens.

"'For once we move,' said I.

"'Yes, we move,' answered my companion.

"At the same instant I heard from the top of the balloon a sound which made me believe that it had burst. I watched, yet I saw nothing. My companion had gone into the interior, no doubt to make some observations. As my eyes were fixed on the top of the machine I experienced a shock, and it was the only one I had yet felt. The direction of the movement was from above downward. I then said—

"'What are you doing? Are you having a dance to yourself?'

"'I am not moving.'

"'So much the better. It is only a new current which I hope will carry us from the river,' I answered.

"I turned to see where we were, and found we were between the Ecole Militaire and the Invalides.

"I now heard another report in the machine, which I believed was produced by the cracking of a cord. This new intimation made me carefully examine the inside of our habitation. I saw that the part that was turned toward the south was full of holes, of which some were of a considerable size.

"'It must descend,' I then cried.

"'Why?'

"'Look!' I said. At the same time I took my sponge and quietly extinguished the little fire that was burning some of the holes within my reach; but at the same moment I perceived that the bottom of the cloth was coming away from the circle which surrounded it.

"'We must descend,' I repeated to my companion.

"He looked below.

"'We are upon Paris,' he said.

"'It does not matter,' I answered. 'Only look! Is there no danger? Are you holding on well?'

"'Yes.'

"I examined from my side, and saw that we had nothing to fear. I then tried with my sponge the ropes which were within my reach. All of them held firm. Only two of the cords had broken.

"I then said, 'We can cross Paris.'

"During this operation we were rapidly getting down to the roofs. We made more fire, and rose again with the greatest ease. I looked down, and it seemed to me we were going toward the towers of St. Sulpice; but, on rising, a new current made us quit this direction and bear more to the south. I looked to the left, and beheld a wood, which I believed to be that of Luxembourg. We were traversing the boulevard, and I cried all at once—

"'Get to ground!'

"But the intrepid Pilatre de Rozier, who never lost his head, and who judged more surely than I, prevented me from attempting to descend. I then threw a bundle of straw on the fire. We rose again, and another current bore us to the left. We were now close to the ground, between two mills. As soon as we came near the earth I raised myself over the gallery, and leaning there with my two hands, I felt the balloon pressing softly against my head. I pushed it back, and leaped to the ground. Looking round and expecting to see the balloon still distended, I was astonished to find it quite empty and flattened. On looking for Pilatre de Rozier I saw him in his shirt sleeves creeping out from under the mass of canvas that had fallen over him. Before attempting to descend he had put off his coat and placed it in the basket. After a deal of trouble we were at last all right.

"As Pilatre de Rozier was without a coat, I besought him to go to the nearest house. On his way there he encountered the Duke of Chartres, who had followed us, as we saw, very closely, for I had had the honor of conversing with him the moment before we set out."

Thus, about twenty-five minutes from take-off, and after traveling about eight miles, reaching an altitude of 3000 feet, the two pioneers again touched the earth.

It must not be thought that this first great aerial undertaking was an obscure event, or even relatively obscure, such as the first flight of the Wright brothers. Thousands of people in Paris saw it, the news traveled across the nation, and even the scientists, who usually are wary of such "stunts," interested themselves in it and wrote accounts of the journey. One of these accounts was prepared by various scientific observers of the French Academy and may be found today in the archives of the Academy signed by the great scientists of that day, including Benjamin Franklin. The great air ocean was now within men's reach. Wings had been tried—flapping wings—and men had jumped from towers with crude parachutes and umbrellas. They had tried rotating helicopter-like blades and even had attempted to be lifted up by large birds. These had all failed. Success remained for this great globe of smoke and heated air in a lavish bag built by the Montgolfiers, two French dreamers, aristocrats, yet manufacturers of paper who represented the gap or the bridge between the idle rich of France and the industrialists. It is perhaps fitting that on the eve of the great French social revolution, a revolution in man's technical prowess should also have occurred. Not everyone could see the use of man's flying, particularly in balloons. But Benjamin Franklin, that brilliant representative of America among the lords of the King's court, said when asked about the possible use of balloons, "Of what use is a newborn baby?"

TWO INTREPID
CHANNEL CROSSERS

Although the French and Italians distinguished themselves predominantly in those early days in aerostatics, the English were not idle. Several aeronauts or balloonists from the Continent visited England and made aerial voyages there, mostly with the hydrogen-gas or "Charles" balloon which was built by the Frenchman Professor J. A. C. Charles about the same time that the early hot-air balloons or Montgolfiers appeared on the scene. But we are not concerned so much here with all of the various balloon ascents in 1784 and the early days of 1785, but with one in particular—the great and noble voyage of a French barnstorming balloonist, Jean-Pierre Blanchard, and a "Dr." John Jeffries, apparently of American descent. Blanchard had made a number of balloon demonstrations throughout England and had been overcome with his own sagacity and virtue. Looking around for new worlds to conquer and capitalizing on the great enthusiasm about aerial voyages which was growing in England, he announced in the newspapers of London and Manchester that he would cross the English Channel from England to France in a balloon.

The English Channel, which has always been a tantalizing object for would-be conquerers and swimmers, was a natural attraction for a balloonist. The dangers of the water crossing and the linking of the two countries in this way would, of course, be a tremendous publicity gain. The accounts of the journey in those days do not tell how Blanchard came into the company of Dr. Jeffries; it is enough to note that strange company often finds itself, and the two prepared for this marvelous journey which depended entirely on the course of the wind.

On January 7, 1785, the two were ready. Blanchard had obtained some support for the building of a fairly large hydrogen-gas balloon and had attached to it a singular gondola which lacked nothing in bold imagination except a little understanding of the science of aerostatics. It had a rear fin or rudder on the gondola and the gondola itself was shaped like an old fashioned bathtub with four dragonfly-like wings, or rather four rudders. It was Blanchard's thought that these rudders and oars could be moved in the air to steer and propel the balloon. He did not realize, as others have since, that a balloon which travels with the wind cannot be steered, unless it is anchored or drags something along the ground to give it resistance. It is entirely a creature of the wind and subject to all of its forces and vagaries.

The two Channel crossers had in their gondola various articles of clothing and food, scientific almanacs, musical instruments, *objets d'art*, letters, and three sacks of sand weighing ten pounds each for ballast.

At 8 A.M. then, on the 7th, above the cliffs of Dover, before a large crowd, the balloon rose. But trouble started at the outset. The two men were not long over the ground when the barometer sank. This meant a change in the weather and winds. Dr. Jeffries, as he said later in a letter to the President of the Royal Society, was enthusiastic about the beautiful spectacle below him with

the numerous towns and villages around Dover and the
charming cliffs and defiles and the long breakers and
waves which had never been seen by man from such a
height. They sailed through the gray sky with the blue-
gray Channel below, seemingly angrily frothing upward
in frustration when for all these centuries it had had the
prerogative of dashing men to death or permitting them
to cross when it felt like it.

The balloon had hardly passed the coast when it sank,
rapidly approaching the water. While Jeffries was gawk-
ing at the scenery, Blanchard, a trained balloonist,
quickly dropped overboard a bag of sand, and the balloon rose once more. They were about one-third across
the Channel when things became more exciting.

The balloon suddenly descended again and Blanchard
and Jeffries, this time working in concert, threw over the
last of their sand ballast. The balloon sank lower. It approached the gray waves that meant certain death for
them. Jeffries and Blanchard now began to argue. Jeffries
wanted to throw over some instruments and Blanchard some
books. While they were discussing this, the gondola hit a
large wave. That united them in action and they threw
over a whole sack of books. They found themselves rising
again and continued across the Channel to about the
halfway point.

Once again they descended with the great brown-and-
blue bag above them flapping in the wind and with
Blanchard frantically pulling at the oars trying to paddle
or row the gondola, turning blue from the exertion.
Jeffries was wiggling the tail and the rudder hoping to
steer the balloon, but all he got for his pains was a sprained
wrist when the rudder stuck at forty-five degrees. As they
were sinking again, they threw over the remainder of their
precious books—treatises on balloonery and several weighty
tomes on that hocus-pocus of science, alchemy, as it was

known in those days. The balloon rose a bit, but not fast enough, and overboard went the scientific instruments, a small telescope, an astrolabe, and a large clock.

Shortly after two o'clock they were about three-quarters of the way across the Channel and in the distance they saw the low green-brown inviting coast of France. Jeffries was so excited he climbed into the rigging, shouting, yelling, and waving, when suddenly Blanchard screamed, "We're sinking again. Stop making an exhibition of yourself or we will never reach it. We must throw more things overboard."

And sure enough the balloon was again sinking slowly. They then threw over their provisions of food and various bottles and Blanchard tore his beloved wings and rudders from the gondola, ripped off the ornaments and other objects. Jeffries, who had carefully and painfully hoarded a large bottle of champagne, was also obliged to throw this overboard, and it fell on the water with a loud smack that sent up a geyser of spray. The water came closer yet.

At this critical moment Blanchard, who had been crawling up into the rigging to postpone his immersion in the cold Channel, threw off his shoes, one of which hit Jeffries on the head. Then he tore his trousers off and his jacket and his shirt and his hat, scarf, and gloves. Jeffries, wild-eyed, began to cut the ropes of the gondola, thinking that if they dropped the entire gondola they could reach the shore in the rigging, like birds in a tree. They were barely skimming over the water in a fast breeze when Blanchard finally deprived himself of his last bit of clothing except for a pair of skimpy drawers, and this on a January day. He came from the rigging into the gondola and almost had a fist fight with Jeffries when he insisted that Jeffries also take his clothes off. Jeffries said if he were going to drown he was going to drown with his clothes on, which would be better than facing the French populace naked.

They had begun to knock the bottom out of the gondola and the gondola itself was hanging by only a few ropes when the balloon rose again.

The voyagers, almost resigned to death by now, except for their squabbling and running back and forth from rigging to gondola, gave out a great shout of joy as the balloon rose slightly only four miles from the coast of France. Jeffries, a bit ashamed by now of his friend's deshabille and sacrifice, threw overboard his boots and socks and a precious belt which he wore. After all, would it not be better to arrive in France with some semblance of self-sacrifice? The two men, sensing eternal glory as the coast approached, became almost feverish and did not notice the freezing temperature, but instead clung to the rigging and what remained of the gondola. They waved frantically to the coast, expecting to see an enormous crowd waiting for them.

At three o'clock that afternoon they passed over the shore halfway between Cape Blanc and Calais. The strong wind changed its direction a bit and Jeffries, hanging onto a strut with both legs, reached down as they crossed a small forest and grabbed a branch of a tree. The valve was opened, gas rushed out of the top of the balloon, and the courageous aeronauts safely reached the ground.

After the successful accomplishment of this daring enterprise they were disappointed that there was no great crowd. However, a number of horsemen, who had watched the balloon as it reached the coast, rode up and gave them a cordial reception. A crowd had not gathered because no one knew exactly where the men would cross. On the following day a great feast was celebrated in their honor in Calais. Blanchard, who had appeared in the village near the landing with a borrowed blanket draped over him, and Jeffries, who had made great noises about his frozen feet and had drawn the requisite sympathy from the spectators, were now dressed in splendid clothes and were given the freedom of the city. The municipal fathers purchased the balloon with the intention of placing it in one of the local churches as a memorial of this experiment; they also resolved to erect a marble monument on the spot where the famous aeronauts landed. Some days later Blanchard was summoned before Louis XVI, who gave him an annual pension of 1200 livres. We do not know what happened to him in the tumultuous days of the Revolution, and about Jeffries we know only that he returned to England, carried on some desultory experiments and lectured about his voyage, and then later returned to America.

So ended this seriocomic voyage and the Channel was bridged. Many predicted in England that this would end the island's insularity and there was talk of establishing a counter-balloon corps, or of setting up flaming-arrow projectiles on the English coast that could shoot down the gas balloons which, some said, would appear by the hundreds and thousands in a war with France or any other country on the Continent. Indeed, Napoleon was advised by several scientists at the peak of his career, when he turned longing eyes toward England, to set up a great balloon corps which would invade England. The science of ballooning in Napoleon's time was not much advanced from the day of our friends Blanchard and Jeffries. One can imagine the experience of these two men repeated thousands of times with hapless French soldiers cast into the wind to land on England, or more likely in the Channel.

Just as in these days men speculate about giant spaceships, so then men speculated about giant balloons for warlike purposes, or balloons which would sail around the world. Some of these monsters were presumed to contain millions of cubic feet of gas and carry shiploads of people, reading and writing rooms, smoking rooms, orchestras and bands, gardens, chickens, cows, etc. However, the charming and obviously gentle disposition of the

balloon never made it useful for warfare; its payload limitations and lack of directional capability prevented its use
for exploration or scientific journeys, except those directly
upward.

Three

A VALIANT TRY

The first excitement about the Channel crossing by Blanchard and Jeffries had hardly died down when the French became enthusiastic again, a thing which is easy for them to do. They realized that this great feat had been undertaken by England, although not by two Englishmen; now a hue and cry arose among French balloonists and savants, and even some of the populace, that England was carrying off "all" the honors in this great new science that had been discovered by Frenchmen and nurtured by them in its early years. Something had to be done to redeem the honor of France, or at least equal that gained by England. Didn't France have intrepid aeronauts who were the best in the world? Did they not have a balloon industry and experience gained by no other nation?

Here now we meet again our old acquaintance, Pilatre de Rozier, who appeared in the first chapter as one of the two first aeronauts. Pilatre de Rozier took the Blanchard flight as a personal affront. He was bitter that he had not gained support previously for just such a flight. He had talked about crossing the Strait of Gibraltar or the Bosporus, but when this Channel crossing occurred he felt it necessary to recoup the honor of France and perhaps a little of his own by making a similar crossing from France to England, a direction contrary to the usual prevailing winds. A vain and quick-tempered but brillant and courageous man, Pilatre de Rozier resolved to undertake this voyage not only against the normal winds and the advice of his friends, but also in a novel balloon which he had designed himself.

One of the problems of the Charles or hydrogen-gas balloons, which were now being used rather widely in 1785, was their lack of ready altitude controllability. The aeronaut could make an ascent by dumping ballast such as bags of sand, or as our two Channel pioneers Blanchard and Jeffries did by dumping overboard not only sand but every movable or removable thing. A descent could be made then by pulling a gas valve on the top of the hydrogen balloon, which would allow hydrogen to escape and thus decrease the buoyancy of the vehicle. If the aeronaut should be so unfortunate as to have a continual rise and descent, and wished to maintain an even keel, he would finally end with nothing removable and even no gas. This would be an embarrassing and frustrating situation indeed. It took decades of ballooning and design experience to produce balloons that responded quickly and reliably to altitude control.

Pilatre de Rozier, aware of the limitations of the "Charles," very cunningly decided to combine the weight-lifting advantages of this hydrogen balloon with the controllability of the hot-air balloon. By stoking the fire of his hot-air Montgolfier he could change the total buoyancy of the two balloons and make them ascend. By reducing the fire he could reduce their buoyancy and thus again lower the bags. He did not trouble himself with the awkward fact that hydrogen is a most unwelcome neighbor of fire and has an embarrassing tendency to burn at the slightest provocation. Professor Charles cautioned Pilatre de Rozier and said that this was like lighting a bonfire in a powder keg, but Pilatre de Rozier was carried away. The honor and glory of France had to be vindicated.

Pilatre de Rozier asked for and obtained from the French government a sum of 40,000 livres for the building of his new machine. He was flagellated by the French court to move fast and do something spectacular, and he was a not unwilling guinea pig. Thus, with an untried machine and under conditions most unfavorable to his enterprise, he prepared to risk his life in an undertaking which was at once dangerous and useless.

On the 12th of June, 1785, the double balloon, with the hydrogen Charles on top and the hot-air balloon below, was alternately inflated and emptied. It had been stored for about two weeks before this in a shed near the city of Boulogne. While it was there it had been chewed by rats so that it had many holes in it and when the inflation began, leaks and rents appeared in the fabric which had to be patched. Furthermore, the already awkward and patchy structure was blown about by violent winds which did not cease for several days. Pilatre de Rozier and his helpers threw up little trial balloons which showed winds far in excess of what they could tolerate for a successful launching. However, on June 15 at four in the morning a little pilot balloon that had been sent up rose and moved toward the coast, showing that the wind was gently blowing in the direction of England. At 11:00 A.M. of that day Pilatre de Rozier, accompanied by M. Pierre-Ange Romain, who had helped him with the construction of the balloon, climbed into the gallery, which resembled that of a regular Montgolfier.

There were many eyewitnesses to the beginning of the journey. People came from far and wide to see this peculiar structure, although some of them had seen other balloons;

still, this one was a French balloon ready to secure the honor
of France. As the launching hour drew near, the excitement
grew, many hearts were palpitating, and shouts of "*Vive la
France*," and "*Vive le Roi*," and *vive* everyone else who
could be glorified rent the air. The balloon was untethered
suddenly. A short, fat little nobleman ran out to climb into
the car after throwing a purse of 200 louis into the gondola.
However, Pilatre de Rozier firmly pushed him back with one
hand in the face and shouted that the experiment was too
unsafe for him to permit the nobleman to risk his life. The
disappointed nobleman fell on his behind uttering laments
of frustration and disappointment.

At last the awkward structure rose. Several nearby cannon
fired and trumpets blew and the voyagers saluted to the
crowd, which responded with shouts and hat-wavings. Two
ladies were observed alternately standing on each other's
shoulders, a most extreme exhibition for ladies in those days.
Not far away was the still gray and ever forbidding Channel. As the balloon rose it reached a height of about 700
feet and traveled about a mile from its starting point, toward the Channel. Suddenly a wind gust changed its direction and moved it back toward the shore. It had now been in
the air twenty-seven minutes.

Suddenly the eyes and faces of the crowd became trans-
fixed. They saw first that the grating or fire pot of the
Montgolfier was being lowered to remove it from the balloon. Suddenly everyone realized it was too late. A blue-
violet flame appeared at the top of the gas balloon and
spread over the entire globe in a brilliant flash and enveloped the hot-air Montgolfier and the hapless voyagers below it. White-yellow streaks of fabric burned and fell off,
tongues of flame shot from all sides, and the mass settled
swiftly to the ground in a fiery streak with the unfortunate
men falling out before it, through the clouds and onto the
earth. They fell about a league from Boulogne and about
three feet from the sea beach. The dead body of Pilatre de

Rozier was found in the burned wreckage of the wicker gallery. His companion was found nearby still breathing, but unable to speak. He died in a few minutes.

This then was the sad climax to the career of that great pioneer Pilatre de Rozier, the first man to ascend by free balloon into the air. It was an unfortunate but perhaps not unfitting end for the dauntless balloonist and his equally enthusiastic companion. They had been building balloons for the past year and Pilatre de Rozier had defied the elements and tradition to make this a historic voyage. He was to be the first of a long group of aeronauts and aviators who gave their lives to further this great and wonderful science and who could not resist the freedom of travel in the air and a sense of dedication and adventure in breaking the bonds which nature had imposed on them.

Oddly enough, Pilatre de Rozier and Romain fell only a few feet from the monument which today marks the spot where Blanchard descended from his Channel crossing. The epitaphs to Pilatre de Rozier point out that he died "a martyr to honor and to zeal." His kindness and amiability and generosity was known to everyone and endeared him to all. He had lived only twenty-eight and a half years and yet in this short lifetime had greatly advanced man's knowledge of aeronautics and had become immortalized through his historic first air journey.

THE FIRST AIR CORPS

The balloon was scarcely ten years old when it was considered time that it go to war.

This was in the fall of 1793. The court of Louis XVI, which had applauded the Montgolfiers' aerial invention, had either fled from their homeland or else perished under the guillotine of the first French Republic. Now ruling was the Reign of Terror led by Robespierre, the new government believing that bloodletting would cure the country's ills. Already weakened by birth pains, the Republic became prey to a coalition of European powers—England, Holland, Austria, Prussia, Spain, and Sardinia—which was tearing at her boundaries. Thus, fear was turning into despair. The French government was willing, even eager, to sacrifice as a matter of public policy those who resisted change or failed the country in the battlefield. With equal fervor the Republic was ready to embrace any idea, however novel, that would be of military help. When Joseph Montgolfier mentioned that on the battlefield the balloon might be useful, the all-powerful Committee of Public Safety ordered that one be built and equipped for service.

"My dear Monsieur Montgolfier," began one of the Committee's officials after the decision had been made, "since you know more about balloons than any man living, we would like you to accept the commission of building such a vehicle for your country."

If he agreed and failed, the balloon maker saw his life ending on the guillotine. If he succeeded, petty jealousies would make much of the fact that he had entertained and found favor with the monarch. He would still be ending his life on the guillotine.

"I would start instantly if I had even half the ability your Committee thinks I have," Montgolfier answered diplomatically. "Remember, though, that the balloons you want have to stay aloft for hours, possibly days at a time, and for this service you will be needing hydrogen aerostats. In such construction I am not proficient. You will recall that the balloons of my brother and myself were fire balloons, sustained only by hot vapors derived from ignited straw. Now to make the hydrogen aerostat you need a scientist, someone familiar with the new lifting gas. To this I cannot lay claim. My suggestion is that you get a chemist, a competent one like my very good friend Jean Marie-Joseph Coutelle." The man was one who came easily to mind; his face was long and narrow, smooth for a fifty-year old, but small for his sturdy torso. When Coutelle was wearing a high-necked coat, there was no shaking the feeling that in the course of dressing he had mounted the wrong head.

"He is willing," said the official. "Guyton de Morveau, do you know him?"

"A good friend of the Republic," Montgolfier was glad to affirm, "a respected chemist, Chancellor of the Academy of Dijon, and if I remember correctly, an ardent searcher for a way to propel balloons."

"That's right," remarked the official. "He said he'd back you or Coutelle, whichever one we picked. In making

Coutelle our choice, which is now clear, we are perhaps leaving the more prudent man behind."

Once the Committee prepared a path, there was haste to use it. Scarcely a week after the political body decided it would have a balloon, its members assumed the vehicle was nearly built. They ordered Coutelle to the battlefields of the North to arrange for its emplacement. The future director of the French armies, Lazare Carnot, gave the balloonist-elect an introduction to General Jean Jourdan, then commander of France's Army of the North.

General Jourdan was brief. "Monsieur Coutelle, I have no trouble finding the enemy or knowing their strength. My trouble is getting rid of them. If you have a balloon that will do that, tell me! If not, do France a magnificent service by persuading the Committee to send me another battalion!"

Well did Jourdan need that other battalion, or two or more battalions. For weeks he had been racing his troops around the northeast corner of France, nervously overresponding to the prods of the English, Austrians, and Dutch there. He had lately been in the Dunkirk area, under orders of General Jean Houchard, veteran French soldier and patriot. Houchard had heard that the Austrian military leader Prince Von Coburg was massing troops for a siege of Dunkirk. Alas, this had been only a rumor. Von Coburg was marching out of the Low Countries along the Sambre River to attack Maubeuge, a French village halfway down what is now the French-Belgium border. At this time the Committee called Houchard back to Paris. Here he was denounced as a coward, despite his thirty-eight years' military service.

"I have six wounds," he shouted at his accusers. "A musket shot has gone through my face, a second through my thigh, a third in the leg, and three saber cuts. Yet you call me 'coward.' After this, death would be sweet." Panic scored a victory. Houchard was guillotined. General

Jourdan was elected to replace him. Now positioned in the Maubeuge area, the officer was enjoying his dubious promotion while facing the main strength of Von Coburg's Army. It was at this juncture that Coutelle arrived for his interview.

"I tell you again, Monsieur," cried Jourdan, "send me soldiers, not a bag of wind!"

When Coutelle got back to Paris, he went at once to see his friend Louis Bernard Guyton de Morveau. With pent-up heat the traveler told of Jourdan's rejection of even the concept of a military balloon. Surprised at his own vehemence, he added, "Here I am, offering a vehicle I don't have, to do work that's never been done, under circumstances I've never experienced. I must be mad. . . . What I need is time; time to make a military balloon and to test it, and then time to organize a corps of balloonists to haul the contrivance out to the battlefield and send it aloft wherever it will do the most good."

Guyton de Morveau patted Coutelle's hand. "You ask for time just as France asks for time, for a breathing spell between blows from her enemies. France will get none, but you . . . I'll do what I can."

In the next meeting a few days later Guyton de Morveau was happy to say, "My friend, you have until spring to prove out your aerostat. It is Carnot you have to thank for this. He came to your defense when the Committee wished to forget the whole affair except to deal in some measure with the man who dared to fail. Carnot said to Robespierre's face, 'Sir, miracles take time, even up to several months. There will be nothing lost if it is given, and much to be gained.'"

Coutelle extended his hand to Guyton de Morveau. "I am most grateful to you."

"Regardless of how the Committee feels today, you cannot count on the same feelings lasting even until supper-

time," warned Guyton de Morveau. "It would be most
inopportune for you to disappoint them."

In early spring the balloon was completed. It was
called the "Entreprenant." When fully inflated, it was spher-
ically shaped and twenty-seven feet in diameter. Its upper
hemisphere was draped in a crisscrossing network of ropes.
These were tied to a girdle hung around the balloon's
equator. From the girdle other ropes were led down to hold
the basket. The bag was made of silk. It was impregnated
with a varnish said to be so impermeable that after two
months' inflation the balloon would retain most of its lifting power.

The art of aerostatics when it was born was beautiful in
its simplicity. Some inconsequential fuel, a tiny flame,
smoke, a paper globule, and there was an invention. Man,
though, seemingly restless to complicate life for his fellows,
let only three months go by before a physicist began levitating balloons by filling them with hydrogen gas. He generated the lifting fluid by pouring sulfuric acid over iron
filings. This scheme was a luxury that ten years later France
could not afford. All the sulfur that the Republic could get
then was being used to make gunpowder instead of the
acid.

To derive hydrogen without consuming critical materials
was a problem that appealed to Guyton de Morveau. After
experimenting for several days in his laboratory he emerged
with the method that Coutelle was to use. Iron turnings
were first raised to white heat in a furnace. Then just before
the metal reached its melting point, a slow but continuous
spray of water was dropped upon it. Thereupon the water
dissociated, oxidizing the iron and liberating hydrogen. Gas
thus freed was led by hose out of the furnace, was bubbled
through water for washing, and then sent to the balloon for
its inflation.

The Committee visited the field where the "Entreprenant"
was about to be flown. The day was calm, barely a leaf mov-

ing in a grove of nearby trees. The balloon's basket was
laded with stone ballast. Above the basket the bag stood
poised without even a quiver, giving little hint to the un-
initiated of its strange power. Few of the Committee members had ever seen an aerostat. Though they had given in
to the arguments of Carnot and Guyton de Morveau, the
rustics could not envision anybody floating in air. When
the ballast was taken from the basket and they saw first one
man, then two, and finally five use their combined weights
to keep the "Entreprenant" from rising, Coutelle became
a magician in their eyes—in the excitement of the moment,
even a savior. After a captive flight to 1000 feet, the balloonist was taken aside by Guyton de Morveau. "You are
later to build balloons sufficient for all fronts."

On April 2, 1794, the first air corps in the history of the
world was formed. It was known as the *Première Compagnie
d'Aérostiers*. Coutelle was commissioned its captain. The
company was organized on strict military lines and its recruits were given military pay, status, and recognition. The
faith of Montgolfier, Guyton de Morveau, Carnot, and
Coutelle had so far been warranted, but still the unit and
its vehicle had to meet the test of fire.

There were twenty-five men in the corps, each being
selected because he was experienced in some form of ar-
tisanry useful to the aerial mission. There were masons for
laying the furnace brick, carpenters for making and keeping the basket in repair, and chemists to regulate the gas-
generating system and to test the varnishes used on the bag.
To help with the riggings, two fishermen were recruited.
At the last minute Coutelle brought his artist cousin into
the ranks because he would be useful for sketching enemy
works as seen from the balloon.

Knowing that their tasks required talents above those of
the ordinary soldier, and that the results of a flight could
mean the difference between victory and defeat, the men
quickly developed a fierce pride in their unit. During free

time they banded together in their search for entertainment. With great heartiness they fought with any company that did not take aerostatics seriously. Coutelle added to his company's feeling of uniqueness by having a uniform specially designed for his men. It consisted of a coat, waistcoat, and breeches of blue material extravagantly piped in red. Each soldier was armed with sabre and pistols. There was no mistaking an *Aérostier*.

The Balloon Corps arrived in Maubeuge late one night toward the end of May. That entire week had been unusually hot and the men's bodies glistened and stank from the sweat of their 150-mile march from Paris. So eager were the soldiers to use their abilities for the defense of France that they raced ahead of their supply carts, one of which carried the balloon and basket while others had brick and mortar for the furnace. Had the men not been so tired, nor tortured by the vermin they had picked up from the fields in which they had slept, they probably would have noticed with more interest the shell barrage that was shaking the town. As it was, any one of the men would have traded a month's pay for a good night's sleep. They staggered to the campus of the college in which they were to be quartered and then most sank in exhaustion to the floor of the first building they entered. Several crawled down to the Sambre River to wash.

Though wishing he could be with his men, Coutelle had first to toast the Republic with the garrison's commander, a General Favreau. The officer had a guest in his quarters.

"Welcome to Maubeuge!" said Guyton de Morveau.

With great surprise Coutelle stared at the man, then asked, "What on earth are you doing here?"

"I'm now the Committee's representative on this battlefield," Guyton de Morveau explained. After a short conversation he came to the heart of his problem. "We're in desperate straits. We need military intelligence almost more than food. The Austrians and Dutch are said to be around us in force. If this is so, then Favreau is right and we should be thinking about a retreat." The speaker was not too eager for this path, as could be seen by his impatient look at the general who was seated next to him. "But if he's not right, then here we'll stay until Jourdan comes. Well, Coutelle, how soon before you can go up and tell us the truth of the matter?"

"As soon as my equipment arrives plus a little time to put it together," Coutelle replied. In a few minutes he excused himself to go away to go to sleep.

Two days later the balloon arrived. The brick and mortar were traveling slower because of their weight. The balloon was spread out along the ground and inspected for holes and bleached varnish. Coutelle's men were glad to have something to do. Inactivity had made them restless, and the taunts of the line troops who could not understand the Balloon Corps' work had already led to brawls. Coutelle took his problem to Favreau, who ordered harsh penalties on any man who interfered with the balloon work. This ruling made things worse for Coutelle's men. Now they were considered favorites and pampered, and even accused of being of aristocratic origin, a dread slander during the Reign of Terror.

"What it amounts to is that my men think that your *Aérostiers* are cowards," Favreau told Coutelle.

"They'll know differently when they see the 'Entreprenant' floating overhead," the balloonist boasted.

The officer slapped at a fly on his cheek. "Maybe."

Heavier than usual artillery fire coming from the north of town roused Coutelle from his sleep the next morning. Shortly, a company of men began passing through an area on the campus reserved for Coutelle and his equipment. In their path was the balloon. The men began walking over it. Coutelle's authority could not stop them. One of the soldiers as he passed the *Aérostiers* cried out in derision, "Don't worry drummer-boys! We'll save you from the

Austrians." Such was the temper of the marching troops and the high disdain with which they held the noncombatants. It was a miracle that Coutelle was able to keep his men from opening up a new front then and there. The next day the artillery fire became louder and steadier, the jeers of passing troops more violent, and the strain on the *Aérostiers'* nerves more intense. A spokesman approached Coutelle.

"Sir, we want to get into it."

Guyton de Morveau, standing nearby, overheard the request. He addressed Coutelle. "There is no other way. Your men must fight."

Ammunition and muskets were distributed. Then to the surprise of Favreau's men, the *Première Compagnie d'Aérostiers* was seen marching to the north. Its objective, Coutelle learned, was to capture some of the houses in the suburbs. The buildings were still beyond the front lines. Therefore, the Balloon Corps was supposed to hold its attack until the main French force had advanced. Coutelle did not have this last bit of information because the sergeant transmitting the orders thought it would be great fun for the *Aérostiers* to learn what fighting was really like.

Coutelle ordered a dash to the first of several houses. Shells splattered all around his men. The air was filled with showering dirt while the noise of explosions strained their eardrums. One moment the troops could see their chief carpenter pressing forward in advance of Coutelle. The next moment a shell burst on top of the artisan and when the smoke cleared he was gone. There was no thought of caution. The men ran to the first house, surrounded it, and then with relish born of frustration and anger killed all who would not at once surrender. They did the same to each succeeding house until they came to the last. This one was filled with Hollanders who had barricaded themselves in and seemed content to return fire for fire. Impatiently, Coutelle's lieutenant cried out, "If they have not learned to live, we must teach them to die." He was fashioning a torch to throw onto the roof when Coutelle grabbed his arm. "Save them for Favreau's men! After all, we're only helping out."

After this incident the *Aérostiers* were accepted by the rest of the troops as equals. "It was an initiation that had to be," Guyton de Morveau said grimly, "even though it cost you a man. Fighting one's enemies is sometimes less fatal than combating the ignorance of one's friends."

Coutelle stared solemnly at the man. "I am neither a warrior nor a politician, so violent death is still a horror to me. I hope for my soul that there will never be a time when I will consider it differently."

"You can think what you like as long as your job is done," said Guyton de Morveau, obviously displeased by Coutelle's added reference to politicians. "You will find that the furnace materials have arrived. That is good because I've been told that the enemy will be attacking Maubeuge any time now. General Favreau must know where the strike is to be made and the strength of the force making it. Therefore, my dear friend, you are being given three days to get your aerostat aloft. You are to arrange a system of signaling from your perch so that we may know at all times the situation and location of our invaders."

Seventy-two hours allowed and it would take forty of them merely to fill the balloon! Thirty-two hours to build and charge the furnace was much short of the time necessary. A week was needed for that task alone, for the mortar even to get its initial set. Yet the Committee's representative had issued a command and it would be fatal not to obey him. Friendship had no place in the house where Terror was master.

Still worn out by their previous day's fighting, the *Aérostiers* gathered their energies to build the furnace. It was no secret how things stood for their commander. Guyton de Morveau was served by an orderly who liked to eavesdrop and then drink and talk. There was also fear in

Maubeuge that the enemy would be attacking quite soon.
It was said that its strength was at least twice their own. It
was also asserted that General Favreau right now was considering a retreat. This would mean that the grand strategy
by which General Jourdan's troops would come up from the
south to join those of General Favreau would be jeop-
ardized. It would also mean, on a lesser though more personal scale, that the besiegers would be able to capture or
kill with ease thousands of fleeing Frenchmen. In the evening Coutelle learned from General Favreau that these rumors were close to the truth.

The real work for the *Aérostiers* had begun. Woodcutters
measured the boards with which the carpenters began to
erect a scaffolding for the furnace. The masons mixed their
mortar and stacked their brick. The blacksmith beat tin
plate into hose. Other men proceeded with their much re-
hearsed duties while Coutelle supervised the job to be sure
it was being done right. While this was going on, the
Austrians and Dutch tested the men's nerves with a barrage
of shell and bullets. The enemy probably felt that the con-
centration of lantern light they saw reflected in the sky
marked important doings in Maubeuge.

While the mortar holding the furnace together was still
green, the inflation of the "Entreprenant" was begun. During this time Coutelle and his men only took naps and they
ate very little. It was a worrisome period even if the enemy
could have been forgotten. The water spray had to be continuously and minutely adjusted to the condition of the iron
beneath it. There was always the danger that the hose carrying the hydrogen would leak as it passed out of the furnace.
Then if a chance spark ignited the gas there would be a
violent explosion. Any fissure in the furnace wall was cause
for alarm because if left unplugged it, too, could lead to an
explosion. With the furnace running so hot, it was difficult
to plug these cracks. Mud rather than concrete was found
to work best.

At the end of the third day Guyton de Morveau and General Favreau came to see how the work had progressed. They watched the "Entreprenant" lift itself magnificently off the ground. Its bag was smooth and taut and its basket seemed ample for whatever task was before it.

"I'm astounded," Favreau said to Coutelle, "to think that men will be going up in that machine. . . . How many will it carry?"

"Two medium-sized ones easily, plus ballast and ropes," answered Coutelle. "The ropes that will be keeping the aerostat from escaping will be twelve hundred feet long. If need be, we can lengthen them to eighteen hundred feet but I don't think that this excessive altitude will be needed."

"I am looking forward with pleasure to your flight," said Guyton de Morveau. "Sleep tonight and make it tomorrow!"

On June 2, 1794, the "Entreprenant" gracefully rose into the air to the accompaniment of the cheers and musketry of the 8000 troops garrisoned at Maubeuge. It seemed as though the men had forgotten all about the war. They watched with expressions of awe as the aerostat went higher and higher into the sky.

Guyton de Morveau tapped General Favreau on his shoulder. "General, we are witnessing history. We are seeing man taking a part of war off the ground and into the air. Someday, he may even do battle in that rarefied medium."

Coutelle had with him an ordnance officer who, being familiar with the area, was the observer. He was now raising a little blue flag, which meant by the prearranged signals that he wished to remain stationary and tied down. The "Entreprenant" was tethered at 1200 feet. If they wished to go higher, then a white flag would be raised, and if they wished to come down, a red one. As it was, they seemed content to stay where they were and spy on the enemy.

Spread out in the fields below them were the besiegers'

tents. There were several thousand of them at the very least; and though the tents were grouped in large camps, they still commanded an area three-quarters of the way around Maubeuge. This agreed with the detailed report that Favreau's scouts had given Guyton de Morveau.

The ordnance officer observed sadly, "It's only a matter of time, a very short time, before Maubeuge is taken. Now that I've seen our enemy's strength, I wonder why they've held off so long.

"What a post this is!" he marveled. "If we had even a modicum of maneuverable force, there wouldn't be an army safe from us."

"I can tell you why they're not attacking," said Coutelle. His face bore a twisted grin as though the joke he was thinking of was a very unfunny one. He motioned in front of him with his binoculars, then handed them to his companion. "Look down there, I'd say about two miles! What do you see?"

"My God!" the officer exclaimed, "the camp is empty of everything but tents." He swung around seeking other areas to study. "Only half the camps are being used. The rest are decoys. Coutelle, this is a trick that only an Austrian would sink to."

The next day Jourdan's troops began arriving from the south and mobilizing on the right bank of the Sambre. Across the water from them lay Charleroi, an enemy town situated thirty miles northeast of Maubeuge and over the French border. At the same time Prince Von Coburg, anticipating Jourdan's move to capture the town, was gathering his strength to surround the French and throw them into Charleroi's defending guns.

On June 12, Jourdan crossed the Sambre at a point just west of Charleroi. He wanted to relieve the siege of Maubeuge so that he could use the troops there to help him with his campaign. The French general realized quickly, though, that by delaying his attack on Charleroi he was playing into the hands of Coburg. Thereupon Jourdan let Maubeuge continue as it had been. He maneuvered his troops into a semicircular position around Charleroi. This position was not easily held. The town's artillery pounded his troops. Also, the enemy besieging Maubeuge turned toward Jourdan and began poking into his army's soft spots. His troops were so harassed and his commanders so lacking in enemy intelligence that he was forced back across the Sambre. Flushed with success, the enemy around Maubeuge, forgetting their limited numbers, began tightening their lines around that town. This maneuver relaxed the pressure on Jourdan's troops. They recrossed the Sambre two days after their retreat and again began testing Charleroi's defenses.

Exactly how much resistance the town could put up, Jourdan did not know. He worried that an all-out attack might see his troops massacred. He worried, too, that if he did not fight soon and take the town, he would be cut down by Coburg's consolidated armies. He had just one other choice, full retreat. Then he would have to explain to the Committee of Public Safety.

One night in the middle of June, Guyton de Morveau returned to Maubeuge after a conference with General Jourdan. The civilian representative sought out Captain Coutelle at his quarters. "The general wants to pull back," said Guyton de Morveau in a tense tone. "I told him that speaking for the Committee I would not hear of it. He said there was nothing else to do unless I wanted to see his army lost. He called in his scouts and they told me the same thing. 'Charleroi is a fortress,' they said. 'It can't be taken without a prolonged siege and we haven't men or time for it. Even now, Coburg is only hours away and soon will be pressing us against the walls of Charleroi.'

"I asked them how they knew all this, and they said that they gauged the strength of the town by the sound of its gunfire, and that they knew of Coburg's coming from the

stories of peasants bringing us the news. Thereupon I told
them they knew nothing; that it takes only a handful of men
to fire the cannon, and that peasants sometimes lie and
sometimes tell the truth, depending on what they think are
their best interests." He jerked his head up to look deep
into Coutelle's eyes. "I told Jourdan to keep his armies where
they are. I told him that you would do his scouting for him.
The general looked at me in amazement. 'Then the blood
is on both your heads,' he cried and left me."

Under Guyton de Morveau's orders the Balloon Corps
prepared to leave Maubeuge. Coutelle could not go out the
road he had come in because there was too much danger
that the "Entreprenant" would be seen. What added to his
problems beyond the fact that he would have to slip through
the enemy's lines was that he would have to carry the balloon fully inflated.

Around the college grounds stood a ten-foot-high stone
wall opening only upon the road that the "Entreprenant"
could not travel. On the other side of the wall was a water-
filled ditch, its black surface now reflecting a quarter moon.
Sixteen ropes hung from the "Entreprenant," the ends in the
hands of the *Aérostiers*. The men leaned ladders against the
stone wall, climbed them, and jumped down and waded
through the ditch onto the outer bank. Wet from the high
humidity of the summer night, slimy from their dip in the
water, plagued by the mosquitoes spawned in the stagnant
liquid, they towed their machine across the field. With
every step they took they feared that their silhouettes would
be glimpsed by the enemy. Three fences lay ahead. In
going over them the men held the aerostat so close to the
ground that its basket scraped each fence top.

When dawn came the *Aérostiers* were safely past the enemy. Coutelle allowed his men a short rest and then had
them move on. Toward noon a light rain fell but it was not
even enough to dampen the road they were traveling. Particles of black dust, characteristic of that region, lifted by

the wind, became glued to the men's faces and half-naked bodies. To the peasants watching them pass, they looked like black devils cavorting with the entrails of some bloated creature. It was no wonder that the soldiers could not get close enough to a native even to buy a few crusts of bread. At nightfall they arrived at Jourdan's camp. Their reputation had preceded them. It seemed to Coutelle that his host's entire army were outside their tents waiting to welcome the balloonists with cheers and hugs. Wine and bread were plentiful; the *Aérostiers* ate and drank. With their mouths filled and grape running from their lips they contorted their faces into appreciative grins. General Jourdan turned to Coutelle and sourly remarked, "My men are turning defeat into victory and they have not yet fought."

On the morning of June 24, Coutelle and Jourdan's aide, General Morlot, went up to 1500 feet. What they saw brought a smile to Guyton de Morveau's face when he heard about it. Charleroi was only moderately armed, obviously undermanned, and certainly not able to withstand a sustained siege.

"I must stay up longer," begged Morlot when Coutelle proposed a descent. "I want to set down every defense the enemy has." The balloon made three ascensions that day, with Morlot standing in the basket making notes for more than eight hours. In summing up for his superior the observer said, "If needed, I could even get you the tent assignments of each of their men."

The balloon had an effect on the morale of the Charleroi defenders that neither Coutelle nor Morveau could have anticipated. The balloon was a sorcerer's eye, witchcraft, an evil against which humans were helpless. The troops at Charleroi trembled in fear. No maneuver could go unobserved; no place was safe to hide in. Charleroi's governor knew the aerostat for what it was—a machine that showed General Jourdan the location of every gun in the city's defense, every soldier in the garrison. There was no escaping the aerial observer.

The day after the ascension the governor's representatives met those of Jourdan. Charleroi surrendered. Jourdan entered the town while its troops were giving up their arms. The French general was finishing a glass of wine in the governor's office when he heard the rumble of a distant cannon.

The governor got up slowly and pushed open the windows facing the sound. "Prince Von Coburg!" he said in a whisper and then faced his captor. "If I had heard that cannon an hour sooner, you would never have entered Charleroi."

Jourdan stared at the half-empty bottle on the governor's desk. "Isn't it strange that a mere bag of wind could snatch victory from your head and put it on mine? Imagine how deadly war will be when every nation has a fleet of such bags!"

"You philosophize as though this war were already over," snapped the governor. "Don't forget that Coburg is out there, probably at this very instant pressing on your camps!"

The next morning the "Entreprenant" ascended from a high point a few miles north of Charleroi. General Morlot was again with Coutelle. The military situation was frightening. French troops were holding their ground at only a few points, elsewhere they were yielding. Coutelle saw the Austrians swarming out of Fleurus, a town several miles northeast of Charleroi. Their lancers rent a mile-wide hole in the French line. The Balloon Corps' position became perilous. Coutelle signaled to his men to haul down the aerostat.

They retreated toward Charleroi. Their way was encumbered by equipment dropped by French troops who had already fled the field. There was little doubt that by the end of the day Jourdan would be chased out of Charleroi and would again be pushed across the Sambre.

"Stop!" yelled Coutelle. "We're soldiers, not rabble. We'll

ascend here and let our commander know what is happening. If the Austrians come, cut us loose!"

Morlot leaped into the basket after Coutelle. They ascended the full 1800 feet. They made their observations, then wrote them on slips of paper which they weighted and let drop overside for immediate delivery to Jourdan. By midafternoon the complexion of the battle began to change. The French defenses were tightening up. In some places the Republic's troops were cutting into the Austrians. Still, from their balloon perch Coutelle and Morlot saw that an Austrian victory, though not now imminent, was highly probable.

Then at five o'clock the observers perceived an astonishing sight. The enemy had ceased their attack and were going back from whence they had come. "It's a hallucination," declared Morlot.

"Not when we both see it," argued Coutelle. He scribbled a note to Jourdan and let it drop. Soon hundreds of French soldiers with renewed heart recovered the weapons in the fields where they had dropped them and became the hunters instead of the hunted. They did not know why, but the French were winning the Battle of Fleurus.

Later it was learned that Coburg had ordered the retreat when he found out that Charleroi had been taken. It was late in the afternoon then and several prongs of the French Army had already made holes in the enemy lines. Coburg saw no point in enduring the pain, perhaps multiplied many times by a siege on a town that he now felt had lost its strategic value.

In commenting about the Battle of Fleurus, Coutelle said with characteristic modesty, "We shall never claim that the aerostat won the Battle of Fleurus. Every French soldier who fought on this memorable occasion made the victory possible. Yet this I will tell you: the 'Entreprenant' was able to point out continuously the movement of enemy troops, distinguish their infantry, watch their cavalry, locate their artillery, and track the movements of the general masses."

The capture of Charleroi and the winning of the Battle of Fleurus finally discouraged the predatory instincts of France's neighbors. The Republic was now freed from the threat of invasion.

Five

HOW TO BE AN AERONAUT

It happened in 1838 on a muggy summer's day in Easton, Pennsylvania, a borough not yet a city, about two days' stagecoach ride out of the port of New York. The townspeople had one date in mind, August 11. It was on this day that John Wise, the famous aeronaut, was going to ascend in his balloon from the public square.

For three weeks there had been advertisements in the local paper as well as in those of nearby towns telling of the flight. Announcements were posted on every tree on Main Street. The time was to be noon. On that Saturday the stores would be closed. The bank would open for business one hour after the ascension.

Shortly after dawn the people started arriving, dressed as though for a county fair. By ten o'clock the ascension place was jammed by over 3000 spectators. Every tree that offered a view was filled with onlookers.

A wagon arrived. The balloon was taken from it, and opened upon the ground. Next came five wooden casks, which with hose made up the inflating apparatus. Hydrogen was to be generated in four of these, each of which had been charged with water, oil of vitriol, and iron turnings. The fifth cask, larger than the rest and filled only with water and a sprinkling of lime, was to be used to cleanse the hydrogen. Finally, the purified gas was to be led through the hose of stout muslin into the balloon's neck.

John Wise, gaunt-faced with deep-set eyes and a cleft chin, taller than most men and thinner, checked every square foot of the balloon's fabric. He did this more hurriedly than usual because high winds were expected. The balloon began taking shape. It started to lift itself off the ground. The citizens pressed forward, not even feeling the few drops of rain that had begun to fall. The people seemed to know that John Wise was planning something special.

At a few minutes before two o'clock the aerostat was released. Seldom in the history of ballooning did ascensions occur when they were scheduled. As Wise went up, he tipped his top hat to the spectators and bowed to them from every station in his wicker basket. Wise was a showman. This was an asset he used most of his life to further the aeronautic art. He saw commercial air routes crisscrossing the United States. He dreamed of making a transatlantic crossing by balloon. For the present flight, though, he had set himself to prove one thing—that a burst balloon is as safe as a filled one. He reasoned that the air rushing by would convert the empty bag into a parachute. The citizens had been right in expecting something different from this ascension.

He entered a mass of thunder clouds. Lightning flashed so close he could smell the electricity in the air. He breathed deeply, but not for courage. He gloried in the storm. Had he been looking for a symbol, he would have said that the heavens were applauding his faith in a new science.

At 13,000 feet his soaked garments began to stiffen. Above him his balloon strained against its net, fabric blisters forming and squeezing through the ropes. The aerostat continued to rise. A mile below, lightning was springing from cloud to cloud. Wise took out his watch and recorded the time in his log book, twenty minutes past two. His pencil was barely off the paper when the balloon exploded. It fell with sickening speed. Air rushed through the network of ropes, whistling a high-pitched song. In less than ten seconds the bag was empty of its gas. Soon the lower half of the bag rose into the upper half. The speed became slow enough to make the descent a safe one. Although Wise was becoming ill from the spiral motions of his new vehicle, it did not matter. He had shown what he had intended to show, and he dreamed of the aerostat he would make for an ocean crossing.

John Wise was thirty years old then. He was a stern man but one who had learned to yield to the forces of nature. In later life he was to learn to yield to the forces of man. He once wrote that as a child in bed at night he would spend hours looking through his window to follow the path of the moon and to count the number of stars it had overtaken. The sight of a meteor streaking through the atmosphere would keep him watching until midnight hoping to see another. His favorite toy was a kite. With this he could reach the sky. He lost count of the number of times he sent frogs and toads upward on a kite's tail. How he envied them their trips and wished the animals could tell him what they had seen! On some evenings his neighbors in the farm community of Lancaster, Pennsylvania, would watch an eerie red or yellow spot of light rising in the sky. The first time the spectacle appeared the farmers thought they were witnessing something supernatural. Later they learned that Johnny Wise had been flying a paper lantern. The boy thought that if he could get his light high enough, he would be able to learn the true color of the stars.

"If a small kite can lift a frog, then a larger kite can lift a chicken," the boy reasoned. Why stop there? He would make a kite large enough and strong enough to bear his own weight. This he began to do, using fabric for the skin, and boughs from young trees for the frame. One afternoon while waiting for a gluepot to warm, he glanced at a newspaper that was lying around. He saw an article about a balloon flight in Italy. Hastily, he scissored out the account. Kite-making was now forgotten.

John Wise thought he wanted to be a minister. He took classical studies at Lancaster High School and began learning theology from the Rev. William Muhlenberg. Very soon, he doubted that he would be wearing the cloth. When the reverend spoke about the firmament, Wise wondered about the motions of the heavenly bodies. When the subject of Noah and his ark was discussed, Wise asked why a balloon was not chosen for the refuge. Then one day John Wise confessed that theology was not for him. He would leave it to those better endowed by God to be its students.

While apprenticed to a cabinetmaker, Wise decided to build a small hot-air balloon. He even had a passenger for it, a cat called Nellie. She probably had more aerial experience than any other animal in the country. Shortly after birth she had ridden one of her master's kites over the church steeple and down into the parish garden. A later experiment found her being lifted into a rain cloud. Two days later she came limping home. The cords that had bound the kite to her body had been cut. Wise pitied the poor farmer who had seen her descend, and wondered whether the man was trying to persuade his neighbors that he had once seen it rain cats and dogs, or at least cats.

To the boy's regret, his attempt at a Montgolfier would not lift Nellie more than a few feet above the ground. Even a deeper saucepan, one that held more of the straw and wood-shavings he used for fuel, was not good enough. He tried his vehicle without Nellie. The balloon took off slowly. Fingers of orange flame poked into the delicate sphere. It rose to several hundred feet. There it burst into flames. The balloon fell rapidly, onto the thatched roof of a nearby cottage. The town's fire bells sounded the alarm. Men dashed across the fields to form fire ranks. Wise fled to his father's cow barn, where he watched the proceedings from a chink in the wall. Although his first experiment in ballooning was not entirely a failure from the scientific point of view, it was not this aspect that presently concerned the boy. The cottage roof was ablaze and he trembled for fear that the building would be burned to the ground. But the buckets flew from the well to the house and the fire was put out before too much damage was done. There was no need to ask whose balloon it was. Wise could see his father, strap in hand, opening the barn door.

By the time Wise was in his middle twenties he was married, had a son, and was part way through building a man-carrying aerostat. "We will use it on Sundays to see the countryside," he told his wife, "like other people use their carriages." His balloon was made of muslin rendered airtight by a varnish of his own devising. The bag was a small one, only twenty-eight feet in diameter, but a big one for a man with so little aeronautical experience. The balloon's netting was fashioned by a woman accustomed to repairing fish nets. The car was a wicker basket able to hold at most two weeks' family wash.

His balloon was finished at the same time his money ran out. If he wished to ascend, he would have to do it as a public demonstration and charge admission. Only in this way could he pay for the chemicals and inflating equipment.

In Wise's youth only a hardy man could be a professional balloonist. It was not storms that a pilot feared or winds that would sweep him into the sea. These emergencies could be met by skill and were proper challenges. Not as easily dealt with was a disappointed audience. They had paid their admissions and a performance they would see. They had no pity for an exhibitionist who failed to ascend. He was a charlatan. A frenzy would seize the mob. The aeronaut would be lucky if he escaped without being pummeled. Wise read of a French aeronaut who failed to go up

as promised. It was in Philadelphia, the city of Brotherly
Love. Though the winds at the time were close to hurricane
force, the people were not to be reasoned with. Ascend he
must or be mobbed. When he failed, he was rushed from
all sides. He was able to run away but his aerial car was
broken up for souvenirs. His silken balloon was shredded
and the remnants waved as banners by the audience as they
paraded triumphantly through the streets. The mansion
from whose garden the ascent was to have been made was
burned to the ground.

Although John Wise made nearly 500 ascensions during
his lifetime, he worried about his audience only at his first.
It had been set for four in the afternoon, April 30, 1835, at
Ninth and Green Streets in Philadelphia. One of his friends
did not hold back his forebodings.

"You're going in among butchers."

John Wise answered, "Butchers are fine people. Look at
the credit they've given me!"

"They'll take a pound of your flesh, blood and all."

"Only if they can fly."

The day arrived, dark and storm-ridden, characteristic of
the type nature seems to whip up when a balloon flight is
planned. Several hundred people, all having paid their half-
dollar admissions, watched as the inflation began. To give
the storm time to pass, Wise was delaying operations as
much as he could. Three hours went by. When four o'clock
arrived, the balloon was not yet full.

"It's that hour," a farmer yelled. "Time to go up."

"He's going to fly like a chicken," another added. "Cock-
a-doodle-doo!"

Everybody took up the mimicking cry. "Cock-a-doodle-
doo!" They flapped their arms like wings and at the end of
each stroke noisily clapped their hands to their sides. They
reveled in the certainty of approaching fun. They knew that
on such a day only a madman would attempt a flight.

Wise turned from his work. He raised his hands for quiet.

"You will see an ascension even if the heavens break open," he said, and hoped that fear would not crack his voice. "Even though this is my first flight, when the balloon is filled I will go up. My only fright comes from your high spirits." An hour later John Wise stepped into his basket. Even though it was still afternoon, the sky was almost black. He called for volunteers to restrain the aerostat for launching. A man wearing a sheriff's badge came close to the balloon. Wise thought he was there to help. Instead, the man unfastened a knife from his belt and slashed through two of the balloon's riggings. "You'll not kill yourself for me to watch," he exclaimed. The flight was postponed for two days.

The day of the new flight dawned clear and calm. By early afternoon the crowd waiting to see the ascension was twice what it had been the day of the storm. Everybody was excited and happy, seemingly eager to have the aeronaut succeed, yet, oddly, fearing for him to go up. Somehow, they had the idea that Wise would prefer not making the ascent. This made the take-off hazardous. The aeronaut was in his machine. Some cried, "Send him up!" and with powerful efforts sought to suit the action to their words. Others, with oppositely directed thoughts and force, attempted to hold the aerostat down. With the help of the balloon the group for the ascension won. Wise shot up into the air as though from a cannon. Speed did not lend him altitude. The balloon was soon grazing the chimneys of neighboring buildings. The car, striking one of them, bobbed like an irresponsible pendulum. Wise descended to the ground 300 yards from where he had taken off. The crowd streamed toward the fallen balloon. Wise handed his instruments, boots, and coat to a nearby spectator, thus lightening the aerostat. He roared at the top of his voice, "Let me go!" All hands gave way. The vehicle rose quietly.

This was one of the happiest moments Wise ever experienced. Up he went almost perpendicularly, until he reached an altitude of several thousand feet. Here a gentle breeze pushed him to the southwest. Below him was the city. It had a voice that Wise described as melancholy and he compared it to the sound of an aeolian harp. To his east was the Delaware River. Above it all floated his balloon, swollen with pride and in equilibrium between heaven and earth.

Practical matters called the aeronaut. The balloon had reversed its direction, had crossed the Delaware, and was rapidly dropping to the New Jersey shore. Landing was imminent. Wise was as sorrowful as though he had been thrust out of the Garden of Eden. He dropped his grappling hook and made a safe landing in a village nine miles from Philadelphia.

He returned home with a plan. He would earn his living as a professional aeronaut. Assuredly, aerial travel was the coming mode of transportation. He would hasten its arrival by building balloons for the new era and proving their safety. Perhaps he would even fly across the Atlantic.

Six

JOHN WISE—BARNSTORMER

John Wise's new vehicle was called the "Meteor," and he could not have chosen a more prophetic name. After a year's professional use his first aerostat had escaped during a storm. He was delighted. He had enough money to buy a new one and this time he would have a bag of silk instead of muslin. Only in New York could he find the material he needed, one of tight enough weave. It had been imported from Paris to line gentlemen's capes and was glisteningly white. Under Wise's close, almost old-maidish supervision the new aerostat was built. Its bag when fully inflated was pear-shaped and eight yards across. Its basket was woven of polished bamboo, and its ropes for riggings and lines were made of long-stranded cotton. "Undoubtedly the prettiest aerial vehicle ever seen," Wise was told.

Its name was derived from two events. In the first, several yards of the silk had been impregnated with sealing oils and then stored in a loft to dry. The material ignited spontaneously and only by good fortune was the flame snuffed out before the building could catch fire. The second event came about in a dream of his wife's. In it she saw the aerostat streaking like a fireball across the night sky.

The "Meteor" was only a few days old when Wise took off on a test flight from his father's farm in Lancaster. All afternoon he had been drifting between two layers of clouds. Occasionally the lower one parted, revealing a hilly terrain studded with trees. Night was coming fast. He had to descend. A yellowish atmosphere closed in on him, quiet and warm as sleep. He played out a 400-foot line, which he soon felt was swishing through the treetops. The line's motion changed, became steadier. The aerostat was traveling over cleared ground. Wise heard voices below him. He yelled but got no answer. He threw out his grappling hook. It bumped along the ground, caught on to what turned out to be a fence, hung on long enough for the aerostat to arc to earth, then uprooted the wooden structure. At the instant of landing Wise released enough hydrogen to keep the basket on the ground.

"Where are you?" a voice called out.

"Over here, by the balloon," Wise answered.

"I know that, I smell it," the voice said. A sixteen-year-old Negro boy materialized out of the fog, and he was wrinkling his nose to show that he was sniffing the air. "It smells like the one I helped a gentleman fill last year in Baltimore." He matter-of-factly added, "You're on Mr. Stump's land."

"And exactly where is Mr. Stump's land?" asked Wise.

"In Harford County, Maryland," the boy said, surprised that the aeronaut did not know. He went on to explain, "It's near Baltimore." While they were talking, the fog had risen to treetop height. Coming toward them was an elderly nightshirted man accompanied by a servant carrying a lantern.

"Keep that light away!" Wise cried out. "There's gas here."

Dutifully, the servant deposited the lantern on the ground and waited while his master went forward to greet the aeronaut. The landowner invited Wise to spend the night at the plantation. But Wise was in a hurry to get back to Lancaster, where in two days' time he had promised to make a public flight. Thus, when Stump offered the help of his servants to deflate and pack the balloon, Wise showered him with thanks.

A light drizzle was falling. Growing weary in the humid atmosphere, Wise held open the balloon's gas valve. Hydrogen flowed out and mixed with the steaming vapors coming out of the earth. The Negro boy who had first greeted Wise was at the lower end of the balloon guiding the loose silk into the car. Another boy was smoothing it out and packing it tight. Standing about twenty feet from the operations and watching intently was Wise's host, surrounded by a score of his servants. The "Meteor" had less than 1000 cubic feet of gas in it when to the aeronaut's horror he saw a little Negro boy running toward him with a lantern.

"Wait!" Wise screamed, but not soon enough. There was a sound like a cork popping. The landscape became brilliantly lit. Wise felt himself lifted high into the air and then dropped. Part of the balloon sped across the field, traveling with a rushing noise and a fiery tail. The other part burned wildly. Wise was enveloped in flames. He rolled in the damp grass to put them out. He cried in pain and was further tortured by the screams of others. His clothes smoldering, he rose to his feet. In the orange light of the burning balloon he saw gray forms picking themselves up and staggering to the plantation house. All at once his sight was gone and he was led off the field.

The rest of the night was spent dressing the wounds of the injured and recounting the terrible happening to a stream of relatives and friends that flowed through the house until dawn. Fortunately, there had been no casualties. Only the balloonist appeared to have a lasting injury. Two days later, though, his sight returned. Against the advice of Stump's physician, the aeronaut left for home. There, after several

weeks, through bloodletting, soothing potions, and a con-
stitution that could survive such medicaments, Wise
emerged with new skin on his face and body. He was eager
to start building another aerostat.

His favorite passengers were old men. The more wrinkled
they were the better he liked them. He told them that they
carried an ocean of air on their shoulders. "Come up with
me two or three miles and the lightened load will round
out your eyeballs," he would say. "You will be able to read
without spectacles. Your face will be as smooth and healthy-
looking as a baby's." He would relate his own health experiences as he passed from novice to veteran aeronaut. "In
the beginning I was suffering from chronic dyspepsia and
a lung infection caused by years of inhaling the dust of the
carpentry shop. By breathing the cool virgin air found only
at great heights, I was cured of all my complaints."

In the summer of 1859 Wise and a companion ventured
on a late afternoon and evening flight. The day was clear.
At an altitude of 2000 feet the scent of honeysuckle was still
strong and poignant. Caught by breezes, scores of little
spiders were wafting by, clutching the spokes of their fluttering webs like sailors hanging onto the riggings of storm-
tossed ships. The glorious day gave way to a moonless black
sky. Toward midnight the men decided to land. A moving
light on the ground caught their attention. They were able
to descend toward it. The balloon was soon hovering over
the heads of three staggering men, one of whom was swinging a lantern. Their voices carried clearly through the night
air. They were very drunk.

"I say we go home," said one.

"I say we go for a ride," said another.

"I say we go get some girls," said a third and he won
agreement all around.

Wise could not miss this opportunity. Cupping his hands,
he intoned, "It is better to go to the house of mourning than

to go to the house of feasting." The men faltered. They looked everywhere to see where the voice had come from. They could not see the balloon because it was cloaked by the night.

"Who said that?" one ventured to ask.

"It's some fool making sport of us," another answered.

Wise heard the sounds of cracking bushes as the men thrashed about trying to find the source of the voice. Looking eerie in the reflected light of the lantern, one of the men turned his face upward and said in chilled tone, "I think it's Him."

Wise's companion then announced, "My son, if sinners entice thee, consent thou not." The three men did not linger to hear more. They scurried across the field like rabbits, paying little heed to the brush underfoot. His voice cracking, the man lagging behind his comrades cried out in a sober voice, "Get thee behind me, Satan!"

In 1843 the telegraph was eight years old and service was being set up between Washington and Baltimore. The Lancaster *Intelligencer,* Wise's home-town newspaper, was telling its readers that a new era was dawning with electric messages and aerial travel soon to become commonplace. The editor saw the balloon bringing England within 100 hours of the United States. He drew a picture of John Wise landing after a transatlantic flight. The editor asked,

Would it not create a stir that would far exceed the reception of a hundred presidents, though every man a Tyler? And then what a sensation he would produce as, coming along the Channel, he made preparations to set down his aerial chariot in the heart of the great London world. Or, missing this, suppose him dropping in on the Frenchmen at Paris or Calais or Bordeau. Or, going still further, suppose him wafted into Constantinople, dashing down unceremoniously and without notice in the Sublime Porte. Why John Wise would become more justly famous than any explorer that comes to mind!

Hundreds of letters came into the newspaper office asking when the flight would be. The excitement of contemplating such a trip spread into the editorial pages of the nation's press, which asked Wise for more details. He acceded by declaring he was presently making plans for his flight. Then, with front-page space provided by the editor of the Lancaster *Intelligencer*, he issued a proclamation to set the world on notice:

TO ALL PUBLISHERS OF NEWSPAPERS ON THE GLOBE

As it is my intention to take a trip across the Atlantic Ocean with a balloon in the summer of 1844, and as the descent or landing of balloons, in my experience, has almost universally created unnecessary alarm and consternation to the people nearby, I therefore give this general notice to the seafaring community of all climes that should they, during any time henceforth, chance to be in the vicinity of a balloon, either on the ocean or in the atmosphere, they need not be under any apprehensions, but should endeavor to give aid to its passengers.

It must not be inferred from this that its success is considered improbable, but merely to be prepared for all emergencies.

Having, from a long experience in aeronautics, been convinced that a constant and regular current of air is blowing at all times from west to east with a velocity of from 20 to 40, and even 60 miles per hour, according to its height from the earth, and having discovered a composition which renders silk or muslin impervious to hydrogen gas, so that a balloon may be kept afloat for many weeks, I feel confident, with these advantages, that a trip across the Atlantic will not be attended with as much real danger as by the common mode of transition.

The balloon is to be 100 feet in diameter, which will give it a net ascending power of 25,000 pounds, which is sufficient to make everything safe and comfortable. A sea-worthy boat is to be used for the car, which is to be depended on in case the balloon should fail to accomplish the voyage. The boat is also calculated on, in case the regular current of wind should be diverted from its course by the influence of the ocean or through other causes. The crew is to consist of three people: an aeronaut, a sea navigator and a scientific landsman.

Therefore, the people of Europe, Africa, Asia, and all other parts, on the ocean or elsewhere, who have never seen a balloon, will bear in mind that it is a large globe made of cloth, enclosed in a network, with a sloop hanging underneath it, containing the latest news from the United States, and for crew the world's most obedient servants.

LANCASTER; June 1843.

The notice was poorly received. "How can a man be so arrogant as to say he knows which course the wind will take?" wrote one journalist.

"We have discussed Professor Wise's plans for his aerostat with several experts," related an editor. "The concensus is that if the aeronaut succeeds it will be more through good fortune than good planning." The title of "Professor" was an honorary one given to all practitioners of the aerial arts.

Meanwhile, Wise approached several financiers for backing. None of them would open their purses to buy what the aeronaut was selling. Discouraged, he told the last man on his list of prospects, "Men believe in great inventions and discoveries after they have been accomplished. But if some people did not believe in them before, civilization would make but slow progress." For the time being, this was the end of his project.

Three years later the United States was at war with Mexico. American strategy called for capturing Mexico City. Before this could be done the Gulf of Mexico port town of Veracruz had to be taken. A half-mile offshore stood San Juan de Ulúa, a fearful fortress built on a coral reef. For American naval forces to be able to attack Veracruz, they would first have to navigate safely through the reef-studded

waters outside San Juan de Ulúa. Then the ships would
have to survive a withering cross fire from the fortress and
from shore batteries. This was the problem that the War
Department had been desperately trying to solve for almost
half a year. The military did not lack help; it had the un-
solicited advice of thousands of amateur strategists. Among
these was John Wise.

In his proposal Wise called for making a 100-foot-
diameter balloon of common twilled muslin. When inflated,
it would carry a net load of 20,000 pounds. It would have
enough buoyancy to stay aloft for several days. Percussion
bombs and torpedoes would be its cargo. The aerostat
would be held by a five-mile line connected to a naval ship
anchored outside the range of Veracruz' guns. Then by hovering a mile high over the fortress, the aerial man-of-war
would be safe from enemy fire. The guns of San Juan de
Ulúa could not bear on an object directly overhead. With
such an advantage, the aeronaut would be able to reduce
the fort as quickly as he could throw bombs over his car's
side.

The War Department, after much prodding by the aeronaut, said it would study his plan. They never said any
more than this, and as far as John Wise could learn, even
after Veracruz was subdued by other means, the Department was still considering his proposal.

For the next thirteen years, Wise performed with his balloon for any town that asked him and whose citizens would
pay the admission. He was looked upon as an entertainer,
the same as a circus performer. His talk of prevailing westerly winds, of updrafts, of air resistance, were considered
part of the show. That these notions would someday form
the basis of a new science was as inconceivable as were the
products of such a science. Imagine then the laughter that
greeted the aeronaut's forming the Trans-Atlantic Balloon
Company! Its charter called for carrying mail and passengers from the United States to principal European cities.

For this purpose, a balloon was built, fifty feet in diameter and sixty feet high. It carried a wicker basket to hold passengers and crew, and beneath the basket a wood-and-canvas boat. The aerostat was christened "Atlantic."

On the first day of July in 1859 a trial ascension was scheduled. An enclosure had been erected around the city common of St. Louis. The Gaslight Company opened one of its supply lines in the street for the inflation. The American Express Company, forerunner of the Railway Express Agency, gave Wise one of its overland mailbags for air transport to New York. It was filled with letters and newspapers from the Pacific Coast. With transcontinental mail rates being several dollars an ounce, this was indeed a valuable cargo. It was also the world's first air post.

At a quarter of seven in the evening the ropes holding the "Atlantic" were cut, freeing it for its maiden trip. The aerostat was carrying a thousand pounds of sand ballast and a well-stocked larder. There were cold beef sandwiches and chicken sandwiches, roast game birds from the mayor of St. Louis, a bucket of lemonade, and a hamper of champagne from the publisher of the St. Louis *Republican*. One of the paper's reporters was also a member of the four-man crew. He was known simply as Mr. Hyde. John Wise was the crew's director-in-chief. The other two members were the balloon's fabricator, John Lamountane, and the scientific observer, Oscar Gager.

Night came soon after take-off and with it a temperature drop to the freezing point. Bundling himself in a tarpaulin, Wise settled to the bottom of the car for a nap. Lamountane took charge. There was a light easterly wind blowing. He ordered ballast thrown overboard. He was seeking the stronger westerly wind. The balloon began filling out as it slowly ascended. Hyde made some remark about an "ethereal" atmosphere and Gager nodded agreement. Then, in fascination, the men listened to John Wise's snores.

"Who'd ever believe we'd have steamboat whistlings at

12,000 feet?" Lamountane asked. The balloon fell in with a
westerly. The machine was almost full now and still rising.
A hose fastened to the balloon's neck—the safety valve that
equated the bag's internal gas pressure to the atmospheric
pressure—began rising from over the car's side. When the
balloon was finally fully distended, the hose had been
pulled entirely within the car and was swinging pendulum-
like over Wise's face. The aeronaut began breathing in hydrogen. His snoring became convulsive. Lamountane, busy
testing the riggings, called over his shoulder, "Our steamboat's pulling into its pier." While Gager and Hyde were
busy arguing the merits of air versus sea transportation, the
snoring stopped. Lamountane called to Wise to help with
the navigation. He got no answer. It was then that Hyde,
turning casually away from his companion, saw the hose
hovering over the aeronaut's nose and heard the deadly
hydrogen gas swishing into his face. With a cry of alarm the
newspaperman pulled Wise to his feet. Opening the man's
mouth, Hyde poured into it some of the contents of a bottle
of champagne. After a few desperate moments the aeronaut
opened his eyes and smiled.

"What a wonderful dream I was having!" he said. "It was
of great diving-bell experiments and of interplanetary balloon voyages. Why did you wake me?"

Until early the following afternoon the "Atlantic" sailed
calmly and uneventfully in a northeasterly direction. The
crew had already finished their lunch and were at ease
with their environment. They were three-quarters across
Lake Ontario and pitying the surface vessels they saw below them which so laboriously had to hue their way through
the water. "How foolish, when air travel is here!" Hyde
exclaimed. Hardly had he spoken when a storm came
sweeping across the lake. Its suddenness amazed the crew.
Trying to take the machine above the weather, Wise
shouted for full ballast discharge. There was not enough

sand left to lift the aerostat more than 200 feet. The balloon then began dropping toward the lake.

"Throw out everything you can lay your hands on!" yelled Wise. Overboard went ropes, sandwiches, a jug of lemonade, and the champagne, except for one bottle rescued in time. "We won't want to go to our graves thirsty," Wise explained. They were near the sea's surface. Water thrown up from the waves was drenching the "Atlantic." Above the aerostat tongues of lightning darted out of the heavy sky.

"Give me the hatchet!" Lamountane cried. "I'll cut the boat loose." As he was slashing through one of the lines, the aerostat dropped to a few feet above the water. The boat was dashed down violently. Water poured into it, making it an anchor. With the aerostat so restrained, the wind used the balloon as a punching bag, knocking it again and again onto the lake's surface. Wise saw a hat rolling on the crest of a whitecap. "Lamountane's gone!" he shouted. A voice behind him said, "Let's not tarry, Professor! Bury me!" Wheeling around, Wise was amazed to see the missing man safely on board but sadly watching his hat sink into the sea.

Three of the four lines attaching the boat to the car had been cut. A sharp updraft sucked the "Atlantic" several hundred feet into the air. The boat, emptying its water into the lake, twisted at the end of its remaining line like something alive. Wise set the craft free. Then he braced himself for the final plunge into the sea. It never came. The storm had passed over as quickly as it had come.

Poor visibility kept the men from distinguishing land until it was almost upon them. Wise was dismayed at seeing how small the beach was and the nearness of the forest behind it. Landing would be tricky. The aeronaut jerked open the gas valve. The "Atlantic" hit squarely on shore, then bounced into the air.

"The grapnel, quick the grapnel!" Wise yelled to Lamountane. The iron claw flew out over the side, caught itself on a tree bough. The branch tore off. Propelled by the swift wind, the "Atlantic" went crashing through the forest, breaking off tree limbs as though they were twigs. Several times the aerostat was stopped in its fearful journey but each time it leaped to freedom. It was beyond belief that the passengers could survive the tossings and tumblings they were getting. Once more the "Atlantic" found a perch, then slipped out of it to go crashing into a spruce. Here a sharp branch ripped open the balloon and freed its gas. The men dangled in their basket sixty feet above the earth. With the aid of the grapnel line they lowered themselves to the ground. Wise was the last to descend. He carried with him the surviving bottle of champagne.

Passers-by had seen the descent, approached, and told the men they had landed in the township of Henderson, New York. This was in the Watertown area and not far from the Thousand Islands. Wise calculated that the "Atlantic" had traveled 1200 miles, or a direct span of 800 miles. He broke open the champagne and offered it around. "We're drinking to the longest balloon trip the world has ever known, and to my hearty and hardy companions." One of the local citizens was raising the bottle to his lips when a spectacled elderly woman struck down his tippling arm.

"You drinking," she asked in a dismayed voice, "you, a Son of Temperance?"

After downing his fill the man explained to his earnest companion, "My vows do not include Manna from Heaven."

Two years later the American Civil War broke out. To help the Union cause, the fifty-three-year-old aeronaut organized a group of men from Lancaster, drilled them for several weeks in the manual of arms, and volunteered their services. Toward the end of this period a high-ranking Army officer from Washington called upon Wise and asked him to estimate the cost of a military balloon and the fee for his services. He replied that there would be no fee and that the balloon could be made for $850. Ten days after the meeting

Wise was informed that he had been appointed military balloonist. He was instructed to build his machine and bring it to the capital.

The aeronaut got to Washington on Wednesday, July 17, 1861, four days before one of the bloodiest battles in American history was fought. A few hours after his arrival Major Albert Myer, Chief Signal Officer in the Regular Army, arrived at Wise's lodgings. The man was brightly military, from his smart salute to his square bearing and glossy mustache.

"Captain A. W. Whipple has requested that I take you and your balloon to Centreville, Virginia," he told Wise. "It is a twenty-six-mile trip to the west. Once there, you will be making aerial observations for General Irvin McDowell. We leave tomorrow."

The aeronaut's face showed that he was pleased that the military thought enough of balloon observations to want them for the man commanding the Union Army's advance into Virginia. Even so, the aeronaut did not promise to do what he could not, which was to have the aerostat ready the next day. He explained the delay to Myer, who reluctantly agreed to leaving Friday morning. However, military slowness in furnishing provisions held up the departure until the weekend.

A detail of twenty men and their officer emerged at two o'clock Sunday morning from the Columbian Armory, where the balloon had been inflated. Overhead, the aerostat danced in the light breeze. The men jockied the mooring ropes to coax the huge machine past the telegraph poles and wires lining Pennsylvania Avenue. A bright moon outlined the detail's way through Georgetown and across the Aqueduct Bridge, which spanned the Potomac River. When they reached the Virginia shore, the men began following the Chesapeake and Ohio Canal. Their path was narrow, heavily arched by overgrown shrubs and tree branches. The ropes became entangled in the foliage. Soldiers hacked the way clear so that the balloon could move on. Occasionally, the growth became too thick for the vehicle to penetrate. Then the men took to the water, sometimes wading, sometimes swimming, with the ends of the mooring ropes tied to their waists.

The sounds of battle were clearly heard—the deep-throated thunder of artillery fire, the crack of fusillades, the staccato notes of musketry. The men were getting increasingly eager to join their battlefield comrades. A runner returning to the capital informed Myer that a showdown battle was being waged four miles west of Centreville, in the Manassas area. He added, "Two Federal brigades fought their way over Bull Run River and are now chasing the Rebels back to their plantations." Thus the balloon detail was driven to feverish haste to see action before the battle was over.

The party cut inland to Fairfax Road. Here the men rendezvoused with the wagon and team of horses carrying their supplies, which had crossed the Potomac by boat. Heavy military traffic had prevented the balloon detail from using the same means of travel.

To reach the fight quicker, Myer ordered the balloon tied to the wagon. When Wise saw this being done, he countermanded the major. Enraged, Myer confronted the aeronaut. "By whose authority do you order my men? You, sir, are merely a civilian traveler, and are here only through the courtesy of the United States Army." He motioned to a nearby private and said in a tone severer than he usually used, "Make those ropes fast to the wagon! I'll have your hide if you touch them again. Get those horses up to a smart trot!"

Wise winced as he saw his balloon being forcibly pulled through a stand of trees. The branches compressed the bag so much that the soldiers put their hands to their ears to dull the sound of an expected burst. When freed, the balloon shot forward with enough energy to lift the wagon

1. The landing of the first hydrogen balloon, 1783.

2. The first manned aerial free-balloon launching with a hot-air Montgolfier. M. d'Arlandes and M. de Rozier are pilots. November 21, 1783.

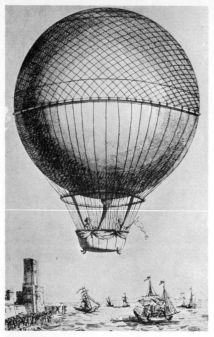

3. English Channel balloon crossing by Blanchard and Jeffries, 1784.

4. The return of Blanchard and Lépinard to Lille, 1785.

5. A French Revolutionary caricature, circa 1790.

6. The French aerostat Entreprenant during the Battle of Fleurus, June 26, 1794, according to an early nineteenth-century poster.

7. Fragment of Confederate balloon made from silk dresses donated by the women of Richmond, Virginia.

National Air Museum—Smithsonian Institution

8. T. S. C. Lowe and his helpers posing for picture during Peninsular Campaign.

National Air Museum—Smithsonian Institution

9. **Balloon** making at the Orléans-Paris railroad station during the Siege of Paris.

10. Launch of the Neptune, first balloon to leave Paris during the Siege, September 23, 1870.

11. Demise of Andrée's Eagle on ice floe, July 14, 1897. Picture taken by Andrée in 1897, but not developed until 1930.

12. Basket and equipment used by Captain H. C. Gray, U. S. Army, in establishing altitude record of over eight miles, greatest height ever attained by an aeronaut in an open balloon basket.

13. Second ascent of Settle (with Fordney) from Akron, Ohio, 1933.

14. "Century of Progress" balloon ready for take-off at Soldiers Field, Chicago, 1933.

15. Doctors Jean and Auguste Piccard inspecting stratosphere balloon gondola, October 1933.

16. Piccard's first gondola being readied for launch.

clear of the ground. Myer was flushed with the success of his idea. He ordered that the horses be made to gallop. The balloon lines lost their slack. The aerial vehicle wheeled from tree to tree in its quickened course. It was stopped once, escaped. It was stopped again, became wedged. The detail urged the horses on, hoping to pull the balloon through. Wise pleaded for the men to stop.

"Out of their way, you fool!" Myer cried. The aeronaut saw the bag gutted by a tree's dead limb. With a huge sigh of exhaustion, the balloon shriveled and dropped to the ground. Field repairs were impossible. "Obviously, your machine can't stand the rigors of wartime use," Myer told Wise.

"Your handling would also prove it could not stand the rigors of peacetime use, either," Wise indignantly retorted. Myer said the aeronaut might be right, and left the wagon and half the detail to help get the aerostat back to Washington for sewing and inflating. The other half of the detail followed Myer to Centreville, where the officer distinguished himself for his bravery. On Wise's return to the capital he learned that instead of a victory at Manassas, the Northern Army had suffered a monstrous defeat.

Within a week of the Manassas holocaust Captain Whipple again requested Wise to bring his balloon to Virginia for reconnaissance work. This time the aeronaut was in full charge of the march. At daybreak a contingent of soldiers took the balloon out of Washington and again to the Aqueduct Bridge for the trip south. As soon as the detail reached the crossing, a swift wind began blowing downstream. The balloon jumped like a frenzied bird. The men could barely hold onto their lines. Seeing that they were handicapped by the military equipment they were carrying, Wise called out to the sergeant, "Have your men put their knapsacks and rifles into the car!" While the command was being carried out, the balloon mooring lines neared the telegraph wires overhead. Soon the lines' rough twisted-hemp strands were rubbing across the wires.

"Take the balloon away!" Wise yelled. The men pulled valiantly but to no avail. The sawing action of the telegraph wires hastened. The lines shredded and parted. The aerostat flew free. It headed for Confederate territory. Wise ordered the men who still had their rifles to fire at the escaping machine. The shots brought others from troops stationed across the river. The last seen of the balloon was its deflation and descent about two miles distant.

Later in the day John Wise met Captain Whipple at Centreville. The officer was highly disappointed at what he called Wise's second failure. He accused the aeronaut of being "irresponsible and perpetrating a fraud on the United States government." Whipple added, "It's almost as though you were in the pay of the Rebels—particularly, at Manassas."

"The balloon part of that disastrous affair," Wise replied, "was just about as good as the fighting part." Two weeks later he resigned from the Army. He received no pay for his services, no allowances for his rations and quarters, no money for building and then rebuilding his balloon.

When John Wise was sixty-five years old, he saw his life's dream about to come true—he was preparing to sail across the Atlantic by balloon. All that remained that August in 1873 was varnishing the bag's skin and finally a favorable weather report.

New York was the take-off point. "To Europe in Sixty Hours," proclaimed one banner headline. "Notice to Mariners—Look Out for the Balloon!" another warned. Sponsors for the trip were the Goodsell brothers, publishers of a young picture newspaper struggling to be heard, the New York *Daily Graphic*. John Wise was the attention-getter the Goodsells were exploiting.

As an assistant to accompany him on the voyage, Wise had chosen Washington H. Donaldson. He was a neophyte aeronaut, young and spirited, best known for performing gymnastics on a trapeze suspended beneath an aerostat. His flight experience totaled two years.

The publishers had agreed to Wise's terms that the vehicle's construction would not be hurried nor would the aerostat be put on public display. They had advertised their good intentions quite early in the program. In a front-page editorial they told their readers, "As soon as the aerostat is ready the party will sail without unnecessary publicity." They piously added, "This voyage is one of scientific inquiry and not for private gain."

A little later they wrote, "The *Daily Graphic* concedes to public pressure to allow witnessing of preliminary inflation of the balloon, which will depart between September first and twelfth, depending on the weather." The strain of virtue had been too much for the Goodsells. They now unabashedly opened the floodgates of commercialism. Any tie-in was acceptable, as long as the price was paid. Wise cried out in anger when he saw a huge banner strung across a downtown Broadway street. In printing a foot high the streamer boasted, *Domestic Sewing Machines* Were Used Exclusively in Putting Together the Transatlantic Balloon.

Over the aeronaut's strenuous objections, including threats to abandon the project, his vehicle was moved from the Brooklyn Navy Yard to a fair site, the Capitaline Grounds in Brooklyn. That the balloon's skin was still wet with varnish did not concern the Goodsells.

"It'll dry in the sun," they told Wise.

"The sun will bake it," Wise explained. "It will lose its elasticity and let the gas through."

"So be it!" The Goodsells had their minds focused on all the people who would be paying fifty cents a head to see the transatlantic balloon. The publishers made a circus of the venture. They advertised, "During the evenings of exhibition of the balloon, illuminated balloons will be sent up provided with fireworks, which will be let off at various altitudes constituting a brilliant pyrotechnical display."

From the 1st of September to the 11th, each day was successively announced to be the take-off time. Each promise was broken, but not before thousands of customers had been beguiled to the grounds in hope of seeing the ascension. Wise could do nothing about the chicanery if he wished to make the trip. Already the Goodsells, as though expecting the aeronaut to rebel, were pointing up the virtues of Donaldson. Wise showed his temper in a note he sent to a friend. "This is the most trying time of my life. A whole season of hope and exertion is to be hung on a mountebank proposition. 'Read the *Graphic* today!' 'Ground and lofty tumbling in the *Graphic* show for four days and four nights!' 'Balloonacies served up at the counter to suit taste!'"

Wise did not quit, though he had sufficient provocation. Donaldson was the one being interviewed and quoted, and nearly every day his opinions stretched for columns in the *Graphic*. He was called "fearless" and "thoroughly accomplished in the aeronautic arts." In contrast, at the height of the Goodsells' dissatisfaction with Wise and his quest for scientific order, the veteran and by this time white-bearded aeronaut was defamed in the newspaper's pages.

"Mr. Wise's course from the outset is marked by incapacity, cowardice, and excessive demands for money." These were the days of relaxed libel laws.

Without notifying Wise the Goodsells on September 12 began inflating his balloon. When the aeronaut arrived, he saw Donaldson standing by and the bag nearly filled. Untrained workmen were manipulating the carefully planned riggings. An ominous bulge began forming above the balloon's equator. Wise turned to Donaldson, who was watching helplessly.

"That bubble wants nothing but a trimming of the ropes."

"It wants something else," said a Goodsell who until that

moment had been unnoticed by Wise. "It wants a balloonist not afraid of his own design."

Wise walked away, but not before prophesying, "In a few minutes it'll tear open—right at the bubble."

Outside the Capitaline Grounds, the aeronaut padded slowly away. He did not pause even after he heard the sound of rending fabric and the serpent hiss of escaping gas.

He returned to Lancaster and told his friends, "I am ready for anything of a practical nature in line with my profession." He added wistfully, "My profession, I wonder if I have one."

In later years there were many aeronauts who owed their lives to John Wise. With thankfulness they affirmed that indeed he did have a profession. For instance, there was Commander Charles Rosendahl. He was in grave danger when the U. S. Navy's airship "Shenandoah" was broken in three parts by high winds over Ohio. Using Wise's free-ballooning techniques, the commander was able to land the section he was on, thereby saving several of the crew.

There was Hugo Eckener. He was commanding the "Graf Zeppelin." Shortly after the start of a transatlantic flight, serious engine trouble developed. With Wise as his mentor, Eckener sailed the ship and her passengers back to land.

Many years after Wise's aborted transatlantic flight, other men in different machines proved his theory of prevailing eastbound air currents to Europe. Perhaps these men were a bit braver because Wise had lived to beat a path for aerial flight.

Wise was nearly seventy-two years old when he and George Burr, a teller at the St. Louis National Bank, ascended from Lindell Park in St. Louis to the tune of "Pinafore" and other lively airs played by the fairground's band. That night the operator of a train depot along the Indiana shore of Lake Michigan exclaimed, "There goes a balloon!" It was in black outline, eclipsing the moon. He watched the vehicle for five minutes before it was lost in the darkness. Neither John Wise nor his aerostat were ever seen again. However, nearly a month after the flight the body of George Burr was found washed ashore near where the balloon had disappeared.

Seven

AN AIR FORCE IS BORN

When John Wise failed in his mission to Manassas, he was replaced by the aeronaut T. S. C. Lowe. There was no official order telling of this change and at the time it is doubtful that anyone except Lowe knew that it had happened.

Several weeks before the Manassas battle, Lowe was in Washington trying to persuade the military to adopt his balloon. He reached Captain Whipple of the Topographical Engineers, who said that John Wise had been given the job of military balloonist. During the interview it came out that Wise had underbid Lowe by $200 on the price of the balloon. The captain asked Lowe if he would be willing to help Wise operate the machine.

"This idea of balloon reconnaissance, if it works, mind you, could be the biggest thing we ever thought of," said the officer.

The smugness of the man's remark was not lost upon Lowe, who could have easily pointed out the military use of balloons in the days of the French Revolution. At the moment, though, he was shocked by the fact of Wise's appointment. Why Lowe disliked his older contemporary has never been made clear. Perhaps it was envy at Wise's established aeronautical reputation or perhaps it was snobbishness induced by what Lowe called Wise's "unscientific" methods. Whatever the cause, these sentiments were one of the rare instances of pettiness on Lowe's part. Thus, the officer's suggestion was sharply answered.

"I am unwilling, sir, to expose my life and reputation in a machine made by a person in whom I have no confidence. He has not the least idea of the requirements of military ballooning nor the gift of invention which will make it possible for me to achieve success. I tell you this not out of boast but merely to be informative." In this way the conference ended, with Lowe feeling imposed upon, and with Whipple feeling that he had seen the last of Lowe.

Whipple returned to his post at Centreville, Virginia. Meanwhile, a Confederate Army led by General Pierre Beauregard was being brought together at Manassas Junction, a point less than thirty miles outside of Washington. At the capital public pressure demanded that the Rebels be attacked. Then, "On to Richmond!" was the cry. Soon, 35,000 Union troops under General Irvin McDowell left Washington for a showdown fight with their enemy.

Captain Whipple waited for Wise to show up at Centreville. After two weeks the officer's patience had worn thin. He wired Lowe to bring his balloon to Virginia. After reading the message Lowe blithely assumed that Wise had defaulted in his errand as military balloonist. Whipple said nothing about giving Lowe any Army support. Thus it fell upon him to hire his own helpers and to procure gas-generating facilities.

On the night before the Manassas battle Lowe was in the Columbian Armory inflating his balloon. To his amazement, Wise walked in. He was accompanied by an Army detail hauling a packed balloon and basket. Each man proclaimed himself military balloonist and demanded access to the inflating equipment. The issue was settled by the gas-company representative. "Captain Whipple told me to lend Professor Wise all possible assistance. He said nothing about you, Mr. Lowe."

The next day Lowe learned that his rival's balloon had exploded on its way to Centreville. There was no time to lose. He hurriedly recalled his assistants, filled his balloon without fear of interruption, and set off for the front.

His full name was Thaddeus Sobieski Constantine Lowe, though for economy he signed his papers T. S. C. Lowe. For a while, he told people that the "C" stood for "Carlincourt." He had adopted the sobriquet on his wife's advice. She felt that the name was more distinguished than his baptismal one. However, his father and brother thought the change so foolish that the aeronaut dropped the affectation after only a few years' use.

Lowe was a big-boned, broad-shouldered man, an inch over six feet tall. Yet, surprisingly for one so powerfully built, his skin was almost as delicate and unblemished as porcelain. His eyes were large and deep-set and strikingly blue. He had jet-black hair and a full mustache that swept upward after passing the points of his lips. One of his daughters said in later years, "He was by far the handsomest man I ever knew."

When he was still a boy, he lived at Jefferson Mills, New Hampshire. He was in his teens when one day a traveling magician came to town. In the schoolhouse that evening the entertainer showed the neighbors some tricks and, for novelty, several chemical experiments. Thaddeus was picked from the audience to help. He performed so well that the magician hired the boy as an apprentice. By the time the association was six months old most of the magician's tricks had been replaced by scientific demonstrations, all of which Lowe had devised. At the end of the first year the boy was master of his own show.

A GREAT EXPERIMENT ILLUSTRATING
THE REPEAL OF THE LAW OF GRAVITY.

Lowe started his performance by dipping a pipe into a soapy solution and then blowing bubbles. Eventually, they all floated down to the floor. His climax involved connecting the pipe to a hydrogen generator. He explained that he was using a different kind of air, a type that worked against gravity. Instead of falling, the bubbles this time rose to the ceiling, to the amazement and applause of the spectators.

Throughout his life he remembered with pleasure one particular evening. This was in the spring of 1854 and he was twenty-two years old. He was mingling with his audience as he always did before a performance, when he spoke to a young and pretty girl seated alone in the front row. Her name was Leontine Gachon. Lowe learned that she was nineteen years old and had come from France. Her father had been bodyguard to King Louis Philippe, but had fled to America with his family during the revolution of 1848.

After the show Lowe saw Leontine to her home and met her father. One week later the entertainer married her. She was a remarkable woman, becoming in her middle years a noted scholar in geology and mineralogy. She was also a remarkable wife, fulfilling her husband's wish for a large family by giving him ten children.

The hydrogen-bubble experiments had a meaning for Lowe far beyond that of showmanship. He saw the delicate spheres as balloons in miniature, whose levitating action he hoped some day to build into a machine that would carry him over oceans. This dream he had in common with John Wise. When Lowe was twenty-six years old, he designed and built his own balloon and set himself a year to become expert in its piloting. To meet expenses, he vol-

unteered to ascend at any county fair or circus that wanted
him. In the winter when engagements were few, he taught
his wife and children the theory and practice of aerostatics.
At the end of a year's time to the day, he announced to a
group of Philadelphia financiers that he was now prepared
to make a transatlantic crossing. A few months previously
John Wise had prepared their minds for such a feat by his
St. Louis to New York record-breaking trip. Still, the audac-
ity of Lowe's venture made the men hesitate.

"Do you know Professor Joseph Henry," asked one of
them, "Secretary of Smithsonian Institution?"

Lowe said he certainly knew of the man and of his high
standing in the scientific community. "If you wish, I would
be glad to confer with him."

At Lowe's meeting with Professor Henry the Smithsonian
scientist said, "If I were to tell people that a strange
celestial body were approaching earth and within a matter
of weeks would destroy our planet, they would believe me.
It would be a fact and could be checked. But if I were to
tell them that a balloon could be flown across the Atlantic
Ocean, it would be only my conjecture and they would not
be convinced, particularly since money is involved, until
the trip was accomplished. Yet, partial proof is better than
none. I suggest you take your machine to some spot in the
west, say Cincinnati. Then fly yourself to the east. By all
means start when conditions are apparently the worst for
you! Go aloft when the ground winds are running to the
west! You will still have your upper winds to carry you
back east."

Lowe was ready to start in early April of 1859. He tied
his balloon down in Cincinnati's public square. Only clear
weather was wanted for the aerostat to be sent aloft. It
was awhile in coming. Rain and wind squalls characteristic
of that time of year and location prevailed.

The political stress between North and South was growing more intense. Confederate troops had already fired on

Fort Sumter in Charleston harbor, forcing its garrison to
surrender. Lincoln was calling for a militia of 75,000 to put
down what was being termed "an insurrection." On April
17, five days after Fort Sumter's fall, Virginia troops seized
Harpers Ferry Arsenal and the Norfolk Navy Yard, and
began arming themselves. Then, countering an announcement of privateering by the South, President Lincoln proclaimed a blockade of the Confederacy from South Carolina to Texas.

On the evening of April 19 Thaddeus Lowe was attend-
ing a banquet given in his honor by Murat Halstead, editor
of the Cincinnati *Commercial.* The host arrived after the
first course had been served. "You'd better start praying
that you go north first and then east," the editor warned
Lowe. "Well to the north. The capital is hemmed in by
rebellion. In Baltimore, Massachusetts recruits are right now
having to fight their way down to Washington. There are
killings, heaven knows how many. The secessionists may
even win control in Maryland."

Midnight had barely passed when a messenger ran into
the hall to tell Lowe that the skies had cleared and that a
strong wind was blowing to the west.

"I'll leave in a minute," said Lowe. "Tell my assistant to
start the inflation!"

"He already has," said the messenger.

Lowe thrust half a turkey and a bottle of wine into a
folded tablecloth. "My provisions," he explained. "I'll need
some coffee, too." Halstead grabbed a steaming jug from
the nearest table, and then accompanied Lowe to an
awaiting carriage. "I'll meet you at the field," Halstead
said, "wait for me!" and he ran off.

An hour later the editor appeared at the balloon site.
Under his arm he carried a sheaf of the *Commercial* still
wet from printing ink. It told the story and time of Lowe's
departure. "Be gone quickly, or you'll make a liar of me!"
said the editor, "and Godspeed!"

The balloon was off. The ground wind carried it westward across the Ohio River. The aeronaut dumped ballast overboard in the hope that altitude would give him the eastbound wind he was seeking. As he ascended, the night air became colder and he gained little protection from the tall silk hat and formal frock coat that he was still wearing. At an altitude of 7000 feet the balloon changed its course, first to the east and then to the southeast. The temperature dropped below freezing, generating a miniature snowstorm within the balloon as the water vapor in the gas began solidifying. The snow turned to ice which shot out through the balloon's neck to beat a thunderous tattoo on the top of Lowe's hat. Soon the annoyance was over. Relieved of some weight, the vehicle rose to an altitude of three miles. It remained at this height during most of the trip. Noontime the next day the aerostat was hovering over a cleared field, which lay near a small village. Lowe released some gas for his descent. His car plopped down near a roost of chickens. Probably taking him for some new species of hawk, the fowl scattered hysterically with great cackling and screeching.

What the aeronaut had taken to be a village turned out to be a dozen weathered wooden shacks lining a gutted dirt road. A group of the inhabitants cautiously approached the balloon. There was no color line drawn here. Whites and Negroes were in the ranks, with almost all of them shouldering a shotgun. Their clothes were in tatters and their hair matted by a season's dirt. For the moment, Lowe was more concerned with steadying the car so that he could fully deflate the balloon than he was with the social standing of the community. "You there," he cried, motioning to one of the less repulsive of the men, "give me a hand!" Not a soul moved even though Lowe looked at each man in turn. He was about to empty the balloon himself when a young white woman who stood at least a head taller than any of the men pushed her way through the gawkers to

Lowe's side. She smiled at him and said, "Most of the white men out there are cowards. All the brave ones of the neighborhood have gone to war." She looked over her shoulder with contempt and then turned back to the aeronaut. "Can I help you?"

"Just hold down the side of the car while I get at this valve," Lowe answered appreciatively. He reached up and pulled heavily on the actuating rope. As soon as the balloon began collapsing, the group of onlookers ambled to the side of the car, but none dared lay a hand on it.

"He's a devil," whispered one of the Negroes. "He's come right out of the earth into the sky and now he's fixin' to stay on earth." The crowd began murmuring among themselves and several wondered out loud what would happen to a devil if you filled him full of buckshot.

When the balloon was nearly packed in the car, the men became braver and at the same time more aggressive. To forestall their attacking him and to prove he was human, the aeronaut took from his basket a small cupcake and put it to his mouth. "See! I eat food, just as you do." He choked on a morsel of the cupcake, and he added, ". . . and I cough, too, just as you do."

The men fingered their guns. One of the more outspoken peered into the car and pointed at a bottle. "What ya got there?"

Lowe picked up the narrow-necked container the man indicated. He showed it around. "You drink coffee," he said somewhat impatiently, "well so do I," and he pulled out the stopper while tipping the bottle to let the liquid flow. It was still frozen solid, so Lowe broke the bottle open and held up the mold. This was greeted by a shrill cry from another of the Negroes. "You sure must be the devil, else how could you get dat shape through dat little hole?" There was an immediate conference to decide whether it would be better to shoot him on the spot or hang him from the tree. Before the men could get down to voting, Lowe grabbed a

large Colt revolver from inside the car. It was a weapon his
wife made him carry because her youthful experiences in a
revolution-torn France never freed her from a fear of unpro-
voked attack. With stage-like bravado Lowe swung the gun
around until it pointed at the man he thought was the
ringleader, and said, "The first one who takes a step toward
me will descend into eternity far quicker than I did into
your fields. But if you listen to reason I will accompany
you to your county seat and let the officials there judge my
case. Now which shall it be?"

The girl spoke out. "If any of you is man enough to kill
him why ain't you up north fighting the damn Yankees?"
She put her hand out for Lowe's gun, which he gave her,
and addressed the men again. "We'll be off to Unionville
as fast as you can pack that thing on a wagon," and she
nodded her head toward the balloon and car.

The men did as they were told, while Lowe remarked how
much he admired her courage. "One question, though," he
said. "What state am I in?" She looked at him as though
wondering whether saving his life had been worthwhile
after all. "Virginia." The current had carried him to the
coast even though a contrary wind had been blowing across
the earth.

Two hours later a tall girl, a man wearing a high hat and
a frock coat, and a group of field hands presented themselves to the hotelkeeper at Unionville. Since at one time
he had been a town official, the men had decided that
his opinion regarding the prisoner would be the one they
would accept. When they arrived, explanations were not
needed. The hotelkeeper grabbed Lowe's hand and shook
it excitedly. He said his name was Black, Mr. Black, and
didn't Professor Lowe remember taking him up in a balloon in Charleston just about a year ago. "You should
remember, you charged me five dollars," said Mr. Black.
"And it was worth every penny of it," he told the group.
"You should be honored. We have a very famous scientist

with us." Lowe's captors did not budge, but rather stared
at the balloonist as they might have at Jefferson Davis if
he had paid them a visit. Even the girl regarded Lowe with
increased respect. The aeronaut returned the compliment
by ordering a feast for all, and the next day he set off for
Columbia, South Carolina, en route to Washington or Cincinnati, whichever had train service from the South.

In Columbia he was arrested as a Yankee spy and im-
prisoned in the local jail because he was carrying an abo-
litionist paper, the Cincinnati *Commercial*. The local newspaper ran his story on the front page. This was fortunate
because it brought to his assistance the president and several members of the faculty of South Carolina College.

"He's no more spy than I am," the college president told
the mayor. "He's an aeronaut, a balloonist, and it was the
wind that carried him to us." Whereupon the mayor wrote,

This is to certify that Professor T. S. C. Lowe who fell acci-
dentally in our midst, is a gentleman of integrity and high scientific attainments. I bespeak for him the courtesies of all with
whom he may come in contact, and trust that this letter, to
which I have affixed the seal of the City of Columbia, South
Carolina, will answer as a passport for him through the Confederate States of North America.

With a flourish the official signed his name, *W. H.
Boatwright*, and appended the date, *April 22, 1861*. Four
days later Lowe was in Cincinnati and in conversation with
Murat Halstead.

"I tell you, Halstead, it's no minor uprising going on
down there," Lowe said strongly. "I've just been through
there, from Columbia to Cincinnati, and there's not a town
or a village that isn't prepared for war. I passed thousands
of their recruits and they're all being armed and readying
themselves to march. This is a civil war with all its trap-
pings. Tents are being pitched and armaments stacked at

every Southern railroad station. Brass bands are playing and like the Pied Piper of Hamelin, are luring more men into the ranks. Do you think they're playing 'Yankee Doodle' or 'Hail Columbia?' Not on your life! They call themselves a free nation and their battle hymn is 'Dixie.'"

"Why are you telling me this?" the editor asked. "I'm on your side. If you want to fight, go ahead and do it, and with my blessings."

"I don't want to fight, especially the South, but if I have to I will, and I want more than your blessings," said Lowe. "I want your help to convince the military that the balloon is more than a piece of showman's art but rather is a scientific instrument that can shorten the war. With it we'll have an observation post that can get in one hour's ascension more intelligence than a score of scouts can get in a score of days. But why go on, you know this as well as I do. What I want you to tell me is whom to see and when I can see him."

"There is only one man," the editor quietly said, "the President—and he's expecting you. I anticipated your request."

Confederate troops were already in Manassas Junction when Lowe and his family reached Washington. Thus it was several days before Lincoln was able to spare time for the aeronaut. When he did it was to ask Lowe for a demonstration of his art. For this purpose, a flight was to be made from the White House lawn.

The night before the event Lowe's wife said to him, "The President doesn't want to see you simply go up in a balloon. Even John Wise could do that. What Lincoln really wants is to see something special, something to bring out the balloon's usefulness in war. Perhaps you could have men shoot muskets from it, or drop shells as in a bombardment. The President must be impressed by your imagination." As an afterthought she suggested, "Build a signal fire in the car if you must, but please do something different."

Her signal-fire jest took a practical turn. By noontime the next day Lowe had strung a communications line from the White House to a telegraph key installed in the aerostat. Late afternoon saw the circuit being checked out and the balloon inflated. The time for the ascent came. Lowe bowed graciously to the President and his guests, which included members of the Cabinet and high-ranking Army officers. Ballast was discharged and the ropes holding the balloon were loosened. The vehicle began a slow rise. Sluggish as it was, the telegrapher on board with Lowe had a busy time playing out his wire fast enough. At an altitude of 500 feet Lowe signaled for tie-down. The telegrapher tested his key and nodded he was ready.

"To the President of the United States," dictated Lowe. "From this point of observation we command an extent of country nearly fifty miles in diameter. We could telegraph to the headquarters of the Army or to the White House, giving practically a map of the enemy's position. I have the pleasure of sending you this first telegraph ever dispatched from an aerial station, and acknowledging my debt to you for your encouragement. We hope we have demonstrated how the science of aeronautics can serve our country."

The ground tug on a balloon rope indicated that the message had been received. Even without this signal the excitement of his helpers and the cheerful hand wave from Lincoln would have told Lowe of his success. The President insisted that the aeronaut spend the night at the White House so that more could be learned about the uses of this new science. During supper the men discussed the possibility of a balloon observer directing artillery fire against an enemy, unseen by ground posts. Lowe proposed other uses, such as launching a balloon from a ship out of range of enemy guns, to which Lincoln added some ideas of his own. It was well past midnight before the men retired.

Back home the next morning Lowe showed his wife a sealed envelope bearing a White House imprint. It was addressed to Lieutenant General Winfield Scott. "This is it," said Lowe, waving his arms in excitement, "the start of the Aeronautic Corps of the Army of the United States."

Lincoln's letter was not the *open sesame* that the aeronaut expected it to be. Repeated attempts to see Scott were turned back by the general's aide. A lower-echelon try brought him to Captain Whipple. It was at this meeting that Lowe learned that the Army's choice for a balloonist was John Wise. More days of fruitless anteroom waiting at Army headquarters discouraged Lowe to the point where he told his wife, "They won't listen to their President, so what hope have I? Let's pack our things and leave!"

"*Jamais!*" she cried, reverting to French in anger. Then she pensively tongued her lower lip. "Thaddeus, I have an idea. Even if by some miracle Wise does get his balloon up, the Army will still have need for more than one. There will be many battlefields. Let's fill our balloon and offer it to whatever commander can make use of it!"

Lowe smiled, and though he tried hard not to be patronizing, he was. "Dear, there are rules and regulations that the military must abide by. Since our balloon has no official sanction, it will not be used despite the need." He stopped and reconsidered. His voice became sprightly, not a bit of deprecation in it. "You may be right. The air is still free. If I wish to do a little sight-seeing, nobody can prevent me. And if I see anything of value, I'm sure the military will be as eager to talk to me as I will be to talk to them." He patted her head in appreciation. "You always were the bright one in this family. Let me have a few hours to think your thought through!" He needed only one of them. A message from Captain Whipple told the aeronaut to report with his balloon to Army headquarters in Centreville, Virginia.

On his first attempt to fill his balloon at the Columbian Armory, Lowe was frustrated by the sudden appearance of John Wise. The next day the first battle of Manassas was

fought. Late that same night Lowe went back to the Armory
and filled his balloon. Then with the help of his wife and
several hired assistants he took his machine to Falls Church,
Virginia, a point ten miles west of Washington. Exhausted
by their trip, the group exerted squatters' rights on a de-
serted farmhouse and went to sleep.

They awoke early the next morning in the midst of a
driving rain, which was thickening the roads with mud.
They saw the remnants of McDowell's Army trudging back
to Washington. As the morning wore on, the number of
soldiers passing grew less and their condition more pitiful.
Weakened by their wounds, many of the men fell by the
roadside. The civilians helped as much as their limited supplies and strength would let them, but an Army of mercy
rather than half a dozen individuals was needed. Confederate troops were said to be right behind and it was ru-
mored they would be in Washington that night. By late
afternoon the pickets who had been supporting the Union
forces' rear guard went by the farmhouse. After they passed
there was not a company of Union soldiers left between
Lowe and the Confederate Army.

In the face of what were now high winds and rain the
balloon party began towing their precious cargo on a retreat course to Fort Cocoran, an Army post on the Virginia
side of the Aqueduct Bridge. Only dedication and inspiration could have carried the party safely through that
night. The dedication came from Thaddeus Lowe, who
worked harder than did the horses pulling his wagon of
supplies. The inspiration came from Leontine Lowe, who
would not yield her place when it came her turn to drive
the wagon or slack a rig line or bear part of the wagon's
weight when a smashed wheel was being replaced. Tired,
hungry, wet, dirty, and proud, the party staggered into
Fort Cocoran the next afternoon with their balloon bouncing jauntily overhead. The commanding officer grabbed
Lowe's coat lapels and quizzed him about the Confederate

Army. "Every scout I send out comes back with a different tale," he complained. "Tell me, is Beauregard on his way to Washington?"

"I don't know, sir," said Lowe.

"I didn't expect you would. But maybe in that contrivance of yours you can do something about finding out," the officer said, and then dismissed the notion by walking away.

"When it clears, I'll go up," Lowe yelled after him. The man was gone and the aeronaut turned to his wife. "I think I was given an assignment."

Infected by the panic of McDowell's fleeing troops, the soldiers of the fort trembled in fear at the advance of the Southern Army. Rumor said that the Rebels were irrepressible after the Manassas victory. In the mud flats across the river the capital lay almost defenseless. General Scott was trying to raise troops to protect the city but all he could find were untrained volunteers and scared recruits.

Lowe stood in despair as the rain kept falling. He would go up and he would learn the truth, he told his wife, and he would be believed, but only if the sky would clear up. On the dawn of his second morning at the fort the winds slowed down and the rains ceased. When the clouds began parting, Lowe made a captive flight to an altitude of several hundred feet. From this small height his view was blocked by rolling hills and a stagnant ground haze. He cut the vehicle free. It floated up three miles, where it fell in with a wind that took him over Manassas Junction. Through his field glasses Lowe saw medical details clearing the area of dead and wounded even though three days had passed since the battle had been fought. Directly below him were so many thousands of Confederate tents that instead of counting them the aeronaut simply noted in his log that "a sizable Confederate force is at Manassas and another is encamped several miles to its east." He spotted two infantry regiments in the Centreville area, seemingly on a mopping-up mission.

Since there were no active Union troops around, they didn't have much to do. Lowe wrote that he could see no hostile Army preparing for a march on the capital. Instead, he saw the Southern troops eating, sleeping, and tending to their injuries.

What mystified Lowe was that none of the thousands of soldiers below him had the slightest idea that they were being observed. They recognized Lowe's existence only when he dropped ballast for an ascent. Then they rushed for their muskets and opened fire, but the gesture was futile. It was like throwing pebbles at a soaring eagle. The aerostat reached a west wind and began the return trip. Behind the Union lines, McDowell's troops opened fire on him.

"Hold off!" he cried.

"Show your colors!" they answered. He had no flag so he threw out his shoes, because he had no ballast either. He ascended out of range of his comrades' guns. He attempted a landing in an open field that he hoped was free from friend and foe. A gust of wind whipped his aerostat against a lone tree. Lowe ducked to avoid an onrushing branch but not soon enough. It hit him above his ear and knocked him senseless. A second branch opened the balloon and ended the day's flight.

From a high spot in the fort Lowe's wife had been watching her husband's flight through field glasses. After she saw him fall behind what she knew were Confederate lines she made plans for his rescue. From a nearby farmer she borrowed a wagon and a horse, and from his wife she bought some clothes. Then she loaded the wagon with whatever household goods she could find, which included a rocking chair from the commanding officer. She told him, "Your men would never get past the first Rebel pickets." In a mock Southern accent she added, "Anyway sir, who would want to bother a daughter of the Confederacy who comes a-totin' her belongings to the side of Jeff Davis and Robert E. Lee?" She found the troops who had fired upon her husband.

They returned the aeronaut's shoes with the suggestion that resoling would make them lethal.

"Would you show me where he fell?" she asked.

One of the men, his face young but gray with fatigue, pointed a finger toward the south. "We're not brave any more," he replied to her quizzical look.

By nightfall she found the clearing where her husband had come down. Rays from her lantern highlighted his aerostat, tilted at an angle, half on, half off a hummock. The balloon was neatly packed inside the basket. As she bent over to examine the vehicle, she heard a noise behind her and the soft padding of feet coming toward her. Unhurriedly, she climbed back into her wagon because she had recognized a familiar form.

In a moment a voice whispered, "Aren't you Mrs. Lowe, the wife of that famous aeronaut, Thaddeus Lowe?"

She answered casually, "Yes I am, sir, but I'll soon be his widow unless he gets into this wagon."

Her husband appeared out of the darkness. Above his left eye a large lump marked where the tree branch had struck him, giving him a fierce look.

"Didn't they have any soldiers to send?" he asked angrily. "Did you have to risk your life coming for me?"

"Is there a better cause?" she replied. "Now hurry, do!" She jumped from the wagon. "I'll help with the basket."

"I packed it and I'll drag it," said Lowe. "You just look neat and clean for the Rebels." Soon the aeronaut and his machine were hidden under a tarpaulin laid across the back of the wagon.

Twice they were stopped by Confederate troops. The soldiers were polite and helpful, even turning the wagon around because, "Ma'am, you're headed in the direction of Yankee territory." Then back down the road the woman's wagon would clatter; and then when out of sight of her helpers, onto a field to circle around.

It was after midnight when they drove their wagon

through the gates of Fort Cocoran. Thaddeus Lowe went immediately to the commander to make his report. It was accepted almost as a miracle would have been. "The Rebels are not coming!" Runners and telegraph operators were summoned and told to give out the news. For the first time since he had arrived, the aeronaut heard singing in the barracks.

Evening of the next day Lowe was seated at an old table in the President's workroom at the White House. After telling what he had seen at Manassas, Lowe begged the President to give an aeronautic corps official standing in the Army. "Without it I'm as apt to be shot down by Union forces as by the Rebels." Lincoln asked how he had made out with General Scott.

"I know that man's anteroom better than I know my own home," Lowe said in despair. "When I arrive, the general's either out or too busy to be disturbed."

Lincoln rose from his chair. He observed for his companion that if McDowell had had a balloon at Manassas, the results of that battle might have been different. "Professor, I wish you would try to confer with General Scott again, at once, and let me know what happens." He took out a personal card and scribbled a note on it. "Here, give him this!"

There was no mistaking the message: "Will Lt.-General Scott please see Professor Lowe once more about his balloon?" This was an order.

First thing the next morning Lowe handed the President's card to Scott's orderly. The man returned to say that the general was in conference. "When will he be out?" Lowe asked sharply. The orderly shrugged his shoulders. The general was engaged when Lowe returned the second time; and the third time the man was at lunch. "Where does he have lunch?" Lowe asked. The orderly was going out for his and did not answer. When Lowe made his fourth call, the general was said to be asleep. The aeronaut's anger was feverish. When he reached the White House, he was breathing hard from his haste. He was admitted to the President's study, where he told his story. He ended by observing, "It's the rankest bit of insubordination I've ever heard of." Yet the President seemed not in the least disturbed. He reached for his fuzzy stovepipe hat and bade the aeronaut to come along and find out what was the matter with Old Fuss'n Feathers.

The sentry cried out, "The President!" In General Scott's anteroom the orderly snapped to attention. Without knocking he threw open the general's office door. President Lincoln and Thaddeus Lowe confronted the commander of the Federal forces. A more startled man the aeronaut had never seen. Lincoln said, "General, this is my friend Professor Lowe, who is organizing an aeronautic corps for the Army, and is to be its chief. I wish you would facilitate his work in every way, and give him appropriate letters to the proper authorities with instructions for them to give him all the necessary things to equip his branch of the service in land and water."

The general was slavish in his agreement. He saw great possibilities for balloons, particularly for observation and mapping work. "For this reason," he said, "I am attaching Lowe and his equipment to the Topographical Engineers. You, Professor, are now chief of the aeronautic corps of the United States Army."

Captain Whipple was put in charge of Lowe's operations. This was the officer who earlier had recommended that Lowe help John Wise in his ballooning activities. For this suggestion, Lowe was most unappreciative. Still, he had to work with the captain, if he wanted to work at all. Lowe was subordinate to any officer who cared to give him a command. True, though the aeronautic corps now had the sanction of the Army Chief of Staff, it had been given no official status. Lowe was therefore still a civilian. Even if he did get Army volunteers to help him, he would either

have to give his orders to the men through a line officer
or maintain discipline by the force of his own personality.
Lowe had to be satisfied with this arrangement if he wanted
to prove to the military the value of an organized and
recognized balloon corps.

Lowe needed a detail of men to help him transport and
service his aerostat. Alas, the Topographical Engineers had
no enlisted men. Everybody was an officer, that is, everybody but the Professor. He gave the problem to Captain
Whipple, who in turn passed it on to General McDowell's
adjutant. The request for help was granted but it was
stipulated that the needed men should come from the Topographical Engineers. Whereupon Whipple wrote out a status
report and Lowe continued using his civilian aides.

An opportunity for an early test of his balloon came
when Lowe received a telegram from Whipple. It instructed
the aeronaut to leave Washington within the next few hours
and to be in Virginia the following day. The captain had
been able to arrange for a temporary ground crew of
twenty men. A few miles out of the city a flash summer
storm burst upon the party. Anxiously, Lowe tried to keep
his balloon under control. Screaming so that his voice could
be heard above the wind, Lowe ordered the men to fill the
car with stones. The soldiers were raw recruits, most of
whom had never seen a balloon before. Several let go of
their lines to obey. The balloon momentarily jumped free.
To save it, even though it cost him the mission, Lowe
emptied the bag of its gas. When news of the event was
relayed to Whipple, it had lost much in fact and gained
much in drama. He was told that the vehicle had ascended
several hundred feet with three recruits swinging from its
ropes. Only by the grace of God were the men saved because
the balloon had burst and then settled back to earth. The
captain wrote his recommendations to Army headquarters.
"Any further operations with war balloons must be given
up. They have proved to be more trouble and expense than

they are worth, and I have yet to see one come when it is needed."

The aeronaut took his troubles to Professor Henry, who immediately wrote a letter to Captain Whipple's superior. After a wait of a few days Lowe received a message from Whipple. The aeronaut was told to construct a war balloon of the best India silk available. He was further instructed that the riggings and cordage were to be fashioned from Irish linen and the sewing done by the finest artisans in Washington. Whipple's anguish must have been strong as he wrote out the details: "The United States wants the balloon to be of 25,000 cubic feet capacity. The government will pay for its construction. We will also pay you $30 per day each day the balloon is in use for reconnaissance on the Virginia side of the Potomac."

Lowe replied by return messenger that the balloon would be ready by the end of August, then three weeks distant. He added that he could not accept the thirty dollars a day. He reasoned, but did not put this in his letter, that he would not last long in an Army where he got more pay than did its major generals. He suggested a lesser fee of ten dollars a day, and this figure was agreed upon.

It was relatively quiet along all fronts in the late summer of 1861. During this time the first war balloon built by the United States floated over the Potomac area. While the aerostat was aloft, its observer took notes and drew maps of whatever military conditions he thought important. Before long, Lowe acquired the reputation of being the most fired-upon man in the Union Army. When the Confederate troops first started sniping at the balloon, they had hopes of hitting it. They soon learned that unless they trained their sights on the vehicle either when it was taking off or landing, it would rise out of range. On one sweltering hot afternoon when the earth's sweat boiled up to Lowe even at at a 500-foot altitude and his clothes stuck to him like damp paper, he closed his log book early and began his descent. Meanwhile, a sentry was making his rounds of the camp. He held his nose while skirting a large open cesspool into which the post's sewage was passed and the garbage dumped. He wondered how close to this filth his duty required that he walk. Suddenly, a shell intended for Lowe's balloon landed in the middle of the hole and exploded. The vile wastes scattered in all directions, burying the sentry under untold gallons of muck. He arose shrieking, shaking, and vomiting; and his appetite was gone for a week.

Toward the end of September an incident occurred which, given a slightly different outcome, might have shortened the war considerably. For several days Lowe had been watching a growing force of Confederate soldiers gathering at Falls Church. However, because of the hilly terrain, the batteries at Fort Cocoran could not see their target and under usual conditions would never have attempted a barrage. Conditions, though, were far from usual when Lowe was there. After devising a system of flag signals that would tell the gunnery officers the range and direction of their shells, he took to the air. The first shots were low and to the right. Lowe signaled corrections. The next shots were wide of the mark, to the left and still far short. New corrections were given. By the sixth round the artillery were dropping their missiles on target. Confederate soldiers scurried around like ants swarming out of a torn anthill. Many took haven in a wooded area to which point Lowe redirected the fire. Years later, through the published journal of a Southern general, Lowe learned that one of the clusters of men he was trying to destroy was a group brought together to plan high strategy for the South. President Davis was there and General Lee and several field commanders. The meeting had barely started, after being interrupted at the camp grounds, when a shell burst only yards away from them. An aide and several horses were killed. A second shell passed what seemed only feet above their heads. A third smashed into the ground close by, showering President Davis with so much dirt that his colleagues feared he had been hit. As it was, he had only minor scratches; and the planning session was free to continue its work of promoting the war.

Every man who saw Lowe perform that day knew his value to the Army. The story of the balloon-directed bombardment was passed along from soldier to soldier to show how technology was coming to the aid of the Federal forces. The direct result of this publicity was an order from the Secretary of War commanding the aeronaut to build four additional balloons. He was also told to construct portable inflating equipment that could follow the vehicles on the battlefield. It was a curious state of affairs for Lowe, a civilian, to be "commanded" to do something. No matter, this was the chance he had been waiting for, to put a balloon on every active front. What gave him even greater joy was that the gas-generating equipment he would build would make his balloons available for observation nearly any time a commander desired and weather permitted.

Lowe called upon his father to help in this enterprise. While the balloons were being manufactured, one of the two men was always present to supervise. Lowe completely outfitted his aerostats, including furnishing a trained aeronaut for each one. When a high Army officer said he would prefer soldiers to fly the balloons, Lowe told him, "I would rather cut the balloons to shreds myself than have them worried to death by inexperienced men." This sentiment was backed by the Army's new military chief, General George McClellan, who said that Lowe was to be completely responsible for the balloons, even down to the men who manned them. Within several months the son and his father had the aeronautic corps so well organized that any commander could have a balloon at his post within a day's notice.

When McClellan asked Thaddeus Lowe to make a series

of balloon observations of the shores of the Potomac, the
aeronaut conceived of an aircraft carrier, a seagoing vessel
whose only mission would be to act as a platform for an
aerial machine. Taking the general's letter as authority,
Lowe commandeered the steamship *George Washington
Parke Custis*, which had been deprived of its run between
Washington and Mount Vernon when the war broke out.
Across the forward part of the ship's hull he erected a
thick plank platform. This was to be the launching area.
The center of the deck he reserved for stowing the balloon
and its car. Gas-generating supplies were placed in the
stern and the tank for making the gases in the bow. When
the work was finished, the *George Washington Parke Custis*
sailed slowly down the Potomac, while over the ship in a
bobbing aerostat stood Lowe making his observations. On
a large map in front of him he spotted the artillery batteries
he saw during the day and the campfires he saw at night.
As fast as he gathered the intelligence, he lowered it to
shipboard, where it was taken by special messengers to
McClellan. The general learned that Confederate forces
were weak along the river and that there was only little
danger in sailing transports down it. This was to be the first
maneuver in the Peninsular Campaign.

In the spring of 1862 the brazen Yankee plan began to
unfold. There was a waterway to the door of the Confederate capital. It ran southward from Washington down the
Potomac for fifty miles and then flowed to the southeast
for seventy-five miles. Here the Potomac emptied into
Chesapeake Bay. The path to Richmond followed the Chesapeake southward for seventy miles. At this point, to the
east, the bay opened into the Atlantic Ocean; and across
to the west the Chesapeake waters washed a peninsula
bounded by two rivers, the York and the James. At the
peninsula's tip was Fort Monroe, held by the Union; and
seventy-five miles up the peninsula lay Richmond. From
Washington the overland distance to Richmond was 110

miles, each one of which could be expected to be strewn with dead Union troops if a direct march were tried. McCellan took the route of least resistance. He began shipping the Army of the Potomac on river boats, tugs, and whatever watercraft he could find. In this manner 121,000 men, 14,000 animals, and scores of tons of provisions and equipment loaded on 400 vessels made their way down the inland water route to Fort Monroe. It was a maneuver that would pierce the heart of the Southland.

When the first wave of the Federal Army disembarked, they were already savoring the taste of Southern fried chicken. Their ardor was dampened after a week's rain. Mud roads appeared where dry ones had been expected. The throats and bodies of the men were worn raw with urging stubborn mules and shouldering heavy wagons over the oozing ground. A story was told about a lieutenant who had requested a mule from the quartermaster to replace the one he had lost by drowning in the road.

McClellan's forces trudged twenty miles up the peninsula, where they were brought to an abrupt halt. Confederate earthworks were stretched completely across the land, from the York River on the right to the Warwick River, a tributary of the James, on the left. Yawning wide at the Union troops were the mouths of scores of naval guns that the Southerners had captured from the Norfolk Navy Yard the year before. The South's chief defenses seemed to be centered at Yorktown, the York River area known for Cornwallis' surrender eighty years earlier. General McClellan had to know how strong the Rebel defense really was before he would risk a battle. Scouts took to the woods for the intelligence needed and Lowe to the sky. He logged the encampments he saw and the locations of artillery. He also tried to surmise the number of troops in the area, but the enemy was so much on the move that this was difficult to do. It would have been a useless notation anyway, because McClellan had asked for facts, not estimates or interpretation. These the general wished to make for himself after going over all the data from all sources. His conclusion was that a Confederate Army was present in strength. A direct attack would be too risky to make. McClellan decided to wait for more reinforcements.

In truth, the opposing Army was woefully weak. Confederate General John Magruder had no more than 12,000 men. These were ill-equipped and weary. On the other hand, McClellan already had 58,000 troops, and more were arriving every day. But Magruder was a talented amateur actor and he had confused McClellan through an ingenious trick. The Southern general had ordered his officers to march their troops to the front, withdraw them, and then march them to the front again to give the appearance of continuous reinforcements. It was these moving troops that Lowe had seen and that had caused the Northern scouts to multiply the strength of their Southern host.

Magruder knew that his stage-play tactics could not go on indefinitely. The Yankee balloon that was constantly hovering over his lines might bring down the final curtain. He sent for the longest and most accurate rifles in the South. Their fire was directed on the balloon. The bullets fell short. Next, a cannon was used. Though the balloon seemed in easy reach and though the weapon was loaded at first with shell and then with shot, the target could not be reached. In desperation Magruder called for overloading a large Armstrong gun. It was aimed, the fuse was lighted, the gunnery crew ran for shelter, and the Armstrong gun burst into thousands of pieces. Lowe leaned over the side of his balloon, an interested observer.

A half mile of no man's land separated the enemy camps. One moonless night Magruder ordered thirty-five of his best shots to creep across that area and station themselves as close to the Union outposts as they could get. Here they were to hide until the next morning's ascension of the balloon. They were ordered to destroy the vehicle. At noon the next day only six of the men returned. Ten of their comrades had been captured before the balloon had gone up. The remaining men had been killed or had fallen into Yankee hands before a dozen rounds had been fired. Unaware of the commotion it was causing, the aerostat floated lazily overhead.

If the direct approach would not work, maybe a devious one would. A reward of a thousand dollars in gold was offered to the man who would destroy the balloon. Five volunteers left to try. One came back. He had entered the enemy camp as a lame peddler of tobacco and notions. It was a week before he was able to find the location of the balloon and its aeronaut. Once there, he heard about two Southern spies who had been caught trying to destroy the balloon and were now awaiting execution. This gave him little heart for his task, especially when he learned that the vehicle was housed in a heavily guarded area. The man was about to give up and return when an opportunity came to him. The balloon had ascended, reached an altitude of a thousand feet, and then broken loose from its tie ropes. It swept gracefully over no man's land and the Southern lines. The spy learned that aeronaut Lowe was not in the car. A general had insisted upon the experience of being a pilot. The Southerner prayed that the balloon would descend, but the wind changed direction and brought the Yankee officer and his machine down close to where the spy was standing. A dozen men grabbed the aerostat, the Southerner being one of them. Calmly he took a pipe from his pocket and filled the bowl with tobacco. He reached for a match to light his pipe, hoping that its flame would ignite the gas flowing out of the balloon. It would have if a sergeant had not turned around in time to slap the poised igniter from the spy's hand. "You damn idiot! Do you want to fire the balloon?" The question was never answered.

So Magruder decided that if the Union balloon could not be brought down, then a Southern one surely had to be sent

up. However, there were problems. Where would he get the
silk to make the bag when even cotton fabric was in short
supply? Who would lay out its pattern? Then who would
sew it? An inspiration came to the general. He would ask the
ladies of Richmond to donate their old ball dresses for the
silk. He would ask the city's dressmakers to help with the
patterns. And finally, he would ask the seamstresses to sew
the spherical garment. Once the scheme was revealed,
Army headquarters in Richmond was not large enough to
contain all the dresses that were offered. As though these
were not enough, many women insisted that their crinolines
and pantalets be accepted as well. It was considered a
privilege to contribute to the venture, and a high social
achievement if one's garment were used. Then one day the
citizens of Richmond gathered in their streets to admire a
huge silken ball floating overhead. It wore proudly its gay
flowered patterns squared off by multicolored plaids and
iridescent blues. Every rotation revealed a different aspect
to praise. The balloon was taken to the front lines, where
for several weeks it served Magruder's forces as proudly
as the ladies of Richmond had hoped it would. Then one
dark day the aerostat escaped. It fell into Federal hands and
with it the fairest dresses ever worn in the Southland. The
balloon was unceremoniously cut up and sent to Washington, where its pieces were given to members of Congress.

The month following the stalemating of McClellan's
troops in the Yorktown area found Lowe and his father
averaging only a few hours sleep a night. There was hardly
a commander in the field who did not want to use their
services. When darkness fell, the day was not over for the
aeronauts. They had to patch and repair their aerostat and
then clean or recharge their generating equipment. They
had help, but not the best kind. The soldiers assigned to the
aeronautic corps by sympathetic commanders were changed
almost daily. This gave the enlisted men no time to gain
balloon experience and hence be useful. Lowe could not

change the system. He was a civilian and well he knew it.
Food for himself and his civilian helpers was something that
was left over after the military were fed. Uniforms were the
only clothes issued and these only to soldiers. These tribula-
tions could have been borne with good grace by the chief of
the aeronautic corps were his civilian assistants paid their
wages. The situation was such that if they received a pay
check six months after it was due, they were glad to call it
current. But several of the men had wives and children to
support and could not afford the luxury of fighting while
their families starved. Some of the men left and the Lowes
carried on by working harder themselves.

The time for attack was at hand. The Union officers had
been briefed. Lowe ascended to make what in days past
would have been a routine observation. It was shortly before dawn. The aeronaut looked to the northwest, where
enemy campfires had been marking the Yorktown line.
There were none to be seen. Scouts confirmed Lowe's report
that the Southern troops had retreated. McClellan started
his march to Richmond. His troops pushed to within seven
miles of the city only to be turned back by the Confederates.
He had waited too long to launch the offensive. His enemy
had been given the time they had needed to bring up
reinforcements for the city's defense.

The ultimate retreat of the Federal forces in a campaign
that they should have won is charged to a complex of
reasons: General McClellan was always overestimating his
enemy's strength, largely because of bad intelligence information. Moreover, he suffered constant political harass-
ment from his government, a divided command in the
over-all campaign itself, and large losses from malaria which
sprang from the swamplands over which much of the fighting had taken place. On August 3, 1862, General Henry
Halleck, newly appointed chief of the Federal Armies,
ordered McClellan to withdraw his troops from the peninsula.

During the following months on different fields Lowe and his colleagues made hundreds of balloon observations. The intelligence gained from these undoubtedly saved the lives of thousands of Federal soldiers who might have fallen into ambush or been overrun by superior forces. It is not inconceivable that Lowe also saved the lives of many Southern soldiers by reporting their presence in strength. The aeronaut looked forward to receiving a commission and also gaining military status for his aeronautic corps as his reward. During the Peninsular Campaign, his wishes seemed close to being granted. General McClellan told him that if they both got out of the fight alive, there would be a commission waiting for the aeronaut as soon as the general got back to Washington. After McClellan's defeat Lowe fell seriously ill from overwork. He was hospitalized for several weeks. That fall of 1862 McClellan was relieved of his command. And so faded Lowe's dream of military status.

When Lowe regained some of his strength and was able to return to field duty, he found that a Lieutenant Cyrus Comstock had been assigned responsibility for the balloons. This boy, for that is what Lowe considered him, had never seen an aerostat until he saw the Professor's. Nevertheless, he presumed to instruct Lowe on the rigging of a balloon and the theory of aerial observation. After the lessons Lieutenant Comstock suggested a reorganization of the aeronautic corps. One day Thaddeus Lowe received the following message from Lieutenant Comstock:

I do not think the interests of the public's service require the employment of Clovis Lowe, your father, or of your principal assistant. Please inform me of the date of their departure, which should be no more than a week hence.

It is also in the public interest to reduce your pay from ten dollars to six dollars per day, which pay shall be made in currency instead of gold as before. I also am putting into effect some general rules to be observed by all civil employees connected with the balloons. Chief among these are that no absences from duty without my permission will be allowed, and pay will be stopped for the time of absence. In camp when the wind is still, ascensions shall be made at morning, noon and night, and reports made to me in writing of all that is observed during the day. You, personally, are expected to make these ascensions frequently, and to be responsible that no camp disappears and no new one appears without its being reported to me at once.

Lowe refused to accept the conditions laid down by the lieutenant. The aeronaut refused even to talk to the officer. There was really little that the lieutenant could do to harm Lowe. The officer could not stop Lowe's pay because the aeronaut had not been receiving it. The lieutenant could not fire Clovis Lowe because he was an employee of Thaddeus Lowe, who was a private contractor. All that the lieutenant could do was to send messages to Thaddeus, who promptly tore them up.

When springtime came, there was a lull in Lowe's activities. He sadly wrote his resignation, which patriotism had kept him from doing while he felt his services were needed. Even after he left the Army and was in Washington tending to his personal affairs, he received many forwarded requests for balloon observations from commanding officers who had not known of his departure. Without the Professor's leadership and devotion, the first aeronautic corps of the United States Army disappeared.

In his later years Professor Lowe moved to Pasadena, California. His last ascent in a balloon was a happy one and to make it he traveled all the way to New York. A scientist and his bride wanted to be married as close to heaven as possible. One thousand feet above New York harbor Professor Thaddeus Lowe helped grant the couple their nuptial wish.

SAGA OF THE OXYGEN-STARVED
BALLOONISTS

The Balloon Committee of the British Association for the Advancement of Science decided on what appeared in 1862 to be a simple venture. Its members would send a colleague up twenty or thirty thousand feet—or more if his balloon would go that high—to make scientific measurements.

Less than eighty years earlier the Montgolfier brothers had fashioned the first practical areostat, which rose a mile into the sky. Eager to test the wholesomeness of this novel environment, the inventors sent a sheep, a cock, and a duck into it. The animals ascended 1500 feet, and eight minutes after launch returned unharmed—except for the cock, which suffered a broken right wing caused by a preflight kick from the sheep. Thus, people assumed that the upper atmosphere was a friendly one.

Muttonchop-whiskered James Glaisher, venerable member of the Association and the most experienced scientific observer on the Balloon Committee, volunteered to go up. His enthusiasm for the project gave him little choice. Although he was fifty-three years old, he still nostalgically remembered the delights of his early twenties when as a surveyor he worked in the hills of Ireland. Often he was enveloped in clouds for weeks at a time, first on the mountain Bencor, in Galway, and afterward on the summit of the Keeper Mountain, near Limerick.

During this time he eagerly studied the colors in the sky and the delicate, changing tints of the clouds. He charted the motions of the floating masses and in winter marveled at the forms of the snow crystals. As he grew older he also grew away from observing nature firsthand. He became famous, mostly for publishing a classic set of dewpoint tables and later for founding the British Meteorological Society and helping to establish the Aeronautical Society of Great Britain. This was behind him now, and he was in a way seeking to bring back his youth when he recommended himself as the balloon's scientific observer.

In the nineteen years the Association had been backing balloon flights—through a faltering succession of committees—only a few scraps of worthwhile data had come out of the ascensions. Something always went wrong—with the balloon, the observers, or the weather, and on occasion with all three. As a result, the project gradually lost the interest of Association members, several of whom admitted having the unscientific feeling that the task had been ill-starred since it began.

This attitude changed at a British Association meeting at Leads in 1858. Colonel William Sykes, M.P. for Aberdeen, called for a new balloon committee—"one with enough influence to arrange to send experiments into the sky again." Sykes's motion was ardently seconded by Glaisher and backed by Sir William Fairbairn, a colleague of Lord Kelvin and J. P. Joule and also the Association's president. Once more the Association held high hopes that the balloon would become a powerful scientific probe.

Alas, despite the Committee's earnest efforts the next three years were as disappointing as the earlier ones. Balloons were now the problem. They were universally bad, some struggling up a mile or two but then sagging and returning to earth before useful work could be done. Finally, Glaisher called upon the professional aeronaut Henry Coxwell for help.

When Coxwell was thirteen years old, his father, who had never fully recovered from three broken ribs he suffered in boarding a Spanish man-of-war in the time of Admiral Nelson, died. With this heritage Coxwell attended military school for a few years and from there steered a dogged course through bookkeeping and dentistry to aeronautics. Ballooning became his entire life. When he met Glaisher, Coxwell was forty-three years old and known as the best aeronaut in England.

To forward its scientific use, Coxwell offered to build an aerostat free of charge for the Committee. Waving aside Glaisher's thanks, Coxwell said the balloon would be fifty-five feet in diameter. He recommended taking off from Wolverhampton, thereby narrowing the chance of the aerostat by misadventure being swept into the sea.

The men spoke of the scientific instruments that would be carried, and of the altitude the aerostat could reach. What they did not talk about were the possible effects of this altitude upon themselves!

It was only four generations ago that Glaisher and Coxwell were planning their balloon flights. By that time men realized that the higher they went the more tenuous the air became. For this reason, aeronauts used barometers as altitude-measuring devices. However, what nobody knew was how high a person had to go before the lack of air suffocated him. That critical altitude, like the place where the ancients felt the end-of-the-earth monsters lived, was presumed to be just beyond man's reach.

Glaisher and Coxwell were familiar with the flights of their predecessors. They knew of the three Italians who in

1803 made a night ascent in a hot-air balloon from Bologna. They went so high that two of them began vomiting and passed out. The third passenger maintained that lack of air snuffed out his lantern and therefore he didn't know how high they really did go. He reported it was so cold that three of his fingers turned black and later had to be amputated.

Although the third man's fingers might have been saved had he worn gloves, it was not as evident that his companions were suffering from symptoms of hypoxia, or lack of oxygen. The diagnosis of Glaisher and Coxwell was that the ill balloonists had either ascended too rapidly or else were not acclimated to high altitudes.

Until Glaisher and Coxwell made their fateful ascent on September 5, 1862, no aeronaut was known to have ever reached an altitude of much more than four miles, or 21,000 feet. This is twice the altitude at which modern-day pilots are instructed to don their oxygen masks. They are warned that flying above 10,000 feet without masks strains their respiratory system. To get enough oxygen out of the thin air at 18,000 feet, most people have to breathe about twice as fast as at sea level. They have to breathe three times as fast at 20,000 feet, and above 20,000 feet they are apt to lose consciousness and die.

Black storm clouds started passing over Wolverhampton early that September morning. By noontime what had begun as distant thunder now sounded like timpani playing overhead. Glaisher hurriedly loaded the aerostat's basket with scientific instruments and bags of sand ballast. His bald head glistened with the sweat of his efforts, while the clump of hair perched on the back of his head stuck out like a desert bush. He murmured half to himself, "Damn this weather!"

"For me, too!" Coxwell lipped back to him while watching the balloon overhead fill out to a plum shape. It was being inflated with an especially light gas—the products of the last distillation of coal—which the local illuminating company under Glaisher's persuasion had consented to store for use on this ascent.

Inflation started late because the impending storm made an ascent doubtful. The strong ground wind that was blowing without pause was enough to chasten even the most ardent aeronaut. Yet the two men hopefully waiting to ascend realized that if they wanted official witnesses, the time for the flight was near at hand. It had already been postponed three times. By now the Balloon Committee representatives were impatient to leave in order to return to their own affairs.

Coxwell feared to wait a moment longer. The storm was going to break, destroying the balloon if it were still on the ground. "Glaisher, come on!" he cried as he clambered into the wicker basket they were to ride. The scientist handed a crate of six pigeons to his colleague and swung himself aboard. The aerostat was cut loose as the rain started.

Grabbing the vehicle, the wind swept it like an autumn leaf swiftly across the launching field, the basket's bottom clipping the tops of the high grass. With almost paternal instinct Glaisher hugged his panel of instruments to his chest to keep them from breaking in the event of a crash. Suddenly, the vehicle arced up into a misty gray atmosphere, becoming a part of it.

"Well, we're off the ground," Coxwell joked in relief. He threw sand overboard to hasten the vehicle's ascent. Nodding agreement, Glaisher began reading his instruments and logging what he saw.

Many of the scientific questions he was attempting to answer then were, except for degree, the same ones that were being asked a century later. What are the electrical characteristics of the atmosphere at different altitudes? How does the earth's magnetic field vary? Glaisher was instructed to gather samples of air at different altitudes for analysis. He was told to observe the solar spectrum and note any changes he saw as he went higher. Only one major experiment would have dated his work: his task to compare the readings of a relatively new pressure-indicating instrument—the aneroid barometer, a rugged and portable device—with those of the reliable but fragile mercury barometer.

The most important question was not asked, yet this ascent did much to answer it. How high can a man go before the lack of air kills him?

As the aerostat emerged into a brighter sky, the men saw a huge yellow storm cloud a thousand feet above them. Its forbidding appearance seemed to offer oblivion to anyone rash enough to enter. Meanwhile, the vehicle passed through a small island cloud about 500 feet below the storm. Glaisher observed the two barometers and recorded their readings. Coxwell tugged on the valve line as a check for an emergency. All at once a torrent of rain splashed on the aerostat and poured into the basket. Moments later the vehicle was in the midst of the storm. Violent gusts of wind hammered the balloon. It spun dizzily around its axis, twisting the riggings holding the basket. As though in agony, the ropes squealed with the strain. The balloon and basket unwound, throwing the passengers hard against the basket's side. Lightning darted through the sky while thunder clapped in apparent glee. Glaisher screamed something to Coxwell, but it was a vain effort.

The cloud became lighter. The sun was seen first as a wispy white disk, and then, as the aerostat broke through the top cloud layer, as a blinding burst of light revealing a magnificently blue sky. Below lay a mountain chain of clouds, undulating with valleys and tufted peaks. It was difficult to believe that they contained so much fury. "We're at 10,000 feet," Glaisher called out. "The instruments are fine—thank God!"

"Up we go then," Coxwell said as he gutted a ballast

bag on the basket's rim and let sand stream out. The balloon hurried its ascent, which caused Glaisher to shorten intervals between his readings.

Coxwell was gasping as a result of the energy he had spent lifting the bag of ballast. Ten minutes later he was back at work. He split two more bags open to let their contents pour over the side. His companion was working as calmly and efficiently as though he were still on the ground. Elated when he discovered that the readings of his two barometers were corresponding at all altitudes, Glaisher asked for greater height so that further checks could be made.

At 15,000 feet ice began forming on the working end of the wet-bulb thermometer, making it useless. This meant that humidity measurements could not be made. However the familiar dry-bulb thermometer was working and showed that the temperature was eighteen degrees Fahrenheit. Coxwell drew his jacket collar tightly around his neck to keep his body heat from escaping. The pigeons huddled one against another as best they could in their rocking crate. Glaisher released one of them to see how well it could fly in the rarified atmosphere. The bird extended its wings, then fluttered helplessly toward earth.

At 20,000 feet, the temperature fell to eleven degrees. "Maybe we'll be getting warmer soon," Glaisher remarked facetiously. "In the 5000 feet just past we lost only seven degrees; we lost twice as much in the 5000 feet before that."

Coxwell labored to empty another ballast bag. Glaisher looked back at his instruments and kept his pencil scribbling. He paused only for the time it took to let a second pigeon go. The bird fell a short distance, then lackadaisically began flying downward in a spiral pattern.

At 25,000 feet the temperature dropped sharply. The lack of oxygen was also being felt. Glaisher could barely focus his eyes on the graduations of his instruments. He read his thermometer with the aid of a strip of paper, with which he tracked the falling mercury column. The temperature was minus five degrees. It was an effort to write the number down. Glaisher signaled that two more pigeons should be released. Coxwell opened the cage, leaving the path free for the birds to escape. They were of a different mind, having no desire to go. He shoved them out. One fell like a stone, not even attempting to fly. The second vigorously winged its way to the top of the balloon, where it alighted and was not seen again.

The aerostat kept rising. The mercury barometer indicated an altitude of 28,000 feet. It took the energies of both men to get and record this information. Then they moved on to the thermometer. Its markings jumped before their eyes and could not be read. Glaisher made a sky observation. He saw something else. The cord running to the gas-release valve was out of reach, entangled in the balloon's shroud lines. They could not descend even if they wanted to. There was no way to let the gas out.

Coxwell began to prepare for the climb he would have to make. A number of ropes held the basket suspended beneath a large iron hoop, which he would first have to mount. In a silly manner Coxwell waved good-by to Glaisher and then hoisted himself onto the basket's edge. He paused for balance. The hoop was now at chin's height. Flaring up from it were the shroud lines. With the help of these Coxwell drew himself up over the hoop and crooked one of his legs around it. Then he maneuvered his other leg around the metal ring and his body into a position near the dangling valve line. He rested, his hands tightly grasping the hoop. The air was piercingly cold. The balloon's neck was white with hoarfrost. He knew he had to work fast or he would not have energy left to work at all. He tried to unclench his hands to raise them from the hoop but they could not be freed. They were frozen to the metal.

Glaisher calculated that the aerostat was nearing 30,000 feet. His eyes searched the floor for the pencil he had dropped. When he found it, his arm was too numb to reach for it. His eyes turned upward to Coxwell, then glazed over. He slumped against the edge of the basket, his head thrown backward and his shoulder and one arm hanging loosely over the side.

Coxwell saw his companion resting against the basket's edge. He called out but got no reply. Glaisher's face was as calm as though he were asleep. His body was limp and rolled with the motion of the basket.

The aeronaut tried to wrench his hands from the hoop but it was useless. They had already turned blue with the cold. There was no pain in them because they did not seem to belong to him. He was beginning to get sleepy and knew that insensibility would follow. Overhead, the valve line floated lazily. Coxwell snapped at it with his teeth. A breeze wafted it from him. He lunged again and missed. For leverage, Coxwell leaned his body as far back as his arms would let him. Then launching himself forward, he caught the line in his mouth. He tugged at it viciously only to break a tooth. The valve was stuck.

Coxwell held onto the line, his tongue pushing it to his molars. He pulled again. The line split his lip and cut into his cheek. He paused for breath and to swallow the blood in his mouth. Incipient nausea, which had been with him since the storm, suddenly matured. His lunch spilled out of his partly open mouth and through his broken tooth. When he could retch no more, he pushed himself forward while laboriously edging his mouth along the rope, using his lips for traction. He bit into the sisal fibers, already frozen by drops of saliva and blood. With all the strength he could gather, Coxwell jerked his body backward. The valve cracked open. His hands tore free. Only his legs held him on the hoop. Pivoting around it, he somersaulted into the basket.

The valve line danced in front of him. He again took it

between his teeth, pulled on the cord by nodding his head, and happily heard the soft hiss of escaping gas. It seemed hours later that the aerostat began its descent.

Coxwell looked at the aneroid barometer. Glaisher would want to know its reading. The aeronaut's elation at having opened the valve made him temporarily forget that his colleague might not be alive. Coxwell could not read the instrument face but he could see the pivoted marker. He fixed its location by noting that the hand was in a line with the cords holding the barometer tautly suspended between the basket and the iron hoop.

Glaisher heard somebody talking to him but the scientist could not utter a sound or move a muscle in response. He felt a hand on his brow and then on his cheeks.

"You're alive." It was Coxwell's voice. "Try to move! Do try! Now do!" Glaisher felt as though his limbs were weighed down with lead. His body tingled in every fiber. His sight returned, at first bleary and then translucent. "Are we aloft?" he asked struggling to his feet. "What happened to my pencil?"

Coxwell kicked the implement into sight. "Your hands!" Glaisher exclaimed. Unsteadily he opened a half-filled bottle of brandy and poured part of its contents over the frozen members. Soon Coxwell felt a throbbing in his fingers, and he remarked, "I can show you where the barometer hand was while you were in a faint."

The reading was seven inches of mercury. "Thirty-five thousand feet," Glaisher said wonderingly. "No man has ever gone that high."

"Nor ever will," added Coxwell.

Landing in open country, they could find no means of transportation back to Wolverhampton. Thus they had to walk as far to the city as they said they had ascended into the sky—nearly seven miles.

Many authorities doubt that the men reached 35,000 feet.

They point out that Coxwell had been under a strain while he was on the hoop and undoubtedly had an oxygen deficiency. Therefore, they say, how could he swear to the position of the barometer's hand—even if the instrument were working?

"No," the critics maintain, "such a flight without oxygen is impossible." The classic Tissandier ascent is often cited to prove the point. On April 15, 1875, the famous aeronaut Gaston Tissandier and his colleagues H. T. Sivel and J. E. Crocé-Spinelli made a balloon flight to 28,820 feet. To prevent the effects of hypoxia, they carried with them a nitrogen-oxygen mixture to breathe. This technique had been devised a few months earlier by Dr. Paul Bert, a research physician occupying the chair of physiology at the Faculté des Sciences in Paris. Unfortunately, when it came time for the balloonists to grab the oxygen tubes, the men were too paralyzed to move. The aerostat floated down of its own accord. When it landed, only Tissandier was alive.

Yet Glaisher had carefully checked his aneroid against his mercurial barometer up to 29,000 feet and found only minor differences. He concluded there was nothing wrong with his instrument or with Coxwell's seeing which way a broad marker was pointing.

Glaisher also told his critics at that time that at 29,000 feet his aerostat was ascending at 1000 feet per minute. Thirteen minutes later he was going down at 2000 feet per minute. Glaisher avers that if this information is plotted out, then it is clear that the aerostat must have exceeded a 35,000-foot altitude.

Glaisher died in 1903. In surveying the scientist's career the highly respected British magazine *Nature* and the scholarly *Aeronautical Journal* affirmed—in the words of *Nature*— "Glaisher and the late Mr. Coxwell attained the highest distance from the earth (35,000 feet) ever reached."

Yet if the detractors are right, and 29,000 feet is the

highest Glaisher and Coxwell went, still these intrepid men hold the world's altitude record for a nonfatal ascent without special breathing equipment. From this viewpoint they were not boasting when they said, "No man has ever gone that high . . . nor ever will." They were telling the truth.

Nine

THE SIEGE OF PARIS

Just when Europe thought that there were no more blunders that Napoleon III could make, he amazed everybody with his ingenuity. He called for war against Prussia. The majority in his Chamber of Deputies ignored the desperate pleadings of their colleague Léon Gambetta for peace. Instead they helped their monarch rush into the trap set by the Prussian Prime Minister, Otto Bismarck. On July 19, 1870, they pushed France into war.

Within six weeks the Prussian Armies, augmented by those of the South German states, struck northern France with devastating swiftness. The main French Army was pinned down at Metz, a town 200 miles east of Paris. The remainder of France's Regular Army set out to free their comrades. Alas, Napoleon's forces were intercepted and then defeated a long way from their objective, at Sedan, a little fortress town northeast of Paris and two miles from the Belgium border. With the capture of Sedan the German military net caught the biggest prize of all, the Emperor of France.

The last hurdle for the German Armies was the capture of Paris. How easy this seemed! There were no troops in all of France organized to stop the Germans' victory march.

The Parisians were thought to be so fearful of famine and so intolerant of discomforts that they would not resist. So sure were the German officers of the imminent fall of the capital, they were promising themselves that within the month, "We shall be shooting hares at Creisau." In high spirits the invaders left for Paris on September 4. Yet had any of the German troops been able to listen to the talk in Paris that day, they probably would not have slept as easily that night.

It was that very day in Paris that the Second Empire fell. *Fell* is perhaps not the word to use. *Collapsed* would be a better one, because that is what happened after the monarch was captured at Sedan. Springing to fill the void was the republican Government of National Defense. Its Minister of Interior was Léon Gambetta. He cried for the new government to carry on with the war, now that it was no longer Napoleon's.

"Take it to the provinces, if need be!" he yelled in the Chamber of Deputies. "We will teach those strutting Prussians just how high France holds her honor."

Deputy Jules Favre echoed this view two days later and his words became a rallying cry for the Parisians during the hard months that were to follow. He orated, "It is for the king of Prussia, who has declared that he is making war on the Empire and not on France, to stay his hand; we shall not cede an inch of our territory or a stone of our fortresses."

The citizens were aroused and angered. The fight had now become theirs. An amazing transformation took place. People who only a few days past had looked upon the war with amazing disinterest were parading down the streets and calling their friends to arms. The "Marseillaise" was being sung throughout the city. Its strains were remindful of the glory that once was France's and invoked a fervor not seen since the Napoleonic days. By the tens of thousands the citizens volunteered their services to their new government.

The German forces came up to the city and surrounded it. The officers retired to Versailles to await the Parisians' white flag. They felt it would not be long in coming and they wagered on the number of days. They had drawn the noose tightly. Neither a man nor crust of bread nor word was allowed to pass out of Paris. Even the telegraph wires had been fished out of the Seine and cut. It was as though Paris had left the face of the earth.

Setbacks only fanned higher the flames of the city's resistance. The people cheerfully accepted rationing, against which the Germans thought they would revolt. Women and children as well as men stood guard duty. Ammunition plants were set up. At night men swam the river to repair the cables that had been cut by the Germans the preceding day. The invaders soon learned what was happening and began guarding the Seine as they did the roads.

Gambetta realized that only an organized French Army attacking from the enemy's rear would ever be able to lift the seige. With such an Army on hand the Parisians could initiate a battle that would crush the Germans in a vise. Gambetta chose himself to escape to the provinces to raise the necessary forces.

There were two balloons in Paris, one at Montmartre and the other at Montsouris. Both had spent nearly a decade performing at public fairs. Now they had different errands. Four times during the day and twice at night the balloons and pilots ascended from their public squares. Each pilot wrote down what he saw and put it into a little box. This was attached to a ring which slid down the balloon's mooring cable into the hands of reporters below. Within a few hours the Paris papers were able to tell their readers about the current state of the siege.

There was going to be a dash for freedom. Just after sunrise on September 23, slim, black-goateed Jules Duruof, professional aeronaut, climbed into the basket of the Montmartre balloon, the "Neptune." He stood on 275 pounds of mail which was to be distributed by the postmaster at Evreux. Looking disdainfully at the load, Duruof said, "It's too heavy." That was all he had time to say. Already the balloon was growing weak from the loss of gas through its ancient fabric. "Cast off!" he yelled.

The basket was released. Duruof hastened his ascent by throwing overboard vast amounts of sand. He had to reach altitude quickly if he was to clear the enemy.

The balloon at Montsouris, called the "City of Florence," was aloft and playing its sentinel role. Its pilot reported that Duruof was continuing to release ballast. "It's a glorious flight, with the 'Neptune' following an almost perfect parabolic path, like that of an artillery shell." Forty-five minutes later the message read by the reporters waiting anxiously below the Montsouris balloon was, "Duruof has landed safely in a field several miles beyond the enemy. *Vive la République!*"

That night Paris celebrated. She had won a major victory. She had her voice back. For a while it would be thin, but even this would be strong enough to bring hope and courage to the rest of France.

The members of the Chamber of Deputies toasted the success of the "Neptune" as heartily as the rest of the city. There was even more reason for the delegates to be happy. They saw high commercial as well as military value in what they were now calling the "Air Post." By setting the postage rates a little higher than they had been, the government would be making a handsome profit out of each balloon voyage. And the government urgently needed this money to finance an ingenious plan—a mass production of balloons which could sail an Army over the heads of the Germans.

The flight of the "City of Florence" was delayed an entire day while two dozen carrier pigeons were being selected to go with the balloonist on his trip. This was the Parisian postmaster's idea, born out of his eagerness for a return post and the revenue from it.

When it came time to leave, the balloon rose gracefully to 2000 feet. Here it fell in with a southbound wind. High enough to be out of range of the enemy rifles sailed the "City of Florence." Once, it paused in its flight, long enough for its pilot to unload thousands of copies of a letter that Jules Favre had addressed to the attackers.

"Why do you invade a country that has done you no harm? What will you gain should you live to see Paris fall? There is nothing in this war for you but risk of an early death. Whatever the fate of Paris, France will keep on fighting and resisting, inch by inch, while your blood colors her soil." Childlike, the enemy scurried after the fluttering pieces of paper.

When several of the pigeons returned to Paris, bearing messages of good will and hope from the provinces, the city's citizens put wine on their tables again. The people now had two-way communication with the world.

"This is only the start of French resistance," Gambetta promised them. "I will escape and I will return. When I do return it will be with the Army of France at my back."

Several imaginative plans for escape were proposed to the Chamber of Deputies. The city's Engineers Council met one night with several of the delegates from the Chamber and said, "We can tunnel a passage under the German lines and into the countryside. We have the plans now. We can start tomorrow."

"No, the work would take too long," said Gambetta. He kept shaking his head in the negative. Then to get his reason for not liking the scheme confirmed, he asked, "How long would it take?"

"Four months, yes, we'd say four months at the very least," answered the Council's spokesman. He turned to his colleagues. "Wouldn't we?" They nodded in agreement.

"Time's on the enemy's side," Gambetta told them. "In four months Paris would be starved out."

"A raft—one that would float you, Monsieur Gambetta, and your party across the Seine," proposed another civic group.

Gambetta dismissed this idea with, "Too hazardous! German patrols watching to see if we're going to splice any more cable would be upon us with rifle shot before we were halfway across the river."

Thus were overland as well as underland ways to escape discussed and dismissed. Logic forced Gambetta to turn to the only means left, through the air.

When it was decided that balloons would be Paris' link with the world, the Deputies looked around for a plant in which to make the vehicles. The men did not expect that a suitable one would be easy to find, because it had to be a fairly long place, one able to accommodate the balloon cutting room; and it had to be an airy place and well lighted so that the balloon's finish could be applied smoothly and so it would dry quickly. Several hours after the search began it ended with remarkable luck. Two manufacturing sites were found, both spacious, both lighted by high clerestories, and both obviously out of use until the siege was over. These were the Orléans and the Northern railway stations.

Overnight an enthusiastic handful of aeronauts and their helpers pushed aside the railroad apparatus and changed the stations into pattern-making and cutting rooms, balloon-drying and basket-weaving areas. They began manufacturing aerostats. It did not matter to them that they were working ten, twelve, fifteen hours a day. They brought in their friends to help and soon the first of many aerostats was finished. This one was for Léon Gambetta. It was called the "Armand Barbes."

Throughout the siege the factories operated. When the supplies of silk were used up and the newspapers worried that this meant the end of aerostat manufacture, the factories calmly turned to using calico. In the Northern Railway Station the balloons were produced with the help of machine-sewing. Such work was not considered fit at the Orléans Station, where only hand-sewing was allowed. The fashion industry supplied the seamstresses. Girls whose fingers had worked only the finest materials were now putting together some of the cheapest. The machine-stitched balloons were left white. The handmade ones were tastefully multicolored, reflecting the art and work of the dressmakers turned balloon makers.

When a balloon was finished, it was rubbed down with linseed oil and then dried, which rendered the material gastight. Sailors were felt to be best fitted to rig the aerostats and the jobs were given to them. These men also were given the task of flying the balloons. Sailing in the air was believed not to be too different from sailing on the sea. The balloons were made in a standard size of 70,000 cubic feet. Filled with coal gas, they were able to lift a ton, which usually was divided into 600 pounds of ballast and 1400 pounds of men, equipment, and mail.

The "Armand Barbes" was finished ten days after the factories opened. There had been a race to see which one would have the honor of making Gambetta's balloon. The people at the Orléans Station had won, and on October 5 they inflated the bag. The time was only one month plus a day since the Government of National Defense had been formed.

The "Armand Barbes" was towed through the streets of Paris from the gas-generating plant at Orléans to the launching site at Place St. Pierre in Montmartre. The balloon makers were proud of their work. They had dyed the bag's fabric a vivid red and only the blind in Paris that day were not struck by its brilliance.

"Bismarck, if he is out there, will certainly see you," said a citizen to Gambetta as the Minister stood waiting to go aloft. "For us you will be like the rising sun. But for him, you will be the setting sun."

The "Armand Barbes" was becalmed. On the morning of the third day Gambetta told his pilot, professional aeronaut Alexander Triched, "We will be off this morning even if I have to sit out the siege in the air over Paris." At eleven o'clock in the morning the "Armand Barbes" with its two passengers, Gambetta and his secretary, shot rapidly up to 1000 feet. A cloud hid the sun, the gas in the balloon cooled, and the aerostat's acceleration slackened. The vehicle floated leisurely up another 500 feet before coming to rest. The city lay beneath them, the Seine meandering through it and then circling part way around before wandering off. Looking through a thin haze, Gambetta was able to make out the gardens of Versailles. Between Versailles and Paris there were countless German camps. To his secretary Gambetta remarked, "Isn't it strange that those little groups of soldiers, which I feel I could crush merely by stepping on them, can press so hard on the throat of Paris?"

The "Armand Barbes" began moving northward. The sky had grayed considerably and a soft drizzle started to fall. Responding to the cooling temperatures, the aerostat floated downward. It came to rest at an altitude of 700 feet, where the pilot let it stay because he was short of ballast. At the time of loading Gambetta had insisted that it was more important to carry dispatches than sand.

The reason was never clear but somehow the "Armand Barbes" lurched and then fell rapidly toward earth. It landed in a clearing not far from a German camp and very close to a detachment of soldiers on whom the aeronaut a few moments earlier had with great glee poured a stream of sand. The aroused ones were at this moment charging into the clearing. All hands inside the basket were wildly shoving ballast over its side. The aeronaut threw away his grappling hook. Rifles cracked at the aerial travelers. Languidly the "Armand Barbes" began rising, with excruciat-

ing slowness. The air was filled with shot. Soon cannon
were heard. At an altitude of 500 feet the aeronaut crossed
himself for being alive and in a few minutes the aerostat was
out of range.

The balloon drifted up several thousand feet and then
down. At the end of an hour, the vehicle had again fallen
to 700 feet. It was now over Creil, a German-held town
thirty miles north of Paris. Below the Frenchmen the invaders were pointing excitedly toward the vehicle and
rushing for their rifles. These were stacked in the middle
of their camp. The aeronaut cried out, "Everything overboard! Everything!" Coats were discharged, shoes, lunch
boxes. "The basket of wine!" Rope and lanterns. The aeronaut was reaching for a dispatch file.

"No, better this!" cried Gambetta, and he let his valise
fall. When he drew his hand back it was covered with
blood. A bullet had pierced it. The "Armand Barbes" moved
up and away.

Four hours after the aerostat left Paris it landed in the
uppermost branch of an oak tree, forty miles from the
capital. French road workers helped Gambetta and his
party down. When they learned whom they were aiding,
they eagerly asked for news of Paris and the way of the
war. They begged for weapons with which to fight. Thereupon the Minister wrote a note for his carrier-pigeon post.
"Everywhere the provincials are hailing their new Republic
and are rising to oust the invaders. We cannot lose."

A side light on the story of the "Armand Barbes" was
added, certainly not by choice, by the owner of the tree that
had caught the aerostat. Thomas Morgan had been a royalist member of the Chamber of Deputies. It was his oak that
had cradled the "Armand Barbes" when it landed and that
quickly became a meeting place and political symbol for all
the republicans in the area. During the war, feelings were
running too high for Morgan to chase the patriots away. He
waited until later, hoping that the tree would lose its popu-

larity. Its renown increased. Several years after Gambetta died the Minister of Fine Arts called for the government's expropriating the area and making it a historic shrine. Whence the frustrated royalist went out and hacked down his tree.

In the weeks following his escape from Paris, Gambetta worked almost to exhaustion striving to put together a military force. The job seemed impossible. The enemy did not even consider it worth while to send a company of men to Tours, where the Minister was headquartered, to stop him.

"Why bother?" asked a German general. "Even if he raises a company of men, how is he going to get them guns and ammunition?"

Gambetta toured the countryside and brought together the scattered military companies he found, and organized these remnants into a fighting force. Their weapons were repaired by local artisans, and ammunition was made in every mechanical shop in France, even under the noses of the Germans. While this was going on, the Chamber of Deputies in Paris elected Gambetta their Prime Minister. He thanked his colleagues for this honor by raising, within a few weeks, thirty-six fully equipped Army divisions. They had 600,000 rifles and 1400 cannon. France had now grown a new sting which she was eager to plunge into the body of her invaders.

Then came for the Germans the fog of war. Hitherto unarmed French National Guardsmen were attacking and destroying enemy outposts. Armed citizenry were sniping at German scouts. Whereas before the French peasants had been docile, now they were arrogant. Soon within the German barracks a ghastly fear began taking shape. This came from the rumor that a French Army drawn from the provinces was on its way to crush the invaders against the Army of Paris. France was no longer the weak country of Napoleon III, or the country that Bismarck with braggadocio had told Europe would fall to her feet begging for mercy from her German masters. It was now clear that Paris' spirit of resistance had escaped into the countryside just as Jules Favre had promised, and that the hare-shooting season at Creisau had passed.

Most humiliating of all to the Germans was seeing balloons rise from the center of Paris like soap bubbles out of a pipe and then blithely sail overhead as though there were no siege at all. Each time a balloon passed the invaders emptied their rifles at it. The slow-moving bags seemed so close and yet frustratingly so far out of reach. The German high command set up a complex system to bring down the balloons, which included spotters, telegraphic communications, relays of cavalry, and runners if the underbrush got too thick. It was a joy for the Frenchmen to see the proud Prussians racing across the fields after the aerostats almost like children chasing after butterflies.

Knowing how unhappy the Germans were in having their blockade pierced, the Parisians nimbly turned their minds to increasing the pique and at the same time making the most of the aerial paths they had established. Of great help here was the Paris Pigeon Fanciers Society. This group devised a method of microphotography that allowed their pets to carry more messages than ever before. It was a simple system and one that is in use today. Letters were photographically reduced to a small fraction of their original size before they were given to the pigeons to carry. Once the birds arrived in the capital, the messages were taken from them, enlarged on a photographic screen, and then copied and delivered. In this way, long letters could be brought down to postage-stamp size and a sixteen-page sheaf of dispatches could be processed to weigh less than a gram. Because the charge was small, the equal of half a cent a word, and the pigeon post available to anyone in France who cared to use it, there was always a backlog of messages waiting to be flown into Paris. Yet the postmasters were exceedingly efficient and the revenues exceedingly welcome, and except for periods of bad weather the mail was dispatched quickly and never piled up out of hand.

The system was so annoying to the Germans that they tried to harass it by sending hawks after the pigeons. The practice was dropped when the hawks showed a stronger appetite for field mice, which were easier to capture and perhaps tastier to eat. Still, of the 360 pigeons bearing messages for Paris over a four-month period, only 57 of the birds got back to the city. These, however, did magnificent work, carrying over 100,000 messages to the besieged population.

Since the return post was such a haphazard business, the people in the provinces sought a surer method of communication. To better the odds that their messages would be received, they sent their letters several times over. Return trips by balloon were also thought of but the caprices of the wind made free-balloon traveling to a specific location untrustworthy. Another thought was to carry dogs and sheep out of Paris by balloon and then let them find their way back while bearing messages sewn into their collars. This idea, even if it could have worked, was doomed by the capital's acute shortage of food.

During the first few weeks of the Air Post sixteen trips out of Paris were made, all successfully. On the seventeenth the balloon and its aeronauts landed only fifty yards from an enemy camp. The German soldiers arrived on the scene just as a passing farmer who had been driving a dung cart was helping the aeronauts fold the balloon into the basket. Rudely the Germans undid the work. "Your mail, we must have it," snapped one of them as he wantonly ripped open the balloon in his search for the post.

The Frenchmen gestured with their hands that they could not help, one adding sadly in broken German, "This trip, we had none. *C'est la vie!*"

They were taken prisoner of war, except the farmer. He

was sent on his way, and it was with great effort that he pulled his dung cart with the pile raised a foot higher by several hundred pounds of mail, which he soon delivered to the nearest French post office.

Another time an aerostat landed midway between two enemy camps. The travelers heard a search party beating the brush. Near the Frenchmen was a small stream and this gave them an idea. They hurriedly hoisted their dispatches into the foliage of a tree and then cut down and stripped two thin branches about five feet long. The Germans arrived and found two French peasants, their faces and hair caked by the dust of the land, fishing lazily in the noonday sun.

"Yes, yes *mein Herr,* a balloon did fall out of the sky but not here, no, not here. You say there were people in it? No, we saw no people because we were fishing, no people at all, not at all."

Even this information the German interpreter got with difficulty because the men were hard of hearing. In disgust the search party left, but not before cursing the peasants for idiots for angling in a stream that had no fish.

Naturally, there were balloon disasters. It was strange, though, that with all the flights made there were only two of them. And stranger still that they occurred within two days of each other and in the same way, with the balloons slipping into the sea. The only one of interest is the first flight. It took place one moonless night late in November. A sailor had ascended with a load of dispatches. At dawn the next day, on the north coast of Scotland, the natives saw a balloon far to their west drop into the ocean. What makes this flight remarkable is that the dispatch case which the balloon had been carrying was found a few weeks later floating in the English Channel. It was promptly returned to France and its contents distributed by the French postmasters in the normal way.

Professor Pierre Janssen was a noted astronomer. He had

been commissioned by the French Academy of Sciences to go to Algeria to observe an eclipse that would soon occur there. Algeria was 1000 miles from Paris. The astronomer appealed to the Chamber of Deputies for help. After the delegates debated for several hours they offered Janssen a balloon and a young pilot-sailor to navigate it for him. Early one morning just before dawn the professor's reflecting telescope was loaded into an aerostat and carefully tied down. The flight was being made early, for the double advantage of a smoother ride for the astronomical instruments and for the cloak of darkness should the balloon fall amid the enemy. The aerostat rose to 3600 feet, then dipped sharply as the gas began cooling in the night air. A little while after daybreak the balloon, responding to the warmth of the sun, climbed to 7200 feet. It stayed at this altitude until a descent was made at a coast city near the mouth of the Loire. It had been a 300-mile trip in an escape to freedom and it had been made in less than three hours. The balloon had been traveling at the almost unbelievable speed of 100 miles an hour. Another mark of good fortune was that the delicate instruments had made the journey without damage. Subsequently, Janssen went by ship to the coastal town of Oran, Algeria, where he set up his observatory. The eclipse occurred on schedule, but pity the poor man, a cloud hid the phenomenon from him.

The period of the siege was no time for a Parisian aeronaut to look for balloon experience. One flight out of the city and he was through. Thus, after almost two months of balloon flights there was available in Paris only one experienced balloonist, Paul Rolier. The Chamber of Deputies called upon him to take an urgent military message to Gambetta. So important was the message considered—it told of plans to unite Paris' Army with Gambetta's—that to keep the intelligence from enemy hands it was written on tissue paper, which Rolier was instructed to eat should he be captured.

Though the siege was being stringently maintained, the pendulum of military favor was swinging toward the French. It had been given this impetus when the French Army won a major battle by defeating a Bavarian army corps at Orléans. This rang the alarm in every German post in France. It was now known that there really was a French Army and that it was a fighting one.

The problem of the German Army was that its march through France had been so rapid and so successful that communication and supply lines had been haphazardly constructed and ill-protected. If these were severed, then German blood would really be watering the soil of France. Hence, the attackers weakened their siege by withdrawing men to protect these lines and for service in other parts of the country. In one instance a detachment of troops was peeled off to seek out the French Army and destroy it.

Rolier's balloon was christened "La Ville d'Orléans." Its crew consisted of the aeronaut and a rifleman. Toward midnight on November 24, amid cries of *"Vive la France!"*, "La Ville d'Orléans" darted up 2400 feet. It passed over the Seine, which showed up as a darkened river amid the lamps of Paris. Beyond the capital the campfires of the invaders were spread out in widely separated groups. The aerostat was now directly over one of them. The camp noises could be clearly heard, and it was hard to believe that the vehicle was floating at an altitude of more than a mile. Rolier's companion threw out ballast and the balloon rose to 8000 feet. Rifle fire broke out below, probably from men confused by the sudden downpour of sand.

At 3:30 in the morning the men heard a sudden rushing sound. "A train, and how pleasant!" remarked Rolier. "How good the familiar sounds become when they've been away from you for a while! Even the harsh ones! I wonder why we don't hear the train's whistle." The disturbance stayed with them for a half hour or more, and then fell in volume until it was only a murmur. Dawn opened on a cloudless sky.

The men eagerly peered over the side of their basket to see what land lay beneath them. They looked too soon, because the night was still upon the earth. As the sun rose higher, Rolier looked again and this time he saw what he took to be white splotches on a gray ground. One of them disappeared and then formed again, and soon others did the same thing. Rolier now knew that he was seeing whitecaps.

"That was surf rolling over the beach that we heard last night," he exclaimed. "I wish I knew which surf it was and what beach it was wetting." He was watching the barometer as he spoke and worry crept into his voice. "We'll have no problem as long as the ballast holds out." They were losing altitude and were now down to 1000 feet. They threw some ballast over the side and when there was no reaction, they threw what remained. "La Ville d'Orléans" stopped its downward sweep just 50 feet above the water. Fingers of white spray reached up for the aerostat. The men were drenched. Then what seemed like a giant hand of water formed itself out of the sea and slapped the basket down. It capsized, tumbling the men over each other like mice in a rolling barrel. Food, clothing, a box of mail, everything floatable swirled around and was washed away. Made euphoric by his helplessness, Rolier kicked a coil of rope and a grappling hook into the water. All at once the wind, which had been dribbling the balloon against the sea, paused and then shot the balloon back into the sky. Rolier thought he heard the ocean moan with displeasure as the basket was wrenched from its grasp.

It would certainly seem that the mail that fell into the sea would have been lost. It was not. A news dispatch appearing in the London *Times* a few days later said, "On the morning of November 30, the Dantzic of Christiansand arrived at Leith, Scotland, with a box containing 200 pounds of letters, picked up by fishermen." After giving the circumstances of the rescue the article went on, "The box belonged to the French post office and has been turned over to that agency."

With its load so much lightened "La Ville d'Orléans" rose to 15,000 feet. The thirty-two degrees air temperature dropped past freezing to minus thirty-two degrees Fahrenheit. The men's wet clothing began to freeze on their bodies. The voyagers quickly wrapped themselves in blankets that with foresight Rolier had bundled in tarpaulins and tied to the basket. Rolier felt himself growing dizzy. He saw his companion's nose begin to bleed. Yet the men were afraid to release gas for fear of falling back into the sea, and were equally afraid to stay where they were or go any higher. A mist engulfed the aerostat, grew heavy, then turned into rain. They were still rising slowly. This they knew, not by their barometer, which was not sufficiently sensitive, but rather by an instrument invented by Rolier. It was a simple device, being only a pivoted metal arrow which had been balanced in the horizontal position. It wore paper wings. When through ballasting or release of gas the aerostat moved up or down, the passing air would act on the wings to deflect the arrow, thereby showing the observer the direction of the aerostat's motion. Rolier jerked the gas valve open. "La Ville d'Orléans" began falling.

When the men came out of the mists, the sea was no more. Below them was an expanse of snow dotted by many evergreens. The travelers glimpsed a mountain range in the distance, so extensive that even at altitude they could not see around it. They were nearing the ground fast. Perched on the edge of the basket, they poised themselves for the landing. It came hard, tumbling Rolier outside and the soldier back inside. With the aerostat relieved of one man's weight, it took off again. Hastily the soldier climbed to the riggings and jumped. Luckily, he fell only thirty feet and was cushioned by the snow. "La Ville d'Orléans" took the men's equipment and food back into the sky and soon disappeared into the mist.

After nearly fifteen hours in the balloon Rolier and the soldier found themselves stranded in a strange land. They warmed themselves over a patiently fanned fire made of dead twigs from the evergreens. Then for several hours they trudged knee-deep in snow with their only reference being a hand compass. They followed a southern track, in a foolish way feeling that this would lead to a warmer climate. That night they bedded themselves down on branches cut from the trees. Tired as they were, they had to sleep in two-hour shifts because three gaunt wolves had been following them since an hour before sundown. The next morning the men, racked with hunger and cold and tormented by the canines who were pressing them so closely, stumbled across the track of a sled. One of the wolves dashed in front of them while the other two beasts stood guard at the rear. It was useless to run, because if the men did and fell, the wolves would be upon them. With the courage of desperation Rolier and his companion kept walking the path defined by the sled's ridges. The wolf stood his ground, then grudgingly backed off and circled to the rear. The soldier said, "I know these brutes, and they won't wait much longer."

"I don't think they'll have to if that's a cabin I see," said Rolier. Fifteen minutes later they entered a one-room lodging. The owners were not there, but this was not a time for formalities. The intruders devoured the food that was at hand and only when they finished did they wonder whether they were welcome. They were sipping the last of the contents of their coffee cups, when they heard somebody outside cry "Clas!" They rushed to the door and opened it, only to be stared at curiously by two black-bearded men wearing heavy leather jackets. Using pantomime, Rolier explained that he and his friend had arrived by balloon, but no amount of pantomime was able to tell either group of men the nationality of the other. The cabin's owners were delighted to have company and tried to force upon their guests more of the food. Suddenly, one of the bearded men exclaimed, "Paris! Paris! French!" He had been toying with Rolier's boot and had happened upon the label which told where the item had been made. The bearded ones embraced their guests affectionately and then waited on them as though they were princes. From the markings on a matchbox handed to him by one of the men, Rolier finally learned that he was in Norway. The hosts wrote their names for the Frenchmen, Clas and Harald Strand. They showed by sketch that Rolier was far north and at the foot of one of the highest peaks of the Scandinavian cordilleras, in the Province of Thilemarken. Later in the day the brothers took the men by sled to the neighboring village of Silgjord. Here Rolier was able to send his message to Gambetta.

Rolier and his companion as they traveled through the country were feted by all of Norway. The spectacular distance they had traveled, unofficially said to be over 1500 miles, was called one of the marvels of the ages. Rolier authorized the sale of his picture, the profits of which he said would be given to French widows and wounded. Twenty-five thousand francs were contributed, which the balloonist submitted to his government. To honor his bravery, he was named *Chevalier de la Légion d'Honneur* by Jules Favre, and an Officer of the Order of St. Olaf by the king of Sweden.

The hope of the French people for the defeat of Germany was beginning to fade. Little incidents told this—in farm animals mysteriously disappearing when French troops came to buy them, in campfire wood having to be confiscated instead of being given freely, and in the price of wine to the military going up. Coming to the surface was the Frenchmen's fear of the revenge Germany would exact should she win the war. Almost alone stood the people of Paris in their vigorous opposition to peace. And it was the people of Paris who were suffering the most. It was they who had been forced even to empty their zoos in order to set food on their tables. On this matter one patriotic family, long having lost its squeamishness, turned an elephant hoof recently emptied of its food into an umbrella stand. In a short time even the elephant was gone. "Cellar pigeons" became so popular that soon Paris had consumed its population of rats.

Rolier's message was received at Tours on the day that fifty-five miles away the first of the three battles of the Orléans Campaign was being fought. At Loigny-Poupry on December 2 the second and decisive battle was waged. A German army outnumbered nearly four to one cut through 150,000 French troops, captured Orléans, and split the French Army into two parts. One of these fell back so far that, militarily speaking, it was never heard of again.

There was little doubt that the Franco-Prussian War could have taken a different turn if France had had the military leadership competent to direct the country's defenses, if, for instance, France had had a Joffre or a Foch. As it was, though the French generals had command of troops vastly outnumbering the Germans, the patriots were not able to set up an effective strategy. In the plans they did set up the generals were not capable of enacting them. It was by default, then, that Gambetta was forced to make military decisions. And it was in the nature of the military to resist these decisions because they were made by a civilian.

The French generals asked, "What kind of war can we fight with our armies of raw and half-trained recruits?" Gambetta replied that although the recruits were raw, they had endured almost without complaint the hardships of a bitter winter which had been made even worse by lack of suitable clothing and blankets. He pointed out that the French peasants had cheerfully gone through the fatigue of endless and often pointless marchings which would have corroded the morale of less dedicated men. That Gambetta was right was seen in the deteriorating morale of the German soldiers. Though these soldiers were far better equipped and fed than the French, the Germans were becoming intractable because the war was dragging on longer than had been planned; they were jumpy and fearful because there was no telling when a bullet from a sniper's rifle or a blast from a peasant's shotgun would cut them down, and were mindful of Favre's reported words.

German military leaders, too, were confused by the French resistance. For lack of accurate information, they were willing to accept the truth of even the wildest rumors. For this reason, the German armies fell into tactical errors which, had they been exploited by the French, could have brought about the invader's annihilation.

Toward the end of January a battle was shaping up at Le Mans. French troops numbering 156,000 were about to take the offensive against 40,000 Germans. On January 28, 1871, the Chamber of Deputies overrode the pleas of the Parisian representatives for continued resistance. Peace was declared. It is said that General Antoine Chanzy, leader of half of the French Army which had been split at the Orléans Campaign, cried bitterly when he learned he would have to lay down his arms. He said later, as did many other military strategists, that France had won the war when she surrendered.

France gave up with honor. She had taught her invaders prudence and had punctured the myth of Prussian invincibility. Playing a dominant role in teaching these lessons were the French balloons, which started humbly as carnival affairs and then rose to become a force that nearly defeated the greatest army in Europe. They had also created the first airlift in the world's history.

During the four months of the siege of Paris, of the sixty-six balloons that left the city, only five fell into enemy hands. The slow-moving almost ludicrous bags of illuminating gas carried 167 people to safety. Even more astounding was the work of the balloon post, which flew nine tons of dispatches, or 3,000,000 letters, over the German lines.

The question that still haunts us is that as enlightened and clever as the Parisians were, why did they go no further with the balloon? Why did they not use it as a bombardier's platform to drive their besiegers from their positions around the city? Two years after the fall of Paris the American balloonist John Wise, in commenting about the war, said that the Parisians could have constructed a bag 200 feet in diameter. By using the coal gas available in the city this machine could have lifted over eighty-three tons. About sixty tons of this could have been explosives. Imagine what havoc air-launched explosives would have spread among the German cavalry and troops whose positions were clearly outlined by their campfires! There was no way to retaliate. Such balloons could have been sent out by the score. All provisions needed for them were in the city. On the other hand, the Germans, even if they wished, could not have burdened their supply lines with the equipment needed to send their own balloons up for a counterattack.

Under the treaty of Frankfurt, which was signed on May 10, 1871, France ceded to the now unified Germany a part of Lorraine and all of Alsace. The war indemnity levied by the victors was many times oversubscribed by the French, and the occupation forces soon left the country. When they went they carried with them the plans and materials and chemicals that had been used to make the balloons of resistance in the railway stations in the city of Paris.

TO THE NORTH POLE

Man fashions a tool and hastens to use it, even against outrageous odds. Sometimes he is lucky, but more often not. One such tool was the balloon, and its user was the Swedish explorer Salomon August Andrée who, with two companions, in 1897 sought to conquer the North Pole.

On the 15th of July of that year the Norwegian sailing vessel *Alken* was passing the northeast coast of Spitsbergen bound for her home port. The ship's captain, Skipper Ole Hansen, was on the bridge. For the past half hour he and his mate had been staring at a bird perched head-under-wing on the top of the mainsail riggings. It looked like a mountain grouse, though what it was doing so far north neither of the men could understand. It was killed by the first ball from the mate's pistol. But the captain's mess was not to be graced by the fowl, for it fell fluttering into the sea. Later in the day the ship overtook a whaler. In the exchange of megaphoned messages Hansen learned that the bird might have been one of Andrée's carrier pigeons.

"Let's turn about and find it," the whaler's captain suggested.

"I'll find it alone," Hansen stoutly replied. He went back

to where the bird had been shot, and crewed two boats to search for it. The sea was cold, rough, and limitless. However, fortune was with the seamen, because the bird's white plumage, reflecting the sun's rays, was soon sighted. Wrapped around one of the pigeon's legs was a slip of paraffin-soaked parchment. Nervously, the mate unrolled the paper and read its message to the men in his boat.

From Andrée's Polar Expedition

July 13, 1897; 12:30 midday.
Latitude, 82° 2'; longitude 15° 5' east.
All well on board. This is the third pigeon-post.

Andrée

Philadelphia's World Exposition of 1876 attracted businessmen, adventurers, and the curious from all sections of the globe. Salomon Andrée, a twenty-two-year-old mechanical engineer, numbered among the curious, arrived in New York after a month's freighter trip from Sweden. When he got off the train in Philadelphia, he had three dollars, a textbook knowledge of English, and a strong desire to meet the aeronaut John Wise, whose writings the boy knew as though he had composed them. First, though, there was the problem of getting a job, any job. Andrée went to his consul-general, who referred him to an aide, who referred him to a secretary, who said there was an opening for a porter and cleanup man at the Swedish Pavilion. "It's not the job an engineer would want," he added.

"A hungry one would," said Andrée and he was accepted. He took a room near the Exposition and met a girl. A friendship took root, blossomed, and then died. She had spoken of love and marriage.

"Such things drag down the man who wants to make something of himself," he told her. "They smother him

with responsibilities. Then they trade off his ambition for
an easy chair." At a later meeting his lack of interest was
made even clearer. "My parents sacrificed nothing in raising
me. They wanted the job. The sacrifice would have been if
they hadn't been allowed to have it. As for me, I see other
uses for my talents. Not necessarily better ones, from your
point of view, but other ones."

His friends in Sweden would have expected just such
conversation from Salomon. His family was a sentiment-
free group of five brothers and two sisters. They had learned
from their parents the need for strength, strength of mind
and body, and for self-reliance. It was said that the only
time a kiss was exchanged was at a marriage. Whether this
story was true or not, this much was certain: Papa Andrée
had taught his children that the meek were a long way
from inheriting the earth.

Their bodies and minds reflected their heredity and
training. Angularly built, each offspring looked strong
enough to face the world at the age of ten. Though mentally
there was no touch of genius, there was fortitude and a
Herculean oneness of purpose. And in Salomon Andrée—
square-faced, heavy-nosed, and wispy-haired—these qualities were clearly apparent.

John Wise was going to make an ascension from the
Exposition Grounds. The event had been well advertised.
On the day set Andrée gave up part of his sleep, since he
was on a night shift, to be at the launching area early.
When he arrived, thousands of people were already assembled to see the sixty-eight-year-old aeronaut make his flight.
Many feared that they might not get another chance because John Wise was a man weakened by age and more by
misfortune.

His balloon was old and tired-looking. It lay on the
ground as though glad for the rest and seemed disinclined
to be disturbed by the process of inflation. As the gas
poured in, the bag sluggishly shifted its position and began

taking form. Andrée could see where the sun had bleached its top and weather had streaked its sides. An inspection showed scores of patches on its skin, sealing the scars of time. Casually, the bag lifted itself off the ground. The riggings connecting the bag to the basket began forming a graceful arc in the air.

"Hands away!" cried Wise. The basket was released but it stayed on the ground. He dropped two bags of ballast. The aerostat finally began rising. Andrée and three other porters let run the ropes that held the vehicle captive. Halfway up, Wise began dumping thousands of advertising throwaways over the basket's side. Below him people jumped in the air to catch the papers before they could hit the ground. His job was finished minutes after the holding ropes were stretched to their length. Many of the throwaways were still drifting when Wise gave the signal for haul-down. Andrée wondered what kind of a country America was that forced its foremost aeronaut to earn a living in this fashion.

After the entertainment was over and the equipment packed Andrée introduced himself to the professor. The boy's offer to help the aeronaut take his balloon home was quickly accepted. Once there, Andrée begged Wise for lessons in the theory of aeronautics. At first the man thought the boy was being kind, but when he learned that Andrée was a graduate engineer and had come to America chiefly for instruction from the man who knew ballooning best, he offered the visitor the hospitality of his home and the free gift of his time.

After work, at midnight, Andrée would go to Wise's home. Student and teacher would then study in the basement until dawn poked through the ground-level windows. Andrée learned that there was more to ballooning than simply filling a bag with gas.

"Watch the men who put your varnishes on," Wise warned him. "I've seen the best compositions fail through

inept workmanship." Wise spent much time showing the
boy how to choose proper balloon materials and how to
build mechanisms to test them. An entire week was used
for designing a pattern for a balloon. Early-morning hours
of the following week were detailed to cutting up newspapers in a manner that would give the least waste, had it
been fabric they were using. These newspapers were then
sewn together, while man and boy pretended they were
making a real balloon that soon would be flying. Once they
built a gas generator out of cardboard. For iron filings they
used sawdust, and for acid, water. Soon the demonstration
piece became soggy and collapsed, but not its theory of
operation.

At last the professor told Andrée, "If you stay with me
longer, I can refine what I've taught you, but that's all. I
would have you build on the theory of aerostatics that you
already know; and know, mind you, better than I did when
I began. But then," he said proudly, "I helped develop it,
didn't I?" He looked away from Andrée to stare at the
flaky remains of the gas generator, and his tone changed.
"You're an ambitious boy, Andrée, and I worry about you.
Ambition is what I know most about, even more than about
balloons. It's more treacherous, too, because a burst balloon
brings you to earth slowly, but not a burst ambition."

Andrée answered, "You're still thinking about your transatlantic flight. What a disappointment that must have been!
I admired your courage in first attempting the flight, and
then in the face of a world watching, removing yourself
from it. This act took more bravery than the actual flight
would have. Had I been there, and had the balloon been
made of tissue paper, I know I wouldn't have had the
strength to reject it."

"It really was made of tissue paper, the whole concept,"
Wise said. He added, upon reflection, "No, not really, not
at the beginning. It was a good project and could have
proved to everybody, just from this one flight, the value

and safety of ballooning." His mood changed and he asked Andrée in a sly tone, "Why are you really interested in ballooning? You're too devoted for a passing fancy and too cautious of your time to waste it. What is it you really want from me—my transatlantic plans?"

"Do you think that little of me to believe I'd use stealth to get your ideas?" Andrée asked. He was not hurt as much as he was ashamed of what he thought were Wise's suspicions.

In Wise's eyes there was wonderment and worry, wonderment at the boy's sharp reply and worry that his teasings had been taken so poorly. "If you're going to be a balloonist you're going to need a sense of humor. There are too many trials to take each one seriously."

"I have a sense of humor," said Andrée defiantly.

"So I see," commented Wise, and then to change the subject asked, "What are you going to do with what I've taught you?"

Without hesitating, Andrée answered, "I'm going to the North Pole."

"In a balloon?" Wise sputtered.

"In a balloon!" the boy declared.

"You'll kill yourself," the aeronaut decided.

"Never!" cried Andrée. "The balloon has been around for over a century. It's been proven safe. You helped do that. Now it's time to put the vehicle to work. What better work is there than to send it over the Pole? Listen to me!" he pleaded. "How else but by balloon can man get there? Sleds have failed, and so have ships. The ice was too much for them. But with a balloon . . . ah . . . with a balloon it would be different.

"I'd go during the time of the long day. How much this would help! Can't you see it, sir? The balloon would be in perfect balance. The sun would be heating the gas on one side while the ice reflecting the sun's rays would be heating it on the other. The aerostat could stay afloat for weeks."

"You haven't the slightest idea of weather conditions up there," Wise said sourly. "I say you'll kill yourself."

"I'll make myself," Andrée said vehemently. "Not only that but I'll be giving the world something it's never had before, a knowledge of the Arctic." Andrée thought of the years he had been dreaming of such a trip, ever since he heard that there really was such a thing as an airborne vehicle. Now that he had been taught by his acknowledged master, Andrée saw nothing in the teachings that would prevent the scheme from being successful. He became so excited about it that he forgot that he had only one listener and spoke as though in a lecture hall. He asked rhetorically, "Is there land in the Arctic, or is it merely a mass of floating snow and ice? Will we find life there? If we do, how is it able to adapt itself to the cold? If we learn this, perhaps some day we will be able to populate that region. Oh, there are so many answers locked in that frozen area that I hope I'll have the knowledge and strength to learn even a few of them."

Five years later Andrée saw an opportunity to advance his plan. During the First International Polar Year in 1882, a time set aside by the world's geophysicists to concentrate on learning as much as they could about the polar regions, several countries cooperated in setting up bases in the northern and southern polar tracts. Heading Sweden's expedition was Dr. Nils Ekholm. At a later time he was to join forces with Andrée. For the present, though, Andrée was working for Ekholm as a mechanical engineer. When Andrée had time off, he was busy gathering temperature and wind data, which he felt would be useful should he choose Spitsbergen as the jumping-off place for his balloon trip. An odd circumstance gave him leisure to plan such a journey. The long polar night that the men had endured all winter was drawing to a close. Spring was coming, heralded by a vague lightening of the sky. One midnight the sun peeked over the horizon, its rays so bright they seemed to set the snow on fire. The glare pained the eyes of the men, who had left their lodgings to welcome the first day. They returned to the softer glow of lantern light. After the sun had gone down leaving its twilight behind, the men ventured outside once more. For the first time in months they saw one another in natural light and were startled. Their faces were yellow-green. Or was it, they asked one another, that they just seemed so after the long night? To find out, Andrée volunteered to stay indoors for the coming month. It was during this time that he wrote his first paper proposing a balloon expedition to the Pole. When he emerged, his companion's faces were of normal color but his own, they told him, still had a green hue. "The best specimen of flora I've seen since we left home," observed Ekholm.

When Andrée returned to Sweden, he held back his North Pole paper until he could reinforce his theory with practical experience in ballooning. With no means at hand for this, he had to wait.

The Swedish Patent Office was being reorganized. A post of chief engineer was created and Andrée got the appointment. However, the very qualities that put him in the job, his need for system and to see every facet of a technical problem before making a decision, gave him just the opposite reputation. He was thought to be a dawdler and unorganized. His chief told the trustees of the Office, disturbed by the slowness of patent awards, that it was Andrée's thoroughness that was the cause. In an aside to an associate, the chief said, "To convince him of the novelty of a patent, you have to survey the technical field from the first day of creation. But once his mind is made up, you have to go back to the same day to change it."

This is the way it was with Andrée and his balloon. He was convinced of the need for aeronautical research and he continuously badgered the trustees for money for it. They told him that aeronautics was not their province. "Whose province is it?" he asked them. He followed up his question with a strong memorandum to his chief. "Sweden may let aeronautical research go by, but I assure you that other countries will not; and you and I may live to regret this shortsightedness."

Andrée finally got money for a balloon from the Lars Hierta Foundation, an organization interested in the advancement of science. He immediately designed an aerostat and had it built in France, where he thought the best craftsmen were. When the completed vehicle arrived in Stockholm, Andrée hurried to cram as much flight experience into one year as more patient balloonists gathered in ten. His every spare krone and moment were spent for lifting gas and supplies. He flew over wastelands and seas, in turbulent weather and in calm. Twice he was marooned, once on an uninhabited island in the Baltic and another time in his basket in the open sea. Each time he and his aerostat were rescued by a passing fishing vessel. These experiences taught him that he could be the best balloonist that ever lived but that he still would not reach the North Pole if he depended only on a cooperative wind to carry him there.

While in Spitsbergen, he had dallied with an idea that he felt might solve the problem of how to steer an aerostat. The thought was that a free balloon was always part of the wind and hence a sail would do no good. If the balloon were slowed down though, say by draglines slipping along the ground or across a surface of water, then there would be relative motion between the craft and the wind. Surely here a sail could be used to good advantage. The practical results of his theory were far better than he dared hope. On one of several trips he made with an adjustable sail control, he was able to change his flight path, with respect to the wind's direction, by twenty-seven degrees and on occasions by as much as forty degrees. Salomon Andrée was ready to present his paper to the Swedish Academy of Science.

On February 13, 1895, several score members of the

Academy met in their hall in Stockholm to hear what they expected would be a talk by Salomon Andrée about the workings of the Patent Office. The chairman of the meeting, Baron A. E. Nordenskiöld, polar explorer and discoverer of the Northeast Passage, had assumed that such would be the topic when Andrée volunteered to speak, and this was the information printed in the program notes. Only minutes before the meeting began, when Nordenskiöld asked Andrée about his professional background for an introduction, was the subject of the talk learned. The Baron was the Academy's harshest critic on any proposal concerned with exploring the Arctic. There were as many impractical propositions offered then for going to the North Pole as there were to be at a later time for traveling to the planets. Andrée felt that had the Baron been able to find a substitute speaker, he would have. The chairman could not hide his displeasure when he announced, "Mr. Andrée's paper will be, 'On a Novel Way of Reaching the North Pole.'"

In a voice high-pitched by nervousness, Andrée began reading. "The aeronaut John Wise once said to me, 'If a brave man has not courage to do what has to be done, then who is left to do it?' A parallel is evident. If we of Scandinavia with our history of exploration and our knowledge of the Arctic cannot reach the North Pole, then to whom can the world turn?

"I ask this question simply for its reaction value and to give you an opportunity to note to yourselves the courageous efforts some of our colleagues have made to reach the top of the world. Among these men we count Dr. Nansen, who two years ago purposely locked his ship in a drifting ice mass hoping it would carry him north. There is much doubt that it will. Other dedicated men have tried the trip by sled and dog but only the fortunate have returned and these only to tell us of their failures.

"We can agree then that stark courage alone will not solve our problem. We have lost too many times. But if we

believe, as I do, that every problem has it solution, then
obviously this one does too."

Andrée put aside his notes. His nervousness was gone,
and his enthusiasm made him eloquent. "I propose using
the balloon for the job. Look what we have! A vehicle little
affected by cold, not in the least disturbed by terrain, and
proved safe by thousands of balloonists in more than a
century of flying. How pleasant the trip would be! The
crew, while floating in the atmosphere and using its currents to push them over the Pole, would be making un-
hurried and immensely valuable observations of the region.
They would be rested, well-fed, and warm. What a difference between these men and those who ride the dog sled!

"How cheap such a system would be when we consider
how simple are its needs! The balloon would be of modest
size. One able to lift about 6600 pounds would be ample.
Such a balloon would have a volume of about 212,000
cubic feet. Some of you may remember, at the Paris Exhibition sixteen years ago, an aeronaut successfully ascended
in a balloon with four times the weight capacity of the one
I'm proposing. My balloon would carry three men, scientific
instruments, spare parts, and a four months' supply of food
and equipment. This four months' figure contains a big
factor of safety. The air trip would take nowhere near that
length of time. With a good wind, such as one I experienced
recently in an aerial voyage from Göteborg to Gotland, a
distance of 240 miles, the balloon trip from Spitsbergen to
the Pole would be accomplished in about ten hours. If, on
the other hand, we base our calculations on average
Spitsbergen winds, about sixteen miles an hour, then it
would take two days to reach the Pole and another four
days to cross the Arctic Ocean to a landing off the Bering
Strait. This is only one-fifth the time the balloon would be
designed to stay aloft—I'm assuming some leakage through
the pores of the bag material. During this period the vehicle
would have traveled a distance of 2200 miles.

"Finally, we would need a means to steer the aerostat. This I have worked out." Andrée then told of his experiments with his adjustable sail and his draglines. He described in detail the trajectory of one of his trips during which he was able to deviate his course a large angle from the prevailing wind. The audience's interest was so great that he went on to describe several more of his experimental flights. Questions from the floor, seldom allowed before a talk was finished, were frequent. Finally, with a sidelong glance, Nordenskiöld indicated that Andrée should begin the summing up. The patent officer ended with, "We have shown the feasibility of such a venture. We know its need. What remains is its doing."

Baron Nordenskiöld told the assembly that he thought the speaker still had many problems to work out for himself, such as, what would happen if the balloon were becalmed in the middle of the Arctic? "It could happen, you know. However, Mr. Andrée's scheme has much to recommend it and is far superior to many that I've heard described from this platform." Everyone present realized that Baron Nordenskiöld's closing statement was one of highest praise. In effect it gave Andrée the Academy's scientific approval.

He worked fanatically to raise the money for his expedition. At night he was out lecturing for a fee. During the day he was writing magazine and newspaper articles. Somehow he also squeezed in his Patent Office work. One gray afternoon while Andrée was tallying how much money he had cleared and had discovered that in two months he had made only one per cent of the $36,000 needed, a visitor came to see him. The man was Alfred Nobel. He had read of Andrée's plan and he offered to contribute half the money needed provided the other half were pledged within the next two months. With such sponsorship Andrée was able to get the amount needed, part of which was donated by King Oscar II.

It took two years for Andrée to complete his preparations.

He had to design the balloon and then pick a fabric for it. He had to check the fabric and then watch while it was coated. He had to design the two valves and other mechanisms that went into the balloon. Then there was the problem of buying equipment, testing it, and with all this, being sure he stayed within his budget. Although he had the money he asked for, it was an amount based on the most rigid economy.

The vehicle was only a part of the picture Andrée was putting together. A ship had to be rented and outfitted. It had to be crewed. Yet what Andrée needed most were two qualified men to fly along with him in the aerostat. If he had been looking for ordinary men he would have had no trouble choosing from the hundreds who volunteered; but he did not delude himself that the trip would be easy even though he had inferred this in his talks. From his experience in Spitsbergen he knew how the cold could numb a man's senses and weaken his resistance. He also knew that one bit of awkwardness at the wrong time, one show of bad judgment, and the aerial party could be doomed.

Andrée found only one volunteer who satisfied him, twenty-four-year-old Nils Strindberg, nephew of playwright August Strindberg. The man had worked in science and music, athletics and philosophy. He was chosen because in addition to being mentally and physically qualified, he had two bonus qualities. He was a good photographer and a good cook.

The man Andrée wanted most was Professor Nils Ekholm, doctor of philosophy and member of the faculty of the Meteorological Institute of Stockholm. The professor had not asked to go nor would he make a decision until Andrée had gone over every detail of the project with him. On examining the method of seaming the balloon, Ekholm worried about the possible escape of gas through the thread holes.

"They're covered with a double coat of varnish and then with a fabric strip glued to the skin," Andrée told him. "It's a standard method that's never failed."

"I'm not familiar with it," Ekholm replied, "but then I'm not an aeronaut." Two months of discussions later, the professor consented to be the third man in the aerostat.

On June 7 1896, several thousand people gathered on the docks of Göteborg, major seaport on Sweden's southwest coast, to see the North Pole Expedition ship, the *Virgo*, sail out of their harbor. Three marching bands were entertaining them. The flag of the *Virgo* dipped to salute the well-wishers and they yelled and waved their handkerchiefs in return.

For the past week the townspeople had been entertaining the balloon party and the ship's crew, which was made up almost entirely of engineering students from the technical school at Stockholm. Now, an hour before scheduled departure, the harbor was so choked with vessels carrying sightseers that the *Virgo's* captain feared for his ship's safety. He sent one of his seamen to fetch Andrée for an early start.

Before leaving, Andrée held an informal press conference in the captain's cabin. His face was lined with the fatigue of last-minute work but nevertheless he answered the questions.

"Mr. Andrée," said one of the reporters, "in an Austrian paper yesterday the editor wrote that you are either a fool or a swindler because to cross over the North Pole you would have to stay in the air longer and travel farther than any balloonist has ever done. How do you feel about this?"

"I feel that the editor is unjustified. He is ignoring the possibility of technical progress. If a balloon can hold its gas there is no theoretical reason why it can't stay in the air forever. The trick is to make the bag as airtight as possible. On the record there are many instances of long-distance flights. For these, the travelers descended at night

and resumed their trips in the morning. They did this only
for rest, not because their balloon had to be regassed. Our
North Pole flight is only a variation of this technique. Our
plan is to let two men work while the other sleeps. In this
way there will be no need to descend until our mission is
achieved. I might point out that we will be going over 2000
miles, which, it is true, is some kind of a record. But it can
be easily made because the balloon was designed specifically
for such distance and endurance."

Another reporter rose. "I understand, sir, that you're using
draglines to aid in steering your balloon. What would happen if one of these lines wrapped itself around a piece of
ice and held you fast?"

"Each rope has a weak point in it. This is a section
narrower than the rest. Should an emergency such as you
suggest occur, then the rope would tear away at its weak
point, thereby freeing the balloon. To make up for this loss
we would merely add more rope from our supply."

"Suppose the new rope is now caught."

"The upper part of each dragline is coupled to its lower
part by a screw connection. It can be uncoupled by turning
a winch in the car. The rope would fall and we would still
be safe." At this point the captain interrupted to tell
Andrée that the ship was ready to sail.

Three weeks later the *Virgo* laid anchor at Danes Island,
a place just off the northwest coast of the Spitsbergen
islands. Work was started on a shed to house the balloon
and to protect it against wind blast when take-off time
arrived. The Arctic night was still two months away.

A storm that buried the building materials under several
feet of snow caused three weeks' delay. More time was lost
when a heavy fog moved in, obscuring everything not within
arm's length. Less than a month remained to complete the
half-finished shed, because on August 20 the *Virgo* would
have to sail for home. This was the date Andrée had given

the insurers of the ship. He had experienced one winter in the Arctic and was not eager for a second.

On the last day of July an inflated balloon stood in a completed shed. After the hydrogen generator was discharged, there was a champagne party. One bottle was saved for the christening ceremonies. The aerostat was formally called the "Eagle." Ekholm raised his glass in toast and said, "May your journey be as fast and your path as true as the flight of the bird whose name you bear!" Andrée raised his and said, "May God grant you strength!"

The car of the "Eagle" was made of wicker and Spanish cane. The woods were interwoven, which gave the frame lightness and strength. Wrapped around the car was a heavy tarpaulin which sheltered the interior and insulated it against the outside cold. The covering admitted light through two rectangular portholes. An enclosed room was formed by topping the frame with an arched roof of thick mattress-like material. A small port in the roof gave entrance to the room. A steel ring mounted on jointed railings extended three feet above the roof and formed an observation platform. A dozen buoys hung from the ring. These, bearing messages, would be thrown overboard during the trip. When the buoys were found, they would give information about the drift and currents of the Arctic Ocean. At the last minute a thirteenth buoy was whittled out of a piece of scrap wood. This one, larger than the rest, was to be dropped on the North Pole.

Loading took several days. Three sleds and a canvas boat were being carried. Arms and ammunition were taken for hunting. Strindberg packed a heavy load of camera equipment, which he had spent months designing and building. He intended recording the trip on several thousand plates. Food and scientific equipment were stowed in the car. A Primus stove, newly developed and useful for cooking and melting snow for water, was carefully wrapped in oilskin before it was packed away. This stove was Andrée's toy and he was most proud of it. The loading was finished when a dozen baskets, each housing three carrier pigeons, were hung over the side.

Several times during the first week of August strong south winds blew. These were the ones Andrée needed to carry him north. Each time the crew rushed to their stations to prepare for take-off, and each time the wind died down and reversed itself. After these experiences Andrée sent test balloons aloft to tell more accurately the wind's strength and extent.

At the beginning of the second week in August, Ekholm asked Andrée and Strindberg to accompany him to the balloon shack. He was nervous during the short walk. When the men asked him what was wrong he would not answer. Instead he suggested they climb the scaffolding onto the dome of the balloon. Once there, they heard the soft hiss of escaping gas. Ekholm went to the nearest seam and lifted part of the fabric strip. Immediately the pitch of the issuing gas grew higher, almost hysterical. Andrée simply said, "I'll have the workmen check it."

The next day Andrée called Ekholm and Strindberg to a meeting. He showed them the calculations he had made based upon what he felt was the quantity of gas escaping from the balloon. "If we use for ballast the sleds, some instruments, and some supplies I have listed, then I see no reason why we can't stay aloft for the thirty days we planned on. This means that we will be depending upon a quick rescue at the end of our expedition. The worst thing that could happen is that we'd spend the winter in the Bering Strait region. That wouldn't be easy, but it wouldn't be any harder than surviving in the north of our own country for the same period of time. These are the facts, but it's up to you gentlemen to decide what you want to do." In the discussion that followed, Strindberg said he would live up to his agreement. Ekholm asked for time to think the matter over.

As events turned out, there was no need for Ekholm to reach a decision. The day after the conference Andrée announced that operations were suspended. He felt that there was little chance of getting the proper wind before the *Virgo* had to sail. Two days later he released eight of the carrier pigeons. Each carried the same terse message.

From Andrée's Polar Expedition

Danes Island.
August 13, 1896.
No south wind. Returning to Sweden.

Andrée

His reception back home was much cooler than his send-off. Andrée felt that he had returned a failure. He gave no interviews, wrote no magazine articles. It was as though he had lost all his enthusiasm and only his will to do what he had promised was driving him on. He asked the Swedish government for financing. They gave him the money he needed as well as a gunboat to transport a second expedition to Danes Island. Nobel offered to pay for building a new balloon but Andrée preferred using his old one. He planned to leave in May, which would give him ample time at the island to ready his apparatus and then wait for the best wind.

Nils Ekholm would not make the trip. He said that figures of his own showed that the balloon would be unable to stay aloft a week. He asked Andrée whether he had considered the possibility of an icecap forming on top of the balloon. "Its weight would force the aerostat down," Ekholm said. Andrée did not answer. Ekholm repeated his statement. So little did Andrée disguise his lack of interest that Ekholm cried out, "If you won't think of yourself, think of Strindberg! He wants to get married when he comes back." Ekholm leaned forward. "Will he come back, Salomon Andrée?"

The leader struck out defensively. "Of course he will. If you're saying that I'd deliberately take a man on an impossible adventure, then, Ekholm, I'm stunned at your low appraisal of me. There is danger, we all know that. But there is no more danger than when you volunteered. It's your privilege to back out, but I ask you to do it as a gentleman. Please do not try to rationalize what I can now judge only as your own trepidation."

"I was prepared for that," said Ekholm. "For your sake and Strindberg's, I hope it really is fear and not judgment that has influenced me. One piece of judgment I don't understand, though, is your refusing a new balloon."

"There is nothing wrong with the old one," protested Andrée. "It had a weakness of seams, but these have been repaired. It's been overhauled, tested, and packed. I haven't time to build and search out the faults of a new one."

"Haven't time or won't take the time?" prodded Ekholm. "If I could read your mind, Salomon Andrée, I'd say you don't want to go on your expedition any more than I do."

If Andrée had deliberately tried to replace Nils Ekholm by his opposite he could not have succeeded better than in his choice of Knut Fraenkel. Where Ekholm was an established scientist, Fraenkel was a civil engineer just starting out. Where Ekholm had spent most of his life deskbound except for an occasional expedition, Fraenkel studied when there was nothing better to do, reserving most of his time for hunting and sports. Fraenkel wanted to go on the Polar expedition purely for the adventure.

By the middle of May 1897 Andrée's Expedition was again on Danes Island. By the middle of June, the balloon shed had been built, the balloon inflated and tested, and the car packed. All that was needed was a strong south wind. Twice such a one blew, but each time Andrée said it would not last. Fraenkel grew so impatient that after the second prediction proved false he took Strindberg aside and asked, "Doesn't he want to go? That last wind was perfect for us."

On July 11 Strindberg got up shortly after dawn. He had slept fitfully, his rest being disturbed by thoughts of home. He dressed and went on deck of the gunboat, which the party had made their headquarters. He paused at the rail to scribble a few more sentences in a letter that the captain had promised to deliver to Anna, the explorer's fiancée. Strindberg wrote that the harbor had been calm for a week and that its calmness reminded him of the mountain lakes in Sweden. He told her about Fraenkel and his worry that they would never leave; and about Andrée and his passion to be left alone. While Strindberg was composing this, a soft breeze began ruffling his paper. Soon whitecaps began forming in the harbor, which was now called Virgo Bay. Strindberg stuffed his letter into his pocket. He took out his handkerchief to test the wind's direction and saw that it was blowing to the north. Waves were striking the ship with increasing vigor. By this time Andrée and Fraenkel were on deck and the captain was coming down from the bridge.

"This is it," Fraenkel said excitedly.

"It may not hold up," said Andrée.

"Shall we wait until it's over?" Fraenkel asked sarcastically.

"We'll leave when I say so," Andrée snapped back. "And I'm not saying so, not right now, anyway. But if you're so anxious to get started, why don't you begin by going below for weather balloons?"

Another ship had come into the harbor. Her captain was rowed to the gunboat. On board he told Andrée that he was anchoring until the storm abated. "It's going to be a full-fledged squall," he said, "and will be blowing for the next two or three days."

Fraenkel released two of the weather balloons. They shot

up and to the north. Within minutes they had traveled so
far and fast that they were lost from sight. An hour later
Andrée was on shore directing the demolition of all but the
south quadrant of the balloon shed. The wind blew harder.
Soon all that could be heard above its roar was the biting of
axes into wood and the crash of heavy beams as they
twisted from above into the hard-packed snow below.
Andrée ordered a large canvas erected over the upper scaffolding of the south side. He wanted increased insurance
that his balloon would be protected during launch. The
seamen hurried to obey him. It was a treacherous job. The
canvas jumped about as though alive. The captain's mate
up there with his men was whipped off the scaffolding. He
clutched onto the canvas, was swung around and then
slammed into the framework. His arm was broken. After
this the canvas seemed to relent and was subdued.

On the steel ring above the aerostat's car three ropes were
tied 120 degrees apart. Each was held by four men on the
ground. Several bags of ballast were snipped off the ring.
Relieved of this weight, the aerostat rose a foot off the
ground where it was kept in tow. Andrée walked slowly
around the vehicle, making last-minute checks of the
tightness of the draglines and of other equipment within
reach. Strindberg was busy snapping pictures of all phases
of the preparations. When he had all he wanted, he had
his own picture taken by one of the sailors. The captain
passed by. Strindberg grabbed his arm and put the packet
of exposed film into his hands. Out of his pocket he pulled
the crumpled letter to his sweetheart, wrote a parting sen-
tence on it, and handed this paper over as well. "Tell Anna
I love her, and I'll be home soon!" Fraenkel was leaning
against the gondola and smiling. As though by accord, the
three companions suddenly abandoned themselves to their
emotions and embraced the men they had worked with most
closely. Strindberg was not alone in tears.

Andrée was the first to break away. He hoisted himself

onto the roof of the car and cried out, "Strindberg, Fraenkel, let's go!" The two men climbed aboard. At Andrée's signal the balloon was allowed to rise until its top was just below the canvas sheet. The balloon was buffeted by strong gusts that swirled over the enclosure. Below the aerostat, like tentacles, hung three draglines, three ballast lines, and three restraining ropes. Andrée nodded to Strindberg and Fraenkel. Each unsheathed his knife and poised himself next to one of the restraining ropes. All at once Andrée cried "Cut!" Knives flashed downward. The balloon was free.

Hurrahs and yells broke out from the men on the ground. They watched the "Eagle" tremble fitfully and then, spreading its wings of canvas, soar northward over the bay. Unmindful of the piercing cold and the beginning rain the men ran to the shore line to watch the aerostat's course. Halfway to the mountains on the other side of the bay the "Eagle" began losing altitude. Ballast was seen being dropped. The car swept to within a few feet of the water. Then it hit the surface, bounced crazily, and rose again. Soon the "Eagle" faded from sight. Lying on shore were the aerostat's three draglines. They had become unscrewed during take-off.

Eleven

WHERE IS ANDRÉE?

On May 28, 1898, the following item appeared in a Swedish newspaper:

ANDRÉE'S BALLOON FOUND IN EAST SIBERIAN FOREST

Andrée's balloon has been reported found in a forest in eastern Siberia. The Arctic explorer with two companions ascended near Spitsbergen in July, 1897 in an attempt to reach the Pole. It was the last seen of them. The Swedish government has ordered an investigation of the report.

Then on January 6, 1910, a Canadian newspaper published this story under a Winnipeg, Manitoba, dateline:

FAMED SWEDISH EXPLORER REPORTED SLAIN BY ESKIMOS

The mystery surrounding the whereabouts of three intrepid Swedish explorers who sought to conquer the North Pole by balloon 13 years ago may have been solved by a 71-year-old trapper. William Irvine, 57 years employed by the Hudson Bay Company, says he knows what happened to Salomon Andrée, Nils Strindberg and Knut Fraenkel, who on July 11, 1897, ascended from an island off Spitsbergen and disappeared from the civilized world.

Irvine claims that this past winter he met a band of Eskimos in upper Hudson Bay who had with them some brass instruments, a quantity of brass fittings that they had used for making hunting gear, several cooking utensils of a quality unknown to that land, and some wearing apparel on which was stamped the initials S.A. According to Irvine, the Eskimos told him that several years before they had been hunting on the shores of the Arctic Sea when they beheld an apparition in the sky. Terror-stricken, they watched it land and saw three men jump out. One of the white men opened fire with a rifle. They started a fight in which six of the Eskimos and the three whites were killed.

Irvine said that he would be willing to head a party to search for the Eskimos but that at the time they were far away from home and would be difficult to find.

As the years passed, other stories dealing with Andrée's strange disappearance found their way into the world's press. Some were plausable and some were weird. All had one thing in common: they were incapable of being proved. Then the fickleness of memory took over. The fate of the "Eagle" and her crew faded from public thought just as the aerostat had faded from sight over Virgo Bay.

August 1930. A Norwegian sealing vessel called the *Bratvaag* was feeling its way through the iceberg studded waters surrounding White Island, a piece of land lying thirty-five miles east of the Spitsbergen islands. A map showed the island to be elliptically shaped, with diameters of five miles and twenty miles.

The ship's captain was Peder Eliassen, who for twenty years had been hunting seal in the Arctic seas. He was a calm, courageous man, well-liked by his crew and by the scientists he had on board. These last were headed by geologist Dr. Gunnar Horn of the Norwegian Svalbard and Polar Sea Research Institution. Through the ship owners' and captain's help, the Institution was able to send its men on geophysical trips it otherwise could not afford.

Walruses were sighted on White Island. The ship dropped anchor. Two whaling boats were loaded and sent to shore. Upon landing, one crew went to hunt the animals while the other searched for fresh water to replenish the ship's supply.

The island was covered with a fresh layer of snow. Here and there outcroppings of rocks showed through. On upsloping ground about 100 yards from the harbor two of the men discovered a small brook. They followed it inland hoping it would lead to a larger stream. After ten minute's walk they found one, fast-flowing and a foot deep. As one of the men leaned over to drink, he saw a dull metallic object half-buried in the pebbles on the opposite shore. He stared at it, then pulled it free and wiped it clean. It was a small aluminum lid, which he showed to his companion. The quest for water was forgotten. The men searched the neighborhood for other finds and soon uncovered part of a canvas boat, most of which was hidden in a melting mound of ice. The men looked no more. They ran back to fetch their captain.

Captain Eliassen was on shore talking to Dr. Horn when the men arrived. The seamen told their story, showed the

aluminum lid to prove it. Captain Eliassen simply said,
"Andrée!" A few yards away sealers were loading a bloody
walrus into their boat. Above them circled several sea gulls
looking for a chance to get some of the flesh. When the men
heard the lost explorer's name, they left their work to join
their captain. The sea gulls lazily spiraled down for their
feast. That was the end of the hunting trip.

Silently the men crossed the stream where the first find
had been made. They paused to listen to their colleague,
who told in detail how it had come about. Then they went
on. Thirty-three years ago Andrée, Strindberg, and Fraenkel
had disappeared, a time before most of those present had
been born. Yet each man there knew the adventurers' story
up to the time the "Eagle" took off from Danes Island. Seamen's tales are told and retold in every forecastle and Andrée's story had become part of the Arctic legend.

They came upon the canvas boat. With their bare hands
Captain Eliassen and Dr. Horn began shoveling snow out
of it. They found a brass boat-hook, which the seamen took
to examine. The oldest among them said it had been made
in the late 1800s. A small heavy box was uncovered. Sten-
ciled on its side was the word *Ammunition*. As Captain
Eliassen lifted the box free of the boat, Dr. Horn recited
the words marked on what had been the box's hidden side:
"Andrée's Pol. Exp. 1896." If there had been a question,
this evidence answered it.

Dr. Horn's feelings at the time, he later wrote down for
the Swedish Society of Anthropology and Geography. "We
are here at the spot! Hither had Andrée and his comrades
come, never to leave the place again. The moment was a
strange, a solemn one, and some moments passed before
we began our task anew. We did not speak much—for what
had we to say?—and gradually the whole truth broke upon
us; the story of the tragedy that had been acted here.

"It was strange to stand here and let our gaze wander
over the same landscape and the same sea that Andrée and

Strindberg and Fraenkel looked at for the last time thirty-
three years before. It was as if we saw them before us. They
are coming toward us down there on the ice, pulling their
heavy equipment. Tired and weary they must have been.
. . . It was as if the air still gave the echo of their voices. We
thought we heard the sleds scrape against the stones when,
with a last effort, they pulled them up on the land in order
to encamp in the shelter of the rock beside which we now
stood. And they must have climbed the glacier now and
then to look across the sea, though they could have seen
nothing but ice and ocean. Maybe, one day of clear weather,
they caught sight of Storön's white dome in the west. They
knew that behind it lay Northeast Land, and behind that
again West Spitsbergen, whence there was a path home to
Sweden."

Captain Eliassen found the first body. It was stretched
out on a low-lying ledge overlooking the place where the
canvas boat had been found. The body's skull and upper
torso were missing, probably having been dragged off by a
bear. The part left seemed quite relaxed, almost as though
belonging to a man asleep. The legs were casually crossed
above the ankles and the outline of bent knees was clearly
marked through the stiff trousers. Lower breastbones poked
through the jersey jacket the corpse had on. It was Andrée's
jacket, told by the "A" found sewn on its inside. Also found
protected by the jacket was a large diary and a smaller one,
both carefully wrapped in a native grass. These books were
too frozen to be safely opened. Yet in a few weeks they
were to reveal to the world in Andrée's words his fantastic
North Pole adventure.

Scattered around the body was a collection of eating and
hunting utensils, a rifle buried up to its butt in snow, and a
box which yielded a second store of ammunition. Another
box, this one filled with photographic plates, was uncovered. Some of these had been exposed by the explorers and
wondrously yielded to development in a Stockholm lab-

oratory. Nearby, a Primus stove was dug out. Dr. Horn shook the apparatus. It was half-filled with paraffin. He pumped it up, turned its valve, and ignited the fine spray that issued forth. After thirty-three years' exposure in the Arctic the mechanism was still in fine working order.

A few feet from Andrée's body was a patch of frozen earth singularly free from stones. On the south side it was bounded by the low-hanging ledge; on the west, by the bone of a whale; and on the north and east, by driftwood. Here were concentrated most of the finds—a sleeping sack, a medicine chest, an aluminum cup, Fraenkel's pocketbook, a box of matches, and assorted expedition utensils. There was no doubt this spot marked where the dwelling had been.

While Captain Eliassen and Dr. Horn were freeing Andrée's frozen body for its return to Sweden, several of the sealers were exploring the camp for tokens of their own. About one hundred feet north of the camp site, lying in a wedge between two giant stones and covered by loose rubble, they found a second body. Its feet sticking out from the stones had given it away. A more intense search began. A shoulder bone was found mixed in the rubble and a few feet away a human skull. There was no hiding from the bears. Even a prepared grave, such as this, was no protection. The men carefully removed the stones and lifted the remains out. They were Strindberg's, identified first by a gold locket bearing his sweetheart's picture, which was found where his chest had been; and second, by the initials "N.S.," which though faded could still be read on the jacket and trousers.

The excavations and search came to an abrupt end. The skies had darkened and a storm was brewing. Unless the voyagers hurried they, too, would be stranded on White Island. They gathered their diggings and hurried back to shore and thence to their ship. The waters around White Island were already rough. Only in perfect weather was the land hospitable to navigators. However, what the men had found there was soon told by radio to the world.

Journalists flocked to Skjervo, a small town on the north coast of Norway, to meet the *Bratvaag*. Captain Eliassen and Dr. Horn answered all their questions except one. What had happened to Knut Fraenkel? It was too soon for the scientific commission already appointed by the Swedish and Norwegian governments to have begun their tasks of reading and preserving Andrée's diaries. Where there was no fact, rumors had to do. "Fraenkel had perished before he reached the island." "He had been drowned." "He had been slain by a polar bear." "He had been killed in a fall from the balloon."

Several days before the *Bratvaag* had put into Skjervo, the Swedish journalist Knut Stubbendorff set out on the sealer *Isbjorn* for White Island. He wanted to see the site himself. The weather was ideal, and he had no trouble making the trip or the landing. When he got to Andrée's camp, he saw that he was much better off than he had thought he would be. There was hardly any snow around. Judging from the soaked ground, the reporter surmised that the snow had newly melted. Because of this, there were many remains exposed that had been hidden from the men of the *Bratvaag*. He discovered a third sled, his predecessors having found only two, and not far off, a human backbone, a pelvis, and a thigh bone. He was elated to discover in a container Strindberg's log books and almanac. Scattered around him was more of the expedition's equipment. There were the frozen remains of a bear, from which steaks had been cut; and piled beneath a tarpaulin a small cache of sea gulls. The birds had lain deep in the ice, until the present thaw had come, preserved since the day they had been killed. Near this deposit Stubbendorff found a sun-bleached skull, Andrée's as he later learned.

In the dwelling area the reporter examined what proved to be fabric from the "Eagle." In the lee of the stone ledge close by, from the top of which Andrée's body had been earlier taken, he handled what seemed to be a pile of thawing reindeer hides. It was part of a tent under which lay Knut Fraenkel's remains, except for a backbone, a pelvis, and a thigh bone.

The first entry in Strindberg's notes tells us that take-off was at 1:43 P.M. on July 11 from Danes Island. Oddly enough, Andrée's diaries, though by far the more complete and detailed, say nothing about the loss of the draglines at the beginning of the trip or even about the dipping of the car into the water halfway across Virgo Bay. Strindberg did say briefly, "Draglines lost," but that is all he wrote about them, as he probably felt he could make new ones with the rope on board. This he did but the results were not the same. The ropes were light and not nearly long enough. Thus at the start Andrée had lost much of the mechanism that would have permitted him to steer his balloon. The "Eagle" was practically at the mercy of the prevailing wind. As though this were not enough, the loss of the ropes meant the loss of almost twelve hundred pounds of ballast. And ballast is a balloon's fuel. Its discharge permits the pilot to equalize the loss of lift due to leaking gas. Or it lets the pilot valve gas for a landing and then by lightening the load, take off again. With insufficient ballast the aerostat is condemned to a continuous loss of altitude, except for the elevating effects of occasional thermals, until the amount of gas present falls below that needed to sustain the vehicle.

The first afternoon aloft was a joyous one. The men spliced ropes for new draglines, drank several bottles of ale, and searched the ground beneath for signs of life. Strindberg took a score of pictures, the first few of which, he noted in his log, would be out of focus. Toward the time that ordinarily would be dusk, a light fog surrounded the aerostat. The atmosphere became a fairyland of angel wisps and cotton.

Early evening saw the balloon drifting over a dark-blue sea filled with jigsawed pieces of floating ice. Then a heavy fog moved in. Andrée released ballast, which took the balloon up to 2200 feet where the sky was clear. The aerostat slowly floated down from this altitude as small quantities of gas escaped through imperfections in the balloon material.

Time came for the travelers' first dinner in the aerostat. They had broth heated on the Primus stove, which was lowered over the side to prevent a spark from igniting the hydrogen bag, and sandwiches. When the meal was over, Andrée descended into the car for a few hours' sleep while his companions stood watch. Later, Strindberg replaced Andrée and a sequence was started for each man to get his rest.

While Andrée slept, Strindberg and Fraenkel made and recorded sun observations to determine the aerostat's location. The information was also put inside a buoy which was thrown overboard. Three years later it was found by an old woman scavenging wreckage on a beach off the north coast of Norway. The water-borne message, undamaged by its three-year trip in the Arctic Ocean and across the Barents Sea, was the last the world received from the expedition for three decades. It is now preserved in its buoy in the State Historical Museum in Stockholm. The message says,

From Andrée's Polar Expedition

July 11, 1897; 10:00 P.M. G.M.T.
Buoy No. 4, the first thrown out.
Our journey has hitherto gone well. We are moving on at a height of 830 ft. in a direction which at first was N. 10° E. declination, but later N. 45° E. declination. Four carrier-pigeons were sent off at 5 H. 40 P.M. Greenw. time. They flew westerly.

We are now in over the ice, which is much broken up in all directions. Weather magnificent. In best of humors.
Andrée   Strindberg   Fraenkel
Above the clouds since 7:45 G.M.T.

After midnight Strindberg noted a cloud front directly ahead. He could not see how high it was, though he did observe that its bottom touched the ground. Fast ballasting floated the balloon up to 1500 feet. This was not high enough to top the clouds. The sun disappeared from sight, causing the gas in the balloon to cool rapidly. The aerostat began loosing altitude. In an hour's time it had fallen to within 100 feet of the ground. More ballast was dropped. The balloon stopped its downward flight.

Several hours later a sharp sound like a rifle shot was heard. "It's an ice floe starting to break up," Strindberg explained to Fraenkel. The noise had awakened Andrée. He climbed on deck and ordered draglines hung over the side. They were too flimsy to alter the aerostat's course. Gliding over the ice, their only effect was to set the car rotating. They were hauled up when Strindberg complained about feeling nauseous. He went below.

At breakfast on the morning of the second day the entire crew was on deck. The fog had lifted momentarily and Strindberg had been able to see the sun for another reading. He found that the "Eagle" had traveled 250 miles northeast of its starting point. The men's spirits were amazingly high despite a fine drizzle that had just begun. Suddenly, the aerostat began dropping. Their meal forgotten, the men threw out the last of their ballast and several ropes. This sufficed until midafternoon, when the aerostat again began a downward sweep. The draglines were cut through and let fall. This did little good. A grappling hook followed the draglines to the ground and then some minor scientific equipment. The car was now only a few yards above the ice. Andrée took the Polar buoy, which was to have marked the conquering of the North, and let it drop. It was not enough. The car touched ground and then scraped along it. Andrée flung a tarpaulin onto the ice. The balloon responded by rising 20 feet. The fog increased, its drippings hanging a ringlet of icicles around the balloon's equator.

During the next few hours the situation became increasingly critical. The car was smashing against the ground, rebounding, and hitting a few minutes later. It acted like a stamping machine, leaving its impress on the material beneath. By ten that evening the "Eagle" was so flabby and weak that it dropped to earth from exhaustion. That day the travelers had gone 115 miles west.

At noon of the third day the sun came out, the ice melted off the balloon, the gas expanded, and the North Pole Expedition was again aloft and waiting for lunch. Strindberg prepared the meal and wrote out the bill of fare:

Diner du 13 Juillet

Potage Hotch Potch
Chateau Briand
The King's Special Ale
Chocolate with Biscuits
Biscuits, Raspberry Syrup and H_2O.

While they were eating, Andrée released the pigeon that two days later was shot by Skipper Ole Hansen's mate. Though all the pigeons were sent out one by one during the journey, the bird fished out of the sea for the captain was the only one ever found.

A few hours later fog closed in again. The balloon resumed its stamping across the ice. Strindberg climbed up to the car's steel ring, where he teasingly said he felt safe, and where the bumps were not so sharp. The last buoy and, after a conference, a medicine chest were thrown overboard as ballast. The balloon rose 200 feet. It began traveling as

Andrée meant it to. Its sails billowed out through the agency of two dragropes that had been pieced together and were now doing their job. Fraenkel went to sleep while Andrée and Strindberg stood watch.

A wind came out of the west, forcing the aerostat east in a retrace of the trajectory it had followed the day before. Then a south wind pushed the balloon north. "We'll make the Pole, yet," Andrée exclaimed. His humor was dampened that evening. The fog was heavy. Only a few yards below was the frozen ocean, crisscrossed by leads or channels of water. The balloon crackled as ice formed and then broke. Water showered the explorers when their car splashed into a lead. The aerostat recovered only to bounce off a floe fifty yards farther on. The stamping machine was again at work. Even the release of two dragropes as ballast did not help. The men had no doubt that their balloon trip was nearly over.

The fateful July 14 began with the loss of their last dragrope. It was caught by the snow and had to be cut loose. Thus even the pretense of having a steerable balloon was given up. There was no choice but to look for a stable piece of ice for a landing.

Andrée pulled the valve that set the hydrogen free. The "Eagle" floated down to within a few feet of the ground, then dropped. The balloon portion of the North Pole Expedition was finished. So was their quest for the Pole, still 540 miles away. They ate lunch on a tarpaulin thrown over the ice and planned their strategy. They knew that it would be the next summer at the earliest before a rescue ship could reach them. However, it would never find them where they were. Therefore, they had to head for winter quarters, preferably one of the depots that Andrée had stocked for an emergency such as this.

Danes Island lay 300 miles to their southwest. This area held no scientific interest for them and was discarded. Such an interest was not a trivial influence to the group, who looked upon their predicament as a temporary one. Their records show no note of their hope disappearing, much less faltering.

The second choice was Ross Island, one of seven dots of land stringing northward from Spitsbergen. This island was a minor supply depot only 175 miles away and the nearest land. Why Andrée did not immediately head for it can only be guessed. He may have felt that while Ross Island was untried, Cape Flora, a third choice, had already proved itself a refuge through Nansen's having survived a winter there. Or he may have wanted the increased insurance that Cape Flora's larger stock of provisions offered. Most likely, though, he was driven by his geophysical interest in the place. Whatever the reason, this southern point in the Franz Josef Land island group was their destination, 300 miles to the southeast.

Fog stayed with the men for a week. During this time they outfitted their sleds for the long haul and explored the terrain. It impressed them as being far more formidable than they had judged from their air observations. Summer had turned much of the ice into slush which diffused itself into large pools of open water, some of which were several miles across. Where there was not water or slush there was pack ice, a treacherous mixture of snow and ice which sometimes led a man to think it solid only to have it crumble beneath his feet. Hummocks of this pack ice thrown up by internal pressures extended as far as the men could see. It looked as though an ocean had been frozen at the height of a raging storm. This massive ice area was in eternal motion, driven by winds above and by ocean currents below. When it broke apart, it formed the leads of water, some shallow, some deep, which the men had seen from the air. When winter came, these leads would be bridged by the white polar cement.

Each man packed a 100-pound sled with 350 pounds of food and equipment. The travelers had enough clothes to keep themselves warm, and a stout tent and waterproof balloon cloth for shelter. The men were in good health and morale was high.

Eleven days after their take-off from Danes Island they hitched their sleds to their backs for their journey to shelter. The men sought out the lakes and leads. It was easier to travel here than to pull their sleds over the hummocks. At the water's edge, they would make a raft out of a drifting ice floe. Then with their tent poles they would ferry themselves and their equipment across the water. When the floes were too massive for this operation, they would be maneuvered to make a bridge either to open water where small floes could be found or to a field of ice. The men could move over ice with relative ease, relative in the sense that they could cover two or three miles before they were exhausted. When the only way to go was over hummocks, the men would travel by combining their strengths to pull one sled and then return for the next.

When night came, which they knew by the time shown on their watches, they would raise their tent and prepare supper. To preserve their store of food, they tried to live off the land as much as they could. Raw bear, they said, when salted, tasted like oysters. The brain was good, too, tasting like sweetbreads. Sea-gull meat they compared with chicken, though a bit tougher. This toughness was an advantage, they held, because with so much chewing they did not eat as much and therefore were satisfied without going into their provisions.

After supper Strindberg would prop the picture of his fiancée in front of him and would talk to her and write what he was saying into a snow-stained notebook. Fraenkel would be repairing the sleds and checking and tying down equipment for an early morning start. Andrée, ever the scientist, would be studying the ice formations and wondering what gave them color. For instance, some were yellow, some had a trace of orange in them, and some were on the brown-

ish side. Occasionally, he would find small stones and remnants of leaves. These he would wrap carefully. On the
cover of the packages he would tell in detail where the contents had been found and the state they were in. He was
thrilled when he discovered a thumbnail amount of clay
with plant remains, which, he surmised, had drifted from
the Siberian coast. He double-wrapped this specimen to preserve it with his others for the Swedish Geographical Society.

The men struggled for every yard they gained, for every
lead they crossed, for every hummock they mounted. They
pulled, pushed, and even tried cajoling their sleds in the
race to winter quarters. Despite this effort, at the end of
five days' travel Strindberg reported they had come less
than two miles closer to Cape Flora. They were walking on
a giant treadmill. While they had journeyed to the southeast, the drifting ice mass had been carrying them to the
northwest.

They stopped relaying each sled over the snow. Each man
now had to pull his own load, made lighter by the discard of
some equipment. This had been a hard decision to make but
the only one expected to give them more speed. They also
cut down on time spent in sleeping and eating. When the
ice drift became more favorable or they were on land, they
told each other, they would relax.

Even these sacrifices helped only a little. The drift was
inexorable. The men prayed for a change in its direction.
There were a few days at the beginning of August when the
expedition actually found itself losing ground. That it was a
time of crisis was written in one of Strindberg's letters to his
Anna. "Now we are moving onward so slowly that perhaps
we shall not reach Cape Flora this winter, but shall be
obliged to pass the winter in a cellar in the earth. Poor little
Anna, in what despair you will be if we should not come
home next autumn. And you can think that I am tortured
by the thought of it, too, not for my own sake, for now I do

not mind if I suffer hardships as long as I can come home at last."

On August 4, Andrée announced that they would give up Cape Flora and try for Ross Island. This decision seemed to be all the Arctic had been waiting for. It turned cooperative, giving the party their asked-for southern drift. Within a week the men covered more ground than during the preceding two. After this the ice mass varied its direction of drift but it never moved as consistently against the men as it had at the beginning of their trip.

For a few minutes at midnight on August 31 the sun dipped into the horizon, painting the snow field orange. The polar summer was over. From now on the weather would get colder, and there would be night and there would be day. The days would rapidly become shorter while the nights became longer until there was only night.

The men traveled fast during August and the early part of September, over 150 miles. However, owing to problems of terrain and ice drift, their path became due south. This pointed them between Ross Island on their west and Cape Flora far to their east southeast. They now sought to reach Northeast Land, a major Spitsbergen island seventy-five miles southwest, before darkness set in.

Food and movement were all that counted. Sickness or injuries were of no matter. "Fraenkel fell into the water today, and has diarrhea, and Strindberg has a pain in his foot, and I have diarrhea, but we covered a good distance today in any case," Andrée wrote. "This evening I made fishhooks of pins and will fish with meat and fat. We shall see if I get anything tonight."

The changing season brought with it a raging wind that lasted a week. It carried the drifting ice mass out of reach of Northeast Land and into the sea between that island and the Franz Josef Land islands. The floes were in constant motion. Their direction could not be predicted nor could they be navigated. The water in the leads was like rushing streams. In the attempt to push on, two sleds were broken. The pain in Strindberg's foot moved up to his ankle. He could barely walk. As though this were not enough, the sun was giving light only a few hours a day. The party had no choice. It had to dig in for winter where it stood and pray that its floe drifted to land.

Then on September 17, land was sighted. It was still a long way off. There was no way to send the floe toward it. The men were ice-locked and could count only on the currents for motion. Several days later they got a clearer view of the island. It was dazzlingly white, peaked by a glacier whose top was lost in a drifting mist. Slowly the mist descended until it hid all but the island's harbor, which was brilliantly lighted by a shaft of sunlight. This was Gillis Land, later known as White Island.

The travelers prepared a celebration. There were many reasons for it. Not only had land been sighted but also the snow hut they had been building was finished. It was so warm and tightly constructed that after an hour the Primus stove had to be turned off. Then, too, it was Jubilee Day, the twenty-fifth anniversary of King Oscar's ascension to the Swedish throne. Strindberg made a banquet supper, drawing upon his supplies with childlike glee, and again wrote out the menu for Anna to read.

Banquet, 18 Sept. '97

Seal steak and ivory gull fried in butter and seal blubber
Seal liver
Brain and kidney
Butter and Schumacher-bread
Chocolate with Mellin's Food-flour and Albert biscuits and butter
Gateau aux raisin,
Raspberry syrup sauce
Port-wine 1834 Antonio de Ferrara, given by the King
Speech by Andrée for the King with royal Hurrah!

When the meal was completed, the Swedish flag was hoisted and the national anthem sung.

The ice floe circled halfway around the island and began approaching it from the south. Soon, if they wished, the men could land. They were disinclined to do so. They were comfortable and even had visions of being carried into Franz Josef Land and Cape Flora. The sea and the air furnished them enough food. For variety there were bears, whose tracks the explorers had several times found on the floe.

On the morning of October 2 their plans were terribly changed. It started when the men felt their floe begin to tremble. Then a low rumbling sound was heard followed by a thunderous noise. A fissure appeared beneath their hut. Water streamed in, drenching the men and their supplies. Gillis Land was still a few hours off. They waited, shivering. Fate had evicted them. They had to move.

Here the notes and diaries of these hearty men fade off into pulp. They wrote more, but the ravages of over three decades in the Arctic dissolved all but a few of their last words. These are so scattered in text as to be meaningless. That the men were found and their voices heard at all is more than the world expected. That they were heard in such detail and even seen through pictures they took of themselves has been called a miracle.

Yet even had the diaries been complete, they still could not have told us what killed Andrée and Fraenkel. They undoubtedly would have told about Strindberg for he was found in a grave made by human hands. How he died we can only guess. His body may have been so weakened by his injured foot and by his recurring diarrhea that he perished. Or that shivery night on the floe he may have caught pneumonia. Whatever the cause, he most likely died not long after he set foot on the island, his last almanac entry having been made for October 17.

Through the findings of the *Bratvaag* and *Isbjorn* expeditions, we may have the key to what happened to Strindberg's companions. Let us try to reconstruct the last day of these two explorers. It is after October 17, which date is probably close to the one when Strindberg was buried. It could not have been long after that date because Andrée's second diary, which takes up the adventure after the landing, comprises only a few pages. This is significant in view of the man's record of almost daily observations. Perhaps had Strindberg not died and delayed activities, the camp would have been completely in order. As it was, the site was only partly organized, one sled still waiting to be unpacked. This factor also points to an early death for the two men, because they would have been eager to have been settled for the winter.

We can say that they did not starve to death. Not only did they have ample provisions but also they had the meat from a bear they had killed and flesh from the gulls they had downed. Furthermore, they had plenty of ammunition and an island full of game.

What might seem logical is that they froze to death. This was the surmise many of the seamen made. Yet when the explorers were found they were only lightly dressed. They could have put on more clothes, they were available. Or, if asleep, they could have been using the oversized sleeping bag Andrée had taken along; it would have housed them tightly but not too uncomfortably. Had they needed the bag, the discomfort would have been a small price for warmth.

We may remember that the men's remains, for the most part, were found only a few yards apart, Fraenkel's within the "dwelling place" and Andrée's on a ledge only a few feet away. This is important. In addition, had either of the men died before the other, he would have been buried just as Strindberg had been. This was not done, so we can say that they probably died at the same time.

We see Andrée and Fraenkel inside their tent cooking a

meal. Outside it is not too cold, the temperature being only a few degrees below freezing. The winter's first snow is falling. It throws a mantle of white over the tent, insulating it from the elements. Meanwhile, the Primus stove lights up the inside and keeps it comfortably warm, just the way it did the snow hut on the ice floe. This would account for the men's light dress. Andrée and Fraenkel eat. It gets warmer, almost hot. Suddenly, one of the men faints. The other, realizing what has happened, turns the stove off and then dashes to open a flap in the tent. He is not quick enough. He, too, expires of carbon-monoxide poisoning.

The remains of Andrée and Strindberg and Fraenkel were carried in solemn procession down the streets of Stockholm to the great church of St. Nicholas. Thousands of the explorers' countrymen headed by King Gustaf attended the services. While the city's church bells tolled, the coffins were transferred by guards of honor to the burial place. Here the King welcomed and bid farewell to his country's heroes.

"In the name of the Swedish nation I greet the dust of the Polar explorers who, more than three decades since, left their native land to find answers to questions of unparalleled difficulty. A country's hope to be able to honor them in their lifetimes after a successful journey was disappointed. We must submit to its tragic result. All that is left us is to express our warm thanks to them for their self-sacrifices in the service of science. Peace to their memory!"

Twelve

A VICTIM FOR SCIENCE

As geographical frontiers expanded during the early twentieth century, men turned their sights upward to the sky with the hope of exploring those hitherto inaccessible regions and learning more of the mysterious events that occasionally made their presence known so elusively. Glaisher and others had tried, as we have seen, but with limited success. The airplane was becoming established but had a long way to go before it would be ready to soar to altitudes much over 25,000 feet. On the other hand, the balloon, with over one hundred years of usage, was ready to play a major role in upper-altitude exploration. Developments in instrumentation during the late 90s of the last century, the liquification of air, and the development of pneumatic breathing apparatus all provided means for assisting the aeronauts in their high-altitude flights.

It was known by the turn of the century that altitudes above 10,000 feet could be dangerous to men not properly protected, and deadly if the altitude exceeded 20,000 feet. The years from 1900 on were to show further examples of the price that had to be paid in lives because of failure or inadequacies of oxygen supplies. The effects of low pressure at high altitudes were not yet fully understood and it was to be several decades before aeronauts learned to use pressurized gondolas, or suits that would prevent expansion of their bodies, or swelling, and difficulties with oxygen expanding in their lungs.

Men found other reasons for ascending to high altitudes besides the very act of doing so for record-setting purpose. Evidence was reaching experimental physicists that a new and mysterious radiation impinged on the earth's atmosphere from outer space. McClennan in Canada and workers elsewhere soon looked for means to transport instrumentation to altitudes above those that could be attained by climbing mountains.

Early in this century two German professors, Artur Berson and Reinhard Süring, who had made a specialty of studying the upper atmosphere and who had made a number of ascents, made a flight from Berlin on July 31, 1901. Their giant balloon called "Preussen" (Prussia) rose without incident, launched by many members of the German Army. How many such balloon flights have been made in history with the often unwilling help of soldiers acting as launch crew! The rather large open gondola was loaded with various pieces of equipment, but not with cosmic-ray instrumentation, since little was yet known about cosmic rays.

The two Germans established a world-record altitude of 35,433 feet. They were equipped with crude breathing apparatus; they had on board some steel bottles of compressed air to help them along. Their hydrogen-filled balloon descended a few hours later without incident. However, the good professors had enough difficulties with their breathing equipment and instruments and control of the balloon to discourage them from any further attempt at that time; we hear little more of them in the domain of high-altitude exploration.

The redoubtable French, never far behind in aeronautics and usually ahead, also tried a high-altitude ascent on the

28th of May, 1913. Three aeronauts and scientists, Maurice Bienaime and Jacques Schneider and a M. Senouque, reached an altitude of about 34,000 feet. While this was no altitude record, the flight had several interesting "firsts," one of which was a photograph at high altitude taken of two aeronauts by their third companion. Furthermore, the men were equipped with air-breathing masks coupled to compressed-air flasks. Such experiments helped all phases of aeronautical science, since in the coming war men would fly with airships and airplanes at altitudes where normal breathing was difficult and oxygen help was necessary. Many of the breathing-device systems developed by these high-altitude balloon pioneers were prototypes of devices used later.

The record set by Berson and Süring of Germany was not to be exceeded for twenty-six years. The United States, with its record of ballooning, as illustrious as that of any other nation, was beginning a series of spectacular experiments that was to establish the country someday as a leader in high-altitude exploration.

It had probably no more illustrious aeronaut in those years than Captain Hawthorne C. Gray. This brave officer, born February 16, 1889, in Washington state, had enlisted in the Army in 1915, and after serving as a commissioned officer in the Idaho National Guard, transferred his interests to aeronautics. Early in his career he was irrevocably struck with the bug of ballooning and very quickly established himself as a ranking aeronaut. He entered balloon races and in 1926 won second place in the famous Gordon Bennett competition. That the captain survived several early flights despite plummeting balloons and lack of oxygen are a tribute to his hardiness and skill as an aeronaut.

In the winter of 1926–27 Gray began the first of his series of high-altitude flights with the hope of breaking the German record of 1901. He ascended from Scott Field at Belleville, Illinois, in a hydrogen-filled balloon with open basket, carrying aloft a supply of compressed oxygen. Also included in the equipment was a barograph, an instrument that can record altitude as a function of time. Gray's balloon rose swiftly to about 25,000 feet. But then the elements worked against him. The raw atmosphere and sub-zero temperatures and improperly adjusted oxygen tubes hindered the supply of that precious gas for his breathing and he gradually became unconscious. At about 27,000 feet he was fully overcome, but by great good fortune the balloon descended on its own almost as if it realized the predicament of its aeronaut. At 17,000 feet the denser atmosphere revived Gray; however, he found he was still in great danger, since the balloon was falling at about 1200 feet per minute. Dizzy and intensely cold, he began to throw out sand ballast to slow the balloon's fall. The canvas bags of sand were difficult to handle even though their spouts pointed downward so that the sand could drop out. After the knives that he used became dull from hacking at the sand and canvas, he had to tear the bags with his fingers.

By feverish sand-dumping he checked his descent to about 600 feet per minute and the balloon and gondola finally crashed into some telephone wires near the roadside at Ashley, Illinois, about forty miles southeast of Scott Field. With a great rending and tearing the entire assembly rolled over into a ditch. However, Captain Gray suffered only a sprained ankle, even though his radios were shattered and his basket badly twisted. Strangely enough, there was still oxygen in his supply flasks when he landed, so that it had been a matter of kinking and freezing of the valves and tubes that led to his face mask past his fur-lined helmet and suit.

The difficulties of this flight spurred our hardy aeronaut on to bigger things. He had demonstrated that his oxygen equipment could work reasonably reliably above 15,000 feet and he had shown that frost and unsuitable equipment were greater dangers than any possible failures in the balloon fabric or suspension. Time was now ready for an assault on the still inviolate German altitude mark. He chose a more propitious time with warmer weather and better climatic conditions in May 1927. It must be remembered he was exploring a strictly unknown territory, since very few people had ascended beyond 20,000 to 25,000 feet and then for very short periods and in many cases in a state of unconsciousness from complete lack of oxygen or failure of oxygen or air equipment.

Captain Gray's flights were not specifically made for breaking records, but rather for studying atmospheric conditions at high altitudes and to study the effects of the rarefied atmosphere on the human body and the range of temperature that would be encountered. He also had a stated purpose in wishing to learn data on wind directions between the lower and higher strata of air and other upper-air problems that would be of benefit to science and aeronautics in the future. Nevertheless, the possibility of setting an altitude record was surely a tantalizing extra bonus that spurred on the captain and his superiors.

Gray and his Army Air Corps balloon were ready for ascent over Scott Field on May 4, 1927. The well-trained launch crew released the gray silvery bag without incident and Gray soon found himself ascending rapidly above the more or less critical altitude of 15,000 feet. Gray was in perfect shape and the flight surgeon had pronounced him physically superb; indeed, his excellent condition tended to let him withstand the terrific strain of surviving in the upper altitude without his really appreciating the dangerous situation he was in. The parting words of the flight surgeon were that he, Gray, should cease his flight the moment he felt any pains.

After taking off at 1:33 P.M. in a rather mild temperature of sixty degrees and carrying 3800 pounds of sand ballast, he rose at about 700 feet per minute. He soon reached 25,000 feet, all the time listening to various radio stations in the area—he was able to hear these until he reached 35,000 feet, where a particular station to which he listened signed off. The temperature dropped steadily between 20,-000 and 25,000 feet. The back of his helmet became intensely cold, this uncomfortable situation staying with him until he later descended to 20,000 feet.

Nothing unusual occurred until an altitude of 40,000 feet was reached. The old symptoms of dizziness, the result of lack of pressure or oxygen, were noted. He had great difficulty in reading his instruments because of frost on his face-mask goggles; finally, a small spot the size of a nickel remained clear throughout the flight. The goggles had been treated against this very frost phenomenon and yet did not live up to expectations.

After 40,000 feet the now expanded spherical bag slowed its rate of ascent. He had finally exceeded the official German altitude of 35,000 feet but he was still anxious to reach 41,000 feet, an *unofficial* reading which had been claimed by a Frenchman earlier. Dressed in his warm fur-lined suit and carrying his oxygen tubes with him, he walked around the basket, testing each sandbag to ascertain that no sand remained in them. He found no ballast sand remaining. In order to reach and exceed 41,000 feet he then decided to drop his oxygen cylinder or flask, which had been supplying him oxygen up to this time. The time was 2:05 P.M. He unscrewed the gauge from the flask, and installed it on a new one. The balloon rose quite slowly now and reached an altitude slightly above 41,000 feet. The rate of ascent was almost negligible; at the same time Gray noticed a growing discomfort in his chest as he tested his sandbags for any residual sand.

Bearing in mind the instructions of his medical officers to descend at the first symptoms of distress and pain and having reached an altitude of around 42,000 feet with little further evidence of rising, he pulled the valve that let hydrogen out of the balloon. The aerostat began to descend quickly, and to Gray's surprise rather more quickly than he had anticipated, reaching a velocity of about 900 feet per minute. The bag above him began to flutter and billow, although he could barely make this out because of his frosted glasses. When his ears began to hurt from the rapid descent he applied that classical antidote of aviators of closing his mouth and holding his nose with thumb and forefinger and then trying to blow, building pressure against the stoppage in his nose.

He expected a rapid rate of descent, although not quite as rapid as occurred, and felt no undue alarm until he reached about 20,000 feet. His glasses had now cleared up and on looking at the bag he noticed that it had not begun to billow out like a parachute. During the design of the balloon it had been hoped that a descent with gas escaping from it would leave the bag, now partially empty, in the approximate shape of a parachute. This could considerably ease the descent rate and would be an added safety feature for the aeronaut in case he could not escape from his gondola with his own parachute.

While deciding what to do in view of the strange behavior of the bag, Captain Gray removed his oxygen mask at about 18,000 feet and tossed overboard small parachutes with messages in capsules requesting notification by the finder. The balloon was descending so rapidly that these small parachutes actually seemed to go upward when he tossed them out. If no other fact had convinced him that he was descending too rapidly, the behavior of these small message parachutes was evidence enough that the time was coming when he would have to save himself with his own parachute.

He watched his altimeter changing rapidly and at around 8000 feet he decided to leave the gondola, since he had no way of slowing down the balloon by dropping ballast. A small airplane piloted by Lieutenant Holcomb, carrying a Private Stinson operating a motion-picture camera, followed

17. Explorer I descending rapidly and breaking up, 1934.

18. The crew prepares to enter Explorer II, November 11, 1936.

19. Explorer II just before take-off from "Stratobowl," South Dakota.

20. August 10, 1956. The first manned flight of the Office of Naval Research Project Strato-Lab balloon was launched from Minneapolis, Minnesota.

Official U. S. Navy Photograph

21. May 6, 1958. Setting sun reflects Strato-Lab balloon from surface of water at bottom of iron mine as technicians complete inflation.

Official U. S. Navy Photograph

22. Balloonists ascend to 81,000 feet. Commander Malcolm D. Ross, USNR, and scientist Charles B. Moore of Arthur D. Little, Inc., were aboard the balloon gondola which ascended to a height of 81,000 feet in a Strato-Lab flight from Rapid City, South Dakota, to Manhattan, Kansas, November 1959.

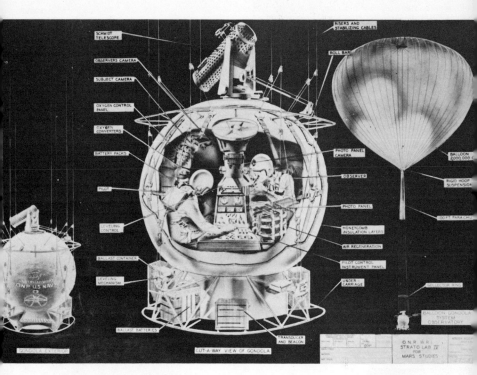

23. Diagram and sketch of a balloon-borne astronomical observatory similar to the one flown by Ross and Moore in 1959.

24. August 26, 1960. Captain Joseph W. Kittinger, Jr., at the moment of his leap from an open gondola at 102,800 feet. Called Excelsior III, this project demonstrated the feasibility of parachute descents from high altitudes.

25. May 4, 1961. Balloon on deck shortly before launching. Strato-Lab High No. 5.

26. May 4, 1961. Lieutenant Commander Victor A. Prather and Commander Malcolm D. Ross in gondola aboard the USS *Antietam*. Strato-Lab High.

27. Man High II launch preparations.

Gray as he jumped from the gondola. Oddly enough, Gray heard Holcomb shouting "He's going to jump!" just as he dived overboard. With his parachute opening perfectly and with the balloon preceding him down with its valve wide open Captain Gray landed in a plowed field away from swamps and a river near the village of Golden Gate, Illinois, about 110 air miles from Scott Field at 3:05 P.M. The balloon and gondola hit the earth with a resounding thud but instruments aboard were not irrevocably damaged and much of the fabric and gondola were recovered.

Thus ended Captain Gray's first attempt to reach the stratosphere and exceed the previous official altitude record set by the Germans. He had learned some new things about oxygen breathing, air pressure on the body, upper air currents, and balloon behavior during rapid descent. He had reached the greatest altitude ever reached by man, but because of the inflexible rules of the International Federation of Aeronautics, was prevented from claiming the official record since these rules demand that the aeronaut be in command of his machine until landing.

He spent that summer scanning records of his flight and in reviewing ways and means to ease the work necessary to maintain instrumentation and life itself at high altitudes. Many hours were spent at Scott Field checking every piece of equipment, testing and retesting to increase reliability and lessen the chance of failures. And why was all this testing and checking going on during the summer of 1927? Captain Gray was determined to try again! After all, the failure of the valve venting system and the balloon itself so near the ground were the only factors keeping him from claiming a world altitude record. True enough, the scientific motivation of the flight was supposed to be paramount, but an adventure of this type would have lacked spice and savor had it not carried with it the element of a new record. Of course, the very breaking of a previous record would in itself be a technical achievement, since the aeronaut would be gathering data in hitherto inaccessible regions.

Several interesting experiments were tried with rats and mice in laboratory vacuum jars that summer. We have here one of the first attempts to duplicate on the ground the conditions to be encountered by a high-altitude aeronaut (*astronaut* today). There are now very large programs in this country and elsewhere with high-altitude chambers that simulate space. The aeronaut or astronaut is placed in these chambers and the air pressure is reduced to correspond with that attained at very high altitudes. So we had in 1927 modest attempts made with small "environmental chambers." As now, these small chambers and animal tests served a very useful purpose. It was quickly established that animals became unconscious between 25,000 and 28,000 feet—the corresponding low air pressures being obtained in the laboratory bell jar. The animals also became unconscious when breathing pure oxygen at an equivalent altitude of 49,000 feet.

The Army Air Corps medical experimenters placed a rat in a jar and pumped into this pure oxygen at pressures that were gradually reduced to correspond with those that Gray would encounter on his expected upward flight. Oxygen was cut off to the rat at a 37,000-foot equivalent altitude. The rat became unconscious and soon stopped breathing entirely, even when air was suddenly fed into the jar. It was impossible to revive the rat, despite artificial respiration in pure oxygen. While it had been known with other experiments with balloons that life is difficult to maintain at altitudes above 30,000 feet without stored oxygen, these tests were the first to give exact readings of pressure versus life activity and also showed the beneficial influence of breathing pure oxygen. It is interesting to note that some animals, like some previous aeronauts who were revived after becoming unconscious, showed no permanent ill aftereffects.

By August, Captain Gray had his balloon readied and was intensively studying the oxygen requirements for his next flight. One thing that had not been duplicated in the laboratory tests at Scott Field were low temperature. While this was expected to have no particular effect on the respiratory mechanism of a living being, it would greatly complicate the handling of delicate valves and instruments and, of course, impede the movements of the bundled-up aeronaut. Gray helped to design a clever oxygen mask, so arranged that it would supply him oxygen even if he fainted or if moisture from his breath froze up the small tube that led into his mouthpiece. Oxygen for much of the flight was used not in a pure state, but mixed with available air. This arrangement greatly lengthened the time of air-mask use; however, it required a mixing valve to properly administer the right amount of oxygen and air to the breathing mask. Here again we see the experimenters and Gray coming up with an ingenious mixing and blending mechanism that was to be of considerable use to him.

Captain Gray was well aware of the extraordinary will power required to accomplish any action in the rarefied atmosphere. Even the simplest physical acts needed mental drive far beyond that needed at the earth's surface, and his awareness of his surroundings and acuity would be much reduced. Therefore, everything was designed for ease of operation and safety. His oxygen tanks had oversized valves on them so that little effort would be needed to open them when necessary for oxygen flow; two of the tanks were mounted outside the basket so that they could be released just like ballast if he needed to obtain more altitude.

Another critical item for his flight was ballast. In previous experiments ballast was contained in bags that were tied to the ribs of his balloon basket. Aeronauts in the past had released sand by lifting the bags, opening their necks, turning the bags upside down, and letting the sand run out as required. Gray believed this required too much exertion, as anyone can imagine who has tried to lift a bag of sand. Therefore, he rearranged the bags so that the open end would point downward with the long canvas neck folded upward and held closed with a pin through holding eyelets. A cordon ring was attached to each of these pins so that simply by lifting his arm and pulling the pins from the eyelets with the cord, the end of the neck of the bag flopped down and the sand would run out. The contraptions looked like so many trouser legs.

All the instruments that were used on the flight were carefully cleaned of oil and grease to prevent gumming and freezing of these materials at the sub-zero temperatures that occur above 25,000 to 30,000 feet. A jeweler spent many hours on the instruments, leaving all parts dry and clean. A rather important instrument, a clock, was also taken along, but for mysterious reasons it was not cleaned of oil prior to the flight and it stopped at 3:17 P.M., undoubtedly because of the congealing of the oil. The other instruments carried aloft, besides various barographs and recording thermometers, were an altimeter and a radio receiver with headphones, trailing antennas, and batteries.

Thus Captain Gray was ready to attempt his new flight with much scientific laboratory equipment, having taken extraordinary precautions to design all instrumentation for minimum effort of adjustment. There was a better design for his valve pull rope and so-called collector ring, the oxygen equipment was doubly checked for adequacy, and the ballast operation was simplified.

At 2:23 P.M. on November 4, 1927, the hydrogen balloon rose with Captain Gray in the gondola. The pilots of several escorting planes were able to keep the balloon in view until about 3:10 P.M., at which time it disappeared in a heavy cloud formation and was not visible again until it was found at Sparta, Tennessee.

Gray kept a log during a large portion of the upper flight. This has proved to be not only an interesting personal document, but also a scientific one. The flight this time seemed to take a longer period to reach a high altitude. In his earlier flight he reached 42,470 feet in an hour and five minutes, while during this last flight his ascent was so slow that it took him almost two hours to reach that height. Although his log does not say so, it could be possible that he slowed his rate of ascent in order to be able to observe carefully conditions that he encountered.

He also spent much time on his radio. At 12,000 feet the entry in his log states, "Tuned in on Station KSD [St. Louis, Missouri]." The low pressure was beginning to effect his reactions. But let us look at some of the entries in his log[1] in order to show graphically the conditions of his flight and the way he battled them. The entries have been simplified and rephrased and the abbreviations eliminated and some small changes have been made for clarity's sake.

"Left Scott Field, Belleville, Illinois, at 2:23 P.M., November 4, 1927. Temperature at ground fifty-one degrees centigrade."

He reached an altitude of 10,600 feet at 2:36, where he encountered a temperature of twenty-four degrees.

"Tuned in on Station KMOX [St. Louis, Missouri]. Listened to the 'Kashmiri Song,' and 'Sympathy.' Emptied two bags of sand as ballast in order to go higher."

"Tuned in on Station KSD [St. Louis, Missouri]. Felt symptoms of rickets [shakiness and fever caused by oxygen want]." He was now over Okawville, which is about twelve miles east of Mascoutah, which in turn is about twelve miles east of Belleville, where the ascent began. "Started taking oxygen."

The dual traverse lever of his barograph marked No. 11 changed its movement after indicating an altitude of 12,000 feet. At 2:10 he dropped an extra handling rope as ballast.

[1] Records supplied through the courtesy of Paul Garber, eminent air historian and curator of the National Air Museum.

"Tuned in on Station KMOX, heard 'Marquita.'" At 3:28 the clock mechanism in this barograph 14 stopped.

At an altitude of 15,000 feet the left lens in his goggles became foggy due to condensation of body moisture. He then began the use of an ingenious device whereby electricity at four volts heated his goggles. By the time he got to 16,500 feet his vision was partly cleared. Meanwhile at about 2:50 P.M. he passed over a red schoolhouse.

At an altitude of 19,500 feet the temperature was zero degrees. Tuning in on Station KMOX he heard a saxophone playing "Träumerei."

At an altitude of 23,000 feet, reached at 3:10, it was snowing. He put on his gloves at a temperature of eight degrees below zero. He tuned in on station KMOX and heard "Thinking of You."

At an altitude of 24,000 feet it was still snowing. At 3:13 he heard "Sunset" played by Ole Oleson.

At an altitude of 27,000 feet (over five miles high), at 3:15, the temperature was twenty-five below zero. He tuned in on WLW, Cincinnati, and heard "Just Another Day Wasted Away."

At an altitude of 29,000 feet, reached at 3:17, the temperature was twenty-nine degrees below zero. He tuned in on point 44 on his radio dial and heard a song about dying and gliding leaves.

Tuning in on Station WLS, Chicago, he heard several pieces and the time. Temperature thirty-five degrees below zero, altitude 30,000 feet; ice was forming on the balloon. The extreme cold congealed the oil in his clock and it stopped.

Tuning in on Station WFIW, Hopkinsville, Kentucky, he heard a march. The temperature was thirty-three below zero.

At an altitude of 34,000 feet he released an empty oxygen cylinder which in falling broke his radio aerial, thus stopping his radio reception.

At 36,000 feet the temperature was forty below. The current used for heating his goggles and oxygen was too strong, so he reduced it to two volts. He now was entering the stratosphere, which is above the atmosphere and where the temperature becomes warmer and remains nearly constant. It had warmed back to thirty-two below zero.

The next entry shows that his senses were becoming less acute, revealing one weakness in his spelling where he wrote "Hair" for "Air." The lack of air density was altering the shape of the balloon by pulling out the lower section. "Vacuum in mouth" may mean either continued alteration in the balloon shape, or personal physical discomfort caused by breathing difficulties. In the original log these entries are in a shaky handwriting. He had climbed to 39,000 feet and the stratosphere was becoming warmer, at twenty-eight degrees below zero.

As one ascends and gets away from the earth haze and dusty air, the color of the sky deepens; sometimes the stars can be seen. Captain Gray in his last entry noted the color of the sky and the brightness of the sun. He had emptied all of his sand ballast and was 40,000 feet high.

One of the more significant entries, at 3:17 P.M., was "clock frozen." This sinister occurrence caused by the frozen clock oil probably was an important element in the events that followed. He had now no means of checking the passage of time and nothing to tell him how much longer his life-giving oxygen would last. Also he could not tell the time remaining for further ascent and whether he would have time to descend to the denser atmosphere with what oxygen he had, to the point where he could breathe the regular air.

Interestingly enough he had to reduce steadily the voltage in the wires that were heating his breathing-inlet tube and his goggles since the rarefied outside atmosphere no longer was able to chill or conduct heat away as rapidly as the denser atmosphere had.

When he reached about 40,000 feet he realized he was approaching the top of the flight and he had to make a decision whether to rise farther either by dropping his remaining ballast or cutting loose his other oxygen cylinder, or to make the descent. He had probably realized that his oxygen supply was becoming limited and he had enough for about an hour and a half.

After the last entry, a little robot recorder, however, still went on—his barograph. This device traced the altitude curve that the balloon followed. Its record shows oscillation or movement up and down—typical of a balloon floating near its so-called equilibrium altitude with no more ballast having been dropped. The barograph's record shows that at about 4:00 P.M. the balloon reached the height of its first oscillation, namely about 42,220 feet. Then it reached a "valley" of about 42,100 feet, and five or six minutes later rose again to 42,220 feet. At this point the battery was dropped for ballast. Unless it dropped by itself, an unlikely occurrence, Captain Gray was still alive to perform this act, but too preoccupied with his survival and surroundings, or perhaps too weak, to enter readings in his log. Shortly thereafter the balloon reached its peak of 42,470 feet as one of the last points on the barograph's curve. Thus Captain Gray and his balloon reached exactly the altitude he had in his previous flight.

But the barograph was to reveal a little more data of considerable interest. For, just after the balloon reached the 42,470-foot mark it began a descent on a downward oscillation. However, instead of oscillating upward again it continued its descent smoothly and evenly. This shows that Captain Gray must have been still able to valve gas, since such a descent curve is typical of a balloon that is losing gas steadily. The balloon descended slowly—but too slowly, for it was not until 4:28 P.M. that 39,000 feet was reached. Suddenly the curve shows a steeper descent. The sudden acceleration downward most likely again was caused by the human hand of Captain Gray valving his balloon, since no other explanation can be found for this sudden soaring and rapid descent. So he was alive at 39,000 feet.

His time, however, was running out. His oxygen was practically depleted; and after he reached an altitude several thousand feet below his ceiling altitude at 4:38, his oxygen flow had ceased. All of Captain Gray's computations show that oxygen should have ceased about that time and all other records verify this fact. The curve of the little recording barograph becomes smooth and even as the balloon descends rapidly. At 5:20 P.M. on November 4 it came to rest in a tree with Captain Gray aboard—dead.

The history of aeronautics and ballooning to that time had already claimed its quota of victims. Airplane pilots were subjected to the inexorable law of gravity when their engines failed, but still the testing and experimentation went on. Balloon pilots had difficulties with breakdown of the bags, often fire in the inflammable coal gas, or, as in the case of Captain Gray, lack of oxygen at high altitude.

Again he was to be denied the official sanction of an altitude record. Although he was in his balloon basket during the entire flight, he had died in the attempt and was not in control of the balloon. Nevertheless his colleagues and the great fraternity of experimenters and aeronauts recognized the great and courageous feat of a fellow aeronaut who anticipated much of the colorful experimentation of the coming years in aeronautics and astronautics with his scientific and careful preparations and ground tests with animals. But as in so many other famous experiments, there was a small but important link in the chain that was to prove his undoing—an oily clock that froze.

Thirteen

THE FIRST SPACE-GONDOLA FLIGHT

On January 28, 1884, in Basel, Switzerland, Jules and Helene Piccard became the parents of twin sons. Named Auguste and Jean Felix, they were destined to enrich the world by their remarkable scientific and exploratory talents. Although both became noted scientists, Auguste in particular was to show the world new methods of reaching the extremities of hitherto unexplored regions, the upper atmosphere and lower depths of the ocean. We are concerned here mainly with Auguste's pioneering attempts to reach the fringes of the upper air—"near space," as it may be called today.

The twins graduated with distinction in natural science and obtained doctorates at the Swiss Institute of Technology in Zurich. Both were distinctive-looking men, lean and spare and yet possessed of charm and a talent for adaptation. Auguste specialized in physics, while Jean went on to organic chemistry. As young men, still living in Switzerland, the boys became interested in balloon aeronautics. In 1913 they flew on a sixteen-hour flight in a balloon from Zurich over Germany and into France. Showing their natural scientific inclinations, they measured the air density and the temperature inside the balloon during the flight. How natural their description of this flight sounds, with no difficulties of international border crossings in evidence! What would happen to adventurous young men today in Europe if they flew a balloon across the jealously guarded frontiers?

Still together, the brothers obtained further balloon experience by serving in the Swiss Army's Lighter-than-Air Service in 1915. Auguste's curiosity about the upper atmosphere and the possibilities of stratosphere ballooning increased with the years. In 1922 he became a professor of physics at the Polytechnic Institute at Brussels University in Belgium. During the early 20s he became more and more engrossed with the scientific purpose of a high-altitude balloon expedition and the requirements for such an undertaking.

While Auguste was making plans of various kinds and becoming increasingly interested in the mysterious rays from space, "the cosmic rays," his brother had emigrated to the United States, where he was to carve out his own brilliant career in engineering and, partly as a side line, but still in a pioneering way, ballooning.

By the late 20s Auguste had finished his design studies on the nature and shape of a high-altitude vehicle and concluded that a pressurized spherical lightweight capsule would be necessary. This radical innovation was the first design of what may now be called a space capsule. He also studied the problems of instrumentation, suspension from the balloon, and launching; it might be noted that both brothers, like good scientists, were very meticulous in their preparations and that their life's work reflected this.

An amusing story is told of Auguste visiting a barber shop in Basel. He asked the barber for a trim and told him to hurry because his hair grew very rapidly. The barber inquired as to what he meant by "rapidly." Auguste said that his hair had been known to grow back within an hour and that this was a thing that had plagued him all his life. The barber indulgently went along with what he thought was a joke, but found himself in a corner when Auguste said he would prove that his hair grew fast and would even take a bet on it. The barber, feeling himself on safe ground, although a little doubtful when he surveyed the tall gangling frame of Auguste, decided to accept the bet for laughs. Auguste promised to return in an hour. And sure enough, an hour later the door opened and in walked the "same" tall individual (his brother); he sat in the chair, and said in the same voice, "A trim, please." The horrified barber, who saw no difference in the head of hair he surveyed from the uncut one he had seen barely an hour before and noting that the hair was natural, was taken aback, to put it mildly. The story does not reveal whether Auguste went along with the gag and collected his bet, or whether he helped the barber out of his fright by appearing himself.

When Auguste had formulated in 1928 his plans for high-altitude exploration, he approached the F.N.R.S. (Fonds National de Recherches Scientifiques), the Belgian government research fund established to support various areas of basic and applied research. With surprisingly little argument, for those days, he obtained the necessary funds to build and equip his first balloon. He tactfully named the balloon "F.N.R.S."

Some months were spent on the balloon, suspension, and gondola designs during 1929. The firm of Lhoir at Liége and a concern called Riedinger in Augsburg, Germany, were chosen to build the aluminum gondola and balloon, respectively. Thus, vehicle, gondola, and instruments were assembled without much delay later in 1929. The most novel element of the project was the aluminum spherical gondola designed by Piccard. This was the first closed pressurized capsule capable of life support at high altitudes. Every other high-altitude and space capsule subsequently was to have some trace of the Professor's design in it.

Then came the selection of a launch site. A balloon high-altitude attempt demands a launch area well away from the oceans and in a locality that has low or steady winds with no gusts. Also needed are repair and servicing facilities and a launch crew. Piccard's balloon required many men to hold down the giant envelope as it became inflated and ready for launch. Such "anchor" crews were familiar sights at all balloon launchings until the coming of plastic balloons, which being of simpler design could be held by a few anchoring ropes.

After weighing various considerations Auguste chose the countryside near the factory that had manufactured his balloon in Augsburg, Germany. He valued having at hand the plant that manufactured the bag, so that both skilled labor and repair facilities would be almost within walking distance of the launch site. Unfortunately, while the site met two of the conditions by having the technical facilities at hand and being distant from the oceans, it was not the best location for low wind velocities, and gusts and winds are the greatest enemies of balloonists who have large fabric bodies to launch.

The Augsburg site demanded that the balloon and cabin with all instruments be transported from Brussels. Here, through his inimical scientist's ability to scrounge, he obtained the services of a German auto factory in Miesse which supplied him with the proper truck for the transport of the sphere. This truck had specially designed springs to minimize the impact of road roughness on sensitive instruments in the capsule.

The "F.N.R.S." was readied for flight early in the morning on the 14th of September, 1930. Although the previous night had been clear, the weather that particular morning began to worsen rapidly. As the morning wore on and the bag became filled, the wind also increased. The launch crew had great difficulty in hanging onto the bag and now a new trouble developed: the bag began to pull on the cabin, which rested on a small four-wheeled trolley that rode on a track. Suddenly, there was a gust violent enough to tip over the cabin, which almost fell on the men who tried to hold it up; the cabin rolled on the ground and damaged several instruments. By now the balloon was at a considerable angle to the ground. The chances of a launch looked dim.

In order to lighten the gondola so that it would not act as too much of an anchor on the bag, several two-hundred-pound sandbags were removed from the outside of the gondola; these bags were to act as ballast for taking off. The balloon could still have been launched despite the removal of these sandbags since there was a method of releasing ballast internally by the use of powdered lead or pellets. The wind increased and the willing crew did everything to wrestle with the aluminum gondola. Piccard was anxiously watching every move, giving suggestions here and there while the managers of the balloon factory became more upset. By late morning it was evident that a launch in this wind could not be attempted. With heavy heart Piccard gave the order to cancel the flight; the gas-dump panel was ripped open at the top of the balloon, the hydrogen gas escaped, and the bag fell into folds on the launch site.

That ended the first attempt and it was necessary to remove the bag to the factory. Sadly Auguste supervised the loading of the gondola onto the little truck and by the end of the day the crew had gone and no sign was left of this inauspicious start.

It was not to be until the spring of 1931 that favorable weather was at hand for the launch. Piccard had decided that another aborted attempt was intolerable and that it would be better to wait for the right weather even if it would take several months. Once again things were ready for a launch on May 25, 1931. However, that day was a holiday in Bavaria and he had difficulty in rounding up a voluntary launch crew. So, impatiently, Piccard had to wait until the 26th, while worrying greatly whether the spell of good weather would continue for another day or two. Various delays held up inflation until the night of the 26th, leaving the morning of the 27th for the launch.

It was planned to take off at 5:30 A.M., around sunrise, that often being a period of low winds. The bag now hung huge and partly filled above the heads of the launch crew as they struggled with ropes and last-minute preparations of oxygen tubes and pipes and electrical batteries, etc. As luck would have it, around that time a sudden rise in the wind speed occurred and the balloon began to flap, pull, and strain. The men again hung onto the gondola, which was still on its little mobile trolley, but to no avail. A sudden burst of wind pulled the gondola off the wagon. As in the previous attempt, it tumbled to the ground, but this time no instrument damage was done.

Piccard and his assistant, a M. Kipfer, who was to fly with him, had cannily tied down all instruments with the expectation that another tumble could occur. With the rise of the wind and the worsening of the weather it was important to work fast. The launch crew outdid itself. The gondola, which had got a small dent in the fall, was righted and the bag was pulled over enough to maintain almost vertical support. In order to hold the balloon more firmly a heavy support line was rigged around the suspension ring. Although this line, through its unique attachment point and extra support by the crew, held the balloon better, it interfered with some of the instrumentation dangling below and was later to give trouble when the aeronauts attempted to open the vent valve on the balloon for descending. It was not possible to remove this rope during launch.

The weather and the attachment of the new line had delayed the launch to midafternoon. Around twelve o'clock Piccard and Kipfer had crawled into the gondola, leaving the circular door open. At 3:30 the major support ropes were pulled through the eyelets by the crew and the balloon now hung free and lifted the gondola several feet off the ground. Piccard closed the hatch and waited for the prearranged start signal indicating take-off. While they were waiting, Kipfer suddenly looked through the window and shouted, "We're slipping by a chimney!" They had started without noticing it and without a signal having been given. Auguste looked out and seeing the faces of the launch crew, sensed their thoughts: "Let's hope that these scholars quickly leave us—they'll soon know when they are ascending." Whether the high wind or a lack of coordination caused the unannounced start, the fact was they were aloft and rising very quickly.

As they rose through clouds farther and farther into the atmosphere, Piccard heard a hissing. Looking down near the foot of the cabin he noticed a hole that he had forgotten. Actually the hole was there by design, since it was the location of a special electrometer-insulation mechanism. He intended to insert a rubber insulating plug containing a quartz rod sometime during the ascent. He had gone to the trouble to go through a drill of inserting this rubber plug, and had learned how to insert it so quickly that he could do the entire installation in thirty-three seconds, a considerable reduction from the forty-five seconds it took him the first time he tried. Confidently he inserted the device, but—it would not fit! The air continued to whistle by the ill-fitting plug and they had now reached an altitude of 15,000 feet. Here their precious air, their very source of life, was whistling through the hole. While Auguste was vainly struggling with the plug, Kipfer came to his help and with a mighty blow tried to drive home the recalcitrant object. But he used too much force and with a resounding crack the quartz rod broke on the inside of the rubber and the device now became totally unmanageable. They noticed also at this time that no amount of trying and pushing could have inserted the plug, since the fall had deformed the small hole and fitting.

The altitude was rising, the external pressure was decreasing, and the air was escaping faster and faster. The internal altitude or air pressure was the same as the external and was at about 18,000 feet. Now came one of those moments that the resourceful Piccard had prepared for. Realizing that the pressurized gondola would act in a reverse way to a vacuum apparatus in a laboratory where many leaks can occur, he had prepared a mixture of tufts and strands of cotton mixed with vaseline. This preparation would be smeared over any leak that occurred in the cabin, with the threads giving the vaseline enough body so that it would not be sucked through the hole. Now, sooner than he thought it would be needed, he had a chance to try the material. He remarked to his companion that a forced descent would be necessary in a few moments unless the leak could be stopped. They quickly smeared liberal doses of the stuff over the hole and to their joy it held. The leakage danger for the time being was over.

But with the cabin altitude above 20,000 feet, sustained life would be very difficult; so Auguste opened one of their liquid-oxygen containers and dumped some of this cold liquid onto the floor, where it ran into crevices and cracks, bouncing and bubbling at its temperature of minus 290 degrees Fahrenheit. If this dumping of liquid oxygen and therefore raising of the pressure would not work, Piccard stated flatly again that they would have to make an immediate descent by pulling the vent-valve cord. Fortunately for his peace of mind, he did not realize that that worthy device would malfunction, being tangled with the aforementioned extra launch rope.

The whistling gradually died down as the vaseline mixture held, and the cabin pressure once again rose until an equivalent altitude of about 12,000 to 14,000 feet was reached. A precious and blessed silence suddenly occurred in the cabin; their affairs seemed to be in equilibrium; they had enough oxygen to breathe at reasonably comfortable pressure and leaks were, for the moment, not a problem.

Half an hour from their launch at Augsburg had now

elapsed and they had reached an altitude of almost 50,000 feet. Most of their ballast of thirty-nine sandbags remained and they debated whether to dump this and reach an even higher altitude. However, Piccard, always the scientist, decided that they would not try to reach some kind of altitude record but rather would begin their cosmic-ray measurements, which were the reason for the flight in the first place.

They had not had a chance to do much measurement because of the leak problem, and Kipfer's preoccupation with getting instruments to behave properly after their shaking around during the launching. They now started to make an adjustment for altitude after dumping a little ballast. Confidently Kipfer started to turn the external drum that held the rope attached to the vent valve at the top of the balloon. He turned, but nothing happened! After several more fruitless tries they peered through the tiny porthole to see as best they could what was wrong. They then made the uncomfortable discovery that the vent-valve rope was not attached to the drum properly and kept slipping as they turned. Its action had been complicated by a mix-up with the extra rope that had been attached during launch. So here they were, around 50,000 feet with no method of valving gas for a descent!

As men experienced in ballooning they knew their danger. Without valving capability they could not pick and choose their own landing spot. The flight could drag on all day, and if for some reason the cabin leaked air, they would suffocate. Furthermore, on descending—an event which would occur if the gas became cooler, as at night—the balloon would lengthen during the drop, like a tear. As the balloon lengthened, the vent or valve line would become shorter and then finally, after all, open the vent. But it would keep it open since no control was possible by the cabin's hapless inhabitants. Their only hope would be that the rapid descent would make the balloon billow out like a parachute and arrest their fall. They also had personal parachutes which they could use in an extremity. However, they were acutely aware of the fact that under any circumstances the landing would not be a pleasant process.

There was not much time to worry about that phase of the flight now. They were up there to measure cosmic rays and this is what they would do no matter what the long-range results would be. Their apparatus required an external pressure of seventy-six millimeters. The barometer showed an external pressure of seventy-nine millimeters. This meant they had to rise some more and they dumped several bags of lead pellets. Soon the external pressure reached seventy-six millimeters and Kipfer began to read the cosmic-ray instrumentation. Aside from not having to go much higher, they were determined to hang onto as much ballast as possible so that, if a rapid descent did occur later, they could drop ballast on the way down and thus slow the rate of descent.

The jammed cord and the ever-present danger of a recurring leak began changing the general feeling of our aeronauts—from scientists preoccupied with their instruments, to men who also had to worry about their balloon system and the maintenance of life itself. Several times the leak seemed to reopen as some of the vaseline was forced out by the internal air pressure, and only concentrated application of the vaseline prevented a catastrophic pressure decrease in the gondola. They were much bothered by the strange acoustics within the gondola which, after all, had no sound-deadening walls and reverberated with every slightest noise, whether that was gas whistling or liquid oxygen bubbling or the ticking and clicking of instruments.

The question now was, would the balloon sink in late afternoon as the sun went below the horizon and the gas cooled? And which direction were they drifting and how fast? Looking through the bottom of their gondola past a small device used for checking drift, they noted they were moving south in the general direction of the Adriatic Sea—

a suspicion they had held for some time. Fortunately, the rate of drift seemed to be quite low and there was no immediate danger of moving into an unacceptable area.

At the time that our aeronauts worried about their drift toward the Adriatic they were diverted by another worry. While fooling with the vent valve in the cabin they had knocked over one of the mercury barometers. The glass container in the barometer broke and the mercury bounced all over the floor and into the crevices of the metal cabin. Now, mercury has a great affinity for other metals and it will find the smallest leak or even make a leak with the least encouragement. Kipfer remarked that it was a good thing the cabin floor and the gondola wall below it were thoroughly painted. Nevertheless, they felt uneasy with a potentially toxic substance like mercury in the cabin, since its vapor is a health hazard. They tried to feel around in the condensed moisture beneath the flat piece of metal floor on which they stood, in an attempt to fish out the small mercury globules. Anyone who has tried to pick up mercury with bare hands, especially in water, can sympathize with the plight of these two men in the narrow and murky confines of their little space capsule.

They realized that one way to get the condensed and trapped water and mercury out from beneath the flat floor would be to suck it up. But no one in his right mind would suck water and mercury and then spit it out. But was there not a vacuum better than many earthbound laboratory vacuums outside the cabin? So they took a piece of rubber hose lying among some other odds and ends, stuck one end down into the "bilge," and coupled the other end to a small faucet or petcock stuck in the wall of the capsule. They opened the petcock and with a great slurping sound the entire mess of mercury and water was quickly sucked out, forming a clever little fountain whose spray they could hear bouncing against the cabin wall on the outside. In a few minutes all was nearly clean and empty beneath the floor. They shut the petcock and resumed their worry about their drifting.

Piccard had time to admire through the small portholes the beauties of the sky above—jet black with no softening of the light by an atmosphere, since the balloon was above much of the earth's gas mantle. This very dark blue or black aspect of the sky had always intrigued the early high-altitude pioneers, and while almost commonplace to the jet traveler of today, is still a vista of remarkable beauty.

Looking downward they now saw hills and then craggy mountains and snow deposits; they were approaching the mountains of the Tyrol in southern Bavaria. Piccard expressed his awe of the magnificent panorama below him, but unfortunately he and Kipfer did not recognize any of the mountains, over which they were flying for the first time. Piccard was now achieving a long-desired wish to fly in a balloon over mountains; unfortunately, in this case he was doing so involuntarily, with no control left over the balloon; also he was flying over mountains that were unknown to him (he did not have a detailed map), in contrast to the Swiss Alps.

Now they were to encounter one of those situations, seriocomic in its aspects, that can result only from the ever-present problems of reliability in man-designed apparatus. What great invention in history, whether submarine or airplane or spaceship, has been free of some unsuspected flaw that often proved embarrassing at a critical moment, subjected the experimenter to a condition he did not anticipate, and sorely tested his mettle? It is evidence of man's triumph over nature and his control of mechanism that in most cases the things that go wrong lead only to improvements and the experimenter survives to make these improvements.

Piccard, with great foresight, had painted the spherical gondola black on one side and white on the other side with the joint running vertically around the capsule, dividing it into two vertical halves. His theory, based on his understanding of physics, was that the temperature in the capsule could be regulated by turning the entire sphere by a motor so that alternately the bright or black side could be pointed toward the sun. He knew from his mountaineering and other balloon experiments that solar radiation at high altitude is very intense and in a short time a body is heated to a high temperature even though the external air temperature may be seventy or eighty degrees below zero. He knew also, of course, that a shiny white surface would reflect much of the solar heat and thus the capsule could probably remain at a comfortable temperature. On the other hand, should the solar radiation be reflected too much from the white side, he could turn some or all of the black side toward the sun and thus heat up the capsule. So much for this theory —it was well thought out and the means of implementation was brilliantly conceived.

However, it seemed that there was some error in the design cycle, as they noticed when they tried to turn the capsule. During their drift over the mountains they felt more and more uncomfortable and realized that the temperature was rising. At first it reached about eighty degrees Fahrenheit, which they thought warm, but not uncomfortable. Then it reached 100 degrees Fahrenheit, which was "decidedly uncomfortable," as Piccard put it. When the temperature reached around 108 degrees Fahrenheit, they realized that something had to be done.

In their preoccupation with the mercury and water and the general problems of measuring drift they had forgotten that the black side must be facing the sun, shining so brilliantly above the horizon. So, it would be a simple matter to simply flip the switch that would start the electric motor that would turn the capsule against the balloon so that after a bit a new orientation would be achieved. The white side would face the sun, the temperature would drop, and all would be well!

Now came the engineering defect. The motor would not

turn! Apparently something had short-circuited or a wire had broken. This brought on a hair-raising situation. They knew the temperature would continue to rise in their closed capsule, although what limit they would be exposed to they could not foretell; they had one solace—the sun was sinking. The temperature soon rose another ten degrees and they decided to slake their thirst. Then they faced another situation not uncommon in new adventures where men are involved —the launch crew had forgotten to supply them with sufficient water. They had only one small bottle, and the larger bottle they wanted was missing. There was not even the solace of the mucky water in the bilge, since there was very little left and even that was mixed with debris and mercury —hardly a palatable mixture. The bit of water in the small bottle was quickly consumed. Now what?

Then again one of those providential events occurred. The cold walls were condensing moisture which ran down the sides: fresh, clear, and cool—really distilled water. Even though the sunny side of the capsule was very hot, the shady side was quite cold. They were able to scrape off the moisture and rime ice with their teeth and get a few swallows of cold water that way.

The afternoon went on. The sun sank lower and now came the time of crisis. The balloon was in equilibrium; this meant that an external change in temperature would change the lifting power of the gas. The sun, the main source of heat at these altitudes, was beginning to disappear below the horizon. They now anxiously watched the barometer, which acted as an altimeter, hanging outside the window in the minus sixty-degree-Fahrenheit thin air. The entangled rope leading to the vent valve flopped tantalizingly outside one of the windows. If they could only reach out and pull this rope, how quickly they would sink. But then how quickly they would lose all air—and life.

Twilight approached and the outside mercury barometer gradually rose. They were descending, but the rise in the mercury was so slow that they estimated it would take them two weeks to reach the ground at that rate. But soon they noticed to their joy that the barometer was rising more rapidly and then they realized that their sink rate was increasing and their enforced stay at altitude would be over.

By eight o'clock in the evening the sun was at the horizon and they had reached the lower levels of the troposphere. They were now approaching an altitude of about 15,000 feet. The ground below was already dark and people could see the shiny balloon still illuminated from the solar rays like a bright star or small moon.

Piccard now began to worry about the actual landing. If they lost their last bit of ballast on landing and dropped most of the instruments, the sudden lightening of the capsule would permit the balloon to rise back up to its equilibrium altitude over 50,000 feet. Therefore, they decided not to jettison any of their instruments, not only because of the ballast problem but also because these were precious and could be used again.

The descent continued. The temperature sank dramatically to more comfortable levels. The aeronauts opened one of the windows, and with a rush the air equalized in pressure.

Lightning events now followed. The sinking was so fast that Piccard was forced to drop ballast, despite his inclinations. They saw huge cliffs and snow fields below. The most important action they could take now was to pull the rip cord on landing. They had located the line and made it ready. The ground rushed up at them. They saw a white glittering glacier; they were now actually below the level of the highest mountains, which seemed to drift away from them like so many black phantoms. They hoped and prayed that they would float toward the glacier with its snow field; their hopes were fulfilled. With a slight bump the capsule touched ground, the bag waved threateningly above them as Kipfer pulled the rip cord. Then the bag flopped over to one side, fortunately away from the capsule instead of falling over it as Piccard feared, at first.

The capsule bumped again and partially rolled over. The clattering and banging of instruments and ballast occurred for a minute or so—then silence. They were on the ground to stay. They clambered out through the manholes and jumped onto terra firma with great care. As experienced Alpinists, having gone to school in Switzerland, they knew that treacherous crevasses in the glacier could finish the job that a hostile stratosphere tried to do.

They flashed their electric torches about them hoping to attract some attention. A few oranges in the cabin provided some nourishment as they spent the night in it, in the cold silence of the glacier. They asked themselves, where are we? They suspected that they were in the general area of the junction of Switzerland, Austria, and Italy. As the night wore on they noticed that no one was coming toward them, so they decided to leave the capsule and wander down into the valley at the first sign of dawn.

They made themselves two alpenstocks out of a piece of bamboo from some of the gear in the balloon. Actually, one of the chiefs of the launch crew, Gerber, had suggested to Auguste that they take along mountaineering equipment and Auguste had replied with some amusement, "Why don't we take along a dinner jacket in case we land near the Lido [Venice]?" Ironically enough, on their next flight they brought complete mountaineering outfits including shoes, but landed in the plains of Lombardy—and then were flown from there by the Italian Minister Italo Balbo to the Lido. There, they were the honored guests at a tremendous banquet, with everyone except themselves in evening clothes.

After much climbing and hiking they came to a small village and were welcomed by the inhabitants, who ran out of their houses to see these strange figures descending from

the mountain. Yes, it was revealed, our aeronauts had been
seen, but no one knew quite where they had landed; there
were already search parties under way. The aeronauts
found they were in the little hamlet of Ober Gurgl in the
Tyrol in Austria. They were made welcome by the astonished villagers, whose hamlet now found a place in history.

Later that day Piccard, who had become restive because
he wanted to get his equipment back, was relieved to see
the commander of the local military district arriving in
the village, and also the civilian representative of the Austrian government. They made arrangements to bring down
the capsule. The sturdy mountaineers from the village and
the adjacent territory soon formed a balloon-carrying bri-
gade that snaked down from the rugged heights. The capsule at first was dragged along, but the difficulties of
transportation were too much. Furthermore, mercury had
permeated many of its metal joints. Piccard reluctantly decided to leave it on the glacier. In its weakened condition
it might not survive transportation without special equipment, which was not available.

Auguste bemoaned the fact later that the capsule in its
worn-out and weakened state was worth more than a new
one, since he had received offers from all over the world to
have the capsule exhibited, which would have paid for the
entire expedition. As it was, the aluminum sphere, denuded
of its instruments and records, had to lie on the glacier for
almost an entire year until the University of Innsbruck
organized an expedition to bring it down, using help of
friendly mountaineers and troops.

So ended one of the great adventures of the air age. Many
interesting results were obtained with the instruments, and
new information was garnered about cosmic rays and upper
altitudes. It was definitely established that cosmic-ray intensity increased with altitude and that they surely had
their origin in some mysterious region of space rather than
in radioactive material in the earth.

Now Auguste Piccard had made history. No matter what anomalies were detected later in the recordings of atmospheric pressure and cosmic-ray intensity (there were some noted), and no matter what the nature of their descent had been, he and his partner had reached an unprecedented altitude in a balloon, in a man-made environment capable of sustaining life, no doubt to even greater altitudes, had they so desired.

After the experiences with the high winds at Augsburg, Auguste decided to begin his next flight from a calmer area near Zurich in Switzerland. This launching was achieved uneventfully on August 18, 1932. He had a new assistant, Max Cosyns, and also a new capsule elaborately instrumented. After reaching an altitude of 53,152 feet the balloon came down quietly near Lake Garda in Italy. Their 850-pound high-altitude capsule was undamaged by the landing and again valuable records were obtained.

Once again a record had been set and the slow and grinding push to the space frontier had been given a large boost by Auguste Piccard. He realized, earlier than many men, that the stratosphere, a region relatively free of violent storms and violent temperature changes, would be a natural medium some day for aircraft travel. In 1931 he predicted twelve-hour flights between the United States and Europe through the stratosphere. Perhaps even he was to be astonished by the unexpected and unprecedented advance in aeronautics which permitted jet aircraft to cross the Atlantic, near the altitudes he had flown in his balloon, in almost half the time that he had predicted, within twenty-six years.

Fourteen

HIGHER AND HIGHER

In early 1933 a number of seemingly unrelated events occurred which were to have a significant impact on the United States high-altitude-balloon research program. The ubiquitous Auguste Piccard gave a lecture on his high-altitude flights before the National Geographic Society in Washington in January of that year.

The Century of Progress Exposition was going on in Chicago and its general manager, General Load, was looking for ways and means to keep the Exposition in the public eye by special exhibits, shows, stunts, and feats of daring.

At the same time, in Akron, Ohio, a young Navy Lieutenant Commander, T. G. Settle, was diligently applying himself to his job as Navy inspector of balloons and other objects being manufactured for the Navy by the Goodyear Aircraft Corporation. Settle, an earnest and indefatigable officer, had not long before returned from a triumphant tour in Europe, where he was a successful contender in the great Gordon Bennett balloon races. He had often thought of the use of the balloon for advanced scientific missions and his curiosity and eagerness had been stimulated by

Captain Gray's adventures and then by the brillant exploits of Piccard.

When he realized that Piccard was lecturing in Washington, he wangled a trip to that city and attended the lecture as more than a casual spectator. After the lecture he buttonholed Piccard and earnestly debated with him the science of ballooning and upper-air research and found Piccard a ready talker, since, as between all balloon men, there was immediate community of interest and sympathy.

Auguste's appearance in this country was motivated not only by the invitation to lecture, but also by the more pragmatic consideration of obtaining funds to do another high-altitude flight. The F.N.R.S. fund in Belgium had apparently dried up, and he hoped to find in the United States some sponsor for continuing high-altitude balloon tests. His brother Jean had helped him with contacts, suggestions, and encouragement.

Hearing of the interest that the Century of Progress Exposition managers had in various adventures that might publicize the Exposition, Auguste went to Chicago in April and discussed with the management the possibility of backing for a high-altitude flight. These hardheaded businessmen, who were obviously not without a touch of that old American spirit of showmanship and daring, acceded to the suggestion, without too many stipulations on their part. They did ask, however, that Piccard launch the balloon from Soldier Field in Chicago, near the grounds of the Exposition. Actually, the Century of Progress Exposition management mainly organized the flight, while the Chicago *Daily News,* the National Broadcasting Company, the Dow Chemical Company in Midland, Michigan, and the Union Carbon and Carbide Company bore the chief cost of the flight.

Piccard, drawing on his experience with his previous balloons and gondolas, laid out the general design for the vehicle and gondola in short order and by the summer of 1933 construction was progressing satisfactorily. The Dow Chemical Corporation constructed a gondola on the lines of Piccard's earlier one, but began an innovation that was to be used in some future U.S. balloon gondolas. They manufactured it of Dowmetal, a metal consisting of 95 per cent magnesium, making it lighter than an equivalent aluminum gondola by about 250 pounds.

In the meantime, Jean Piccard entered the scene very actively. It happened that during the summer of '33 Auguste was called back to Belgium on urgent business, much to his chagrin. Jean offered to take his place as scientific observer.

The little discussion of the previous January in Washington between T. G. Settle and Auguste had resulted in closer acquaintanceship between the two men and the matter progressed to the point where Auguste had suggested that "Tex" (as he was then, and is now, affectionately called) fly the balloon as pilot. Tex was busy at Goodyear, while the gondola was being built, supervising the construction of the balloon that was to carry him and Piccard aloft. He also performed his duty of inspecting the balloon and we may be sure he did so with unusually great care, with the extra motivation raised by the fact he was to fly this balloon.

During July 1933, with Auguste gone, the hitherto quiet waters of this enterprise became heavily rippled by Jean's actions. He fussed and fumed at several changes that were made, and in general by his various deeds and words antagonized a large segment of the sponsors of the flight. He did this with no real intent or personal malice. He was and is actually a very charming and urbane gentleman. However, conformity had never been a strong point for the Piccard brothers, and their mannerisms, usually motivated by scientific rigor, were not always calculated to please everybody. At any rate, a situation developed in late July in which the sponsors refused to have anything to do with the project if Jean flew. That worthy individual, on the other hand, having certain proprietary and legal rights in the venture, refused to sanction the flight if anyone else replaced him as scientific observer. An impasse was reached, and it seemed the flight would not take off that summer.

Then Lieutenant Commander Settle, watching these displays of temperament anxiously from the side lines, stepped in and made a suggestion which was characteristic of the fine feeling he had for diplomacy and tact. Rather than see the project never get off the ground, he suggested that he fly the balloon alone. Since he had been acceptable to Auguste and Jean as a pilot, and was well liked by both sides, the idea was accepted, albeit very reluctantly by Jean, who did want to make the flight. Nevertheless, he realized that all this investment would be wasted or encumbered with legal technicalities, and he stepped aside—this action also being a tribute to his scientific objectivity, which triumphed over his temperament.

With the all-clear signals having been given, the balloon was inflated on August 4 at Soldier Field. Tex Settle had meticulously observed the necessary preparations and had obtained the help of his sister service, the Marines. A group of these sturdy gentlemen, headed by Major Chester L. Fordney, USMC, and various men from the nearby naval station, helped to maintain order at the Field, and to inflate the balloon and ready it for launching. On August 5, 1933, at 3:00 A.M., the balloon with its magnesium capsule, looking very much like that of Piccard's of 1932, ascended from Soldier Field.

The objective of the flight was to obtain an ascent into the stratosphere, with no ceiling being specified except that determined by the endurance of the pilot and the buoyancy of the balloon. Before launching, several troubles showed up with the vent valve on the balloon, as well as friction between the fabric and the cord to the valve at the top of the balloon. Settle first planned to keep the balloon at about 1500 feet above Chicago until several hours after daylight. Later, as the temperature rose, the balloon would rise.

After leaving the ground and meeting a temperature inversion, that is, a rise rather than a decrease in temperature at altitude, he penetrated this inversion region rising at the rate of about four feet per second or less to an altitude of 5000 feet.

The Chicago authorities had been notified about the flight, of course, and Settle could see that the downtown section of Chicago, which was in the pathway of the balloon, had been cleared of traffic in case a forced landing was necessary. This area contained railway yards and open fields permitting an emergency landing, a circumstance not possible later with houses and telegraph lines adjacent.

At about five thousand feet he tried the gas-vent valve. His frustration can now be imagined when it is told that the valve stuck open! Here, after many tests on the ground and improvements on the valve to cure this very condition, it occurred anyway. This at once settled the fate of the flight. Despite his frantic yanking on the rope, the valve maddeningly stayed open and the balloon began an immediate descent. Settle tried dropping ballast to slow the descent and was successful. At 500 feet he let out a long dragline.

The balloon landed about fifteen to twenty minutes after take-off, in a clear area in the yards of the Chicago, Burlington and Quincy Railway near 14th and Canal Streets. To his great relief the landing was easy, with no serious ground winds; no major damage was done to the balloon or to the scientific instruments in the gondola. Since there were stones and concrete in this area, things did not go entirely perfectly and a small dent was made in the gondola when it hit a piece of cement.

Now came a danger that Lieutenant Commander Settle had not foreseen. His balloon bag lay completely deflated on the ground, with the rip cord having been pulled, and he had stepped out of his gondola with the hope of beginning to fold the balloon together. There descended upon him from all sides a shrieking mob of those bipeds that inhabit the downtown regions of many cities. With an avid curiosity born of greed and a fine disregard for the elementary manners shown by animals, they swarmed all over the balloon and started to hack it to pieces. Many Chicago city policemen also arrived, but they not only refused to lend any assistance in controlling the crowd, but helped themselves to small pieces of the balloon!

Suddenly there was a clattering and banging of trucks and automobiles down one of the streets and a detachment of Marines under command of Major Fordney came charging through the crowd. Behind him came a squad of burly Marine sergeants who lost no time performing upon the rabble that exorcism that one hopes they apply much more gently to their raw recruits. Several bloodstains on the bag later testified to the punched noses and jaws suffered by the crowd, which scattered in all directions. Even the doughty and courageous policemen of that great Chicago force scattered. The group, including Tex, worked like beavers and managed to get the damaged balloon bag rolled up and the gondola lifted onto a truck.

Actually, the Marines were also supplemented by Navy and Army officers and Naval Reserve enlisted men, who helped stow the balloon and gondola onto a small truck which they drove to a freight car belonging to the railway. After the gear was stored aboard, the car was transferred to a railroad warehouse.

In a letter to the Chief of the Bureau of Aeronautics dated August 15, 1933, Settle says with his usual modest understatement that the balloon was saved, although "about 1800 patches would be necessary to keep it flying" and that the operation had "generally gone off fairly well."

Settle was not easily daunted and after discussing future plans for sponsorship with the Century of Progress management, decided that the gondola could easily be repaired and that the balloon was still serviceable. So it was that later that year, on November 20, the balloon was again readied, as was the capsule, for another attempt to reach the stratosphere. The 600,000-cubic-foot balloon was still labeled "A Century of Progress," and despite its many patches, which gave it a slightly rakish appearance, was fully airworthy. Settle this time took along Major Fordney, who had so distinguished himself by his help during the earlier launching and who had a scientific background as well as enthusiasm and experience. The legal problems with Jean Piccard had in the meantime been cleared up so that the flight was free and clear of any legal or moral encumbrance to Jean. The backers mentioned earlier again financed the flight, but this time it was started near the Goodyear Zeppelin Airship Dock in Akron, Ohio.

Initial inflation began on November 17, and at daybreak of the 20th the balloon was undocked from the huge hangar in which it had been inflated with gas. A Naval Reserve and civilian ground crew pulled the balloon out, and final rigging was done at the nearby Municipal Airport. This was a unique approach to balloon launchings, with the considerable facilities of the Goodyear Corporation at hand and no large crowds to observe the flight and perhaps interfere, as they had during the Soldier Field launching.

The flight was heavily instrumented with cosmic-ray and optical apparatus to measure various physical phenomena; plant-disease spores were carried aloft to check the effects of high altitude and radiation upon their life cycle. We have here one of the very first life-science experiments being carried into the stratosphere in this manner—many more were to follow in the future years, both with manned and unmanned balloons and then in later days with rockets. A bottle of fruit flies was to have been taken for similar life-science measurements, but the bottle did not arrive in time.

The take-off occurred at 9:30 A.M. after some delay because of high surface winds. Tex Settle kept the hatches open on the gondola until the balloon reached 13,500 feet over East Liverpool, Ohio. Fordney was busy with the large array of instruments that was on board, while Tex was piloting the balloon efficiently. The entire affair had a professional air to it, showing what could be done with sufficient money, preparation, and trained observers. This is not to say that Piccard's flights and others were of lesser importance or stature. Quite the contrary, they had been the pioneers and, as usual, pioneering attempts have an element of drama lacking in later tries, which can benefit from past experience. That this particular flight went so well is, then, to no small extent a tribute to Settle's pilotage, to the rugged construction of the balloon, and to the design of the Dowmetal gondola, reflecting as it did Piccard's experiences.

The flight log compiled by Settle is a brief businesslike document confining itself to the operation of instrumentation, upper-atmosphere winds, and the operation of the balloon. Around two o'clock in the afternoon they reached 51,000 feet. By about three o'clock they had reached peak altitude. Both noted the typical dark-blue overhead sky with a thick haze in the lower atmosphere (troposphere). By four o'clock they were over Pennsylvania in the general vicinity of Greensburg.

During the flight they used elaborate radio equipment, maintaining excellent communication throughout. Fordney talked to operators in Akron, Chicago, Washington, and New York City.

About 4:30 P.M. they decided to descend. Evening was coming on, with its lower temperature, and they had, at any rate, gathered enough data. They were drifting quickly at over sixty miles an hour in the stratosphere, toward New Jersey. On their descent they opened the hatches at 26,500 feet and disposed of ballast and other equipment, since the balloon was now descending fairly rapidly, because the temperature had been sinking as they went lower and the valve had been opened regularly to dump gas.

At 5:40 P.M. Settle leveled off at 800 feet near Bridgeton, New Jersey, in a light northeast wind, and at 5:50 P.M. he landed in marshy terrain. A quick pull of the rip cord vented the remaining gas and the balloon folded itself gently near them on the marsh. It always seems a miracle that balloonists in their confined capsule with limited visibility, even with the hatches open near the ground, are able to avoid high-tension lines and other dangerous obstructions.

The boggy, pitted terrain did not look very hospitable, especially in the growing darkness. The two stratosphere explorers then decided that the better part of valor would be to stay in the capsule for the night; this they did, after tying down all instrumentation and securing external equipment. They made themselves as comfortable as they could and had a light snooze until daylight, at which time the inevitable crowd of visitors came, but with much more restraint than the herd in Chicago. Officials from the local state police, the police themselves, and members of the armed services appeared and the equipment was transferred out of the marshy area without incident.

Lieutenant Commander Settle and Major Fordney were recompensed for their flight by the reward that men of their caliber deserve and want most. They had gathered some new and interesting information about cosmic rays, and upper-atmosphere data, as reported by Arthur H. Compton, the noted American physicist, then at the Ryerson Physical Laboratory at the University of Chicago. What is more, the National Aeronautic Association announced on the 23rd of November that they had reached an official altitude of 61,237 feet—a new world's record. They had achieved, then, the first major U.S. ascent into the stratosphere—an achievement that was to be followed by many others, not all of them so successful.

While Settle and Fordney were making their record-setting ascent over Akron, the U. S. Army Air Corps laid plans for a scientific high-altitude flight of unprecedented scope. Reading the history of these times reminds one almost of the present-day rivalry between the various services in the missile and space arena. The Army's preparations in the fall of 1933 were perhaps not motivated by any sense of rivalry with the Navy; nevertheless, the U. S. Army Air Corps considered itself a natural instrument for exploring the atmosphere. At the same time the members of the Air Corps who were to make two historic ascents were assisted by a guiding scientific committee appointed by President Gilbert Grosvenor of the National Geographic Society. The National Geographic Society was a joint sponsor of the proposed project and lent it redoubted scientific influence and support.

The men who were to make the flight had years of training and experience in scientific and aeronautic endeavors. Captain Albert W. Stevens, a tall and genial Army officer, was picked as the scientific observer for the coming flight and Captain Orvil A. Anderson, also a tall but more powerfully built man with substantial balloon experience, was both observer and copilot. A third man was to be pilot for this flight; he was also an Army officer, Major William E. Kepner, who had more lighter-than-air experience than any other Army man of his age. The Army-National Geographic team was extremely competent and in the short period of about ten months a large gondola and an enormous balloon were designed and built, exceeding in magnitude and scope any other that had been made in the western world to date. Nevertheless, many of the designs worked out by Piccard were, as in Settle's case, reflected in the gondola, which was also made of magnesium.

By the middle of 1933, then, the three-million-cubic-foot rubberized fabric bag for the balloon had been completed. It was then the largest balloon bag ever made, and many new design problems were faced, not the least of which was the proper gluing and stitching together of rubber-impregnated long-staple-cotton cloth—two and a third acres of it.

In order to achieve a trouble-free successful launching, a site had to be chosen with great care so that the balloon would not drift toward the open sea and would be sheltered from surface winds at take-off. A depression or "bowl" (since called the Stratobowl or Stratocamp) in the Black Hills of South Dakota, near Rapid City, was chosen. American balloonists have since used the Stratobowl for several high-altitude flights. This spot is probably one of the best in the country, if not in the world, for its accessibility, distance from nearby inhabited areas, and gentle surface winds.

The summer of 1934 was a busy one for the crew and members of the expedition. With typical American thoroughness, backed by funds and organization, an entire village sprang up near the Stratobowl for the hundred or so inhabitants that formed the general launch and support crew.

The balloon was to be filled with the explosive hydrogen gas that had been used in most flights previously.[1] This required elaborate fire precautions, and a fire department that would be a credit to an average-size town was set up. By July the metal-cylinder hydrogen containers were arriving by the truckload and the crew laid them out like so many cigars on top of each other, connected by manifold piping.

The South Dakota National Guard was a great help to the entire operation, and backbreaking tasks that needed many men were accomplished through the help of these enthusiastic Guardsmen.

By July 9 the gondola, supplies of instruments, launch equipment, and liquid-oxygen apparatus had been shipped to the site. A tremendous 200-foot-diameter disc of sawdust was spread over the ground to a depth of two inches to protect the huge balloon bag when it was spread out for inflation. Everything was now in flight shape. The gondola had been pressure tested. The instruments were checked out, and an innovation was used for the first time on a balloon flight: a dehumidifying apparatus for drying the

[1] Settle and Fordney used a helium-air mixture declared "surplus" by the Navy.

air was included in the capsule. The aeronauts felt, with good reason, that some degree of physical comfort was valuable if they were to do the proper job of monitoring their many instruments. They also planned an extensive program of photography and for that reason waited for clearer weather than a high-altitude flight of this type would normally require.

Now started a long weather watch. A little weather station had been set up on the site and Major Kepner, who had among his many other accomplishments a good background in meteorology, followed all weather news and spent many hours poring over weather charts. Everyone was discouraged by the recurring pattern of clouds and storms that moved around and into the area. The waiting continued. Some felt that the situation looked almost hopeless and it seemed that autumn would arrive with even worse weather before a launch could be undertaken.

Then, suddenly, at noon on July 27, Kepner announced that the weather looked favorable for a launch for the next day. A high-pressure area had drifted over the general region and clear weather seemed ahead. The enthusiastic supporting crews, who had waited so long for this event, became greatly excited and were all for starting immediately. However, it was decided to inflate the balloon that night for an early morning launch.

The conditions looked much like a modern rocket launching at Cape Canaveral. Trucks drove around, a scurry of activity went on, and the hissing of the hydrogen gas could be heard plainly as the inflammable element was passed into the large balloon bag that had been spread so assiduously and carefully on the ground. Wisely, only personnel immediately concerned with the launching and inflation were allowed into the compound. Various men went into the gondola, which sat in its own little shack in order to install instruments and make checks.

The three aeronauts and their supporting personnel were

so well organized for this event that by early morning all instrument installation had been done and the gondola was ready for take-off. At 2:00 A.M. the bag, which had risen in the center like a piece of dough with a small bump like a man's shiny bald pate, had grown into a huge bubble that rose above the ground and was restrained by almost spider-web-thin ropes. The searchlights played on the bag as they do on today's rockets, illuminating the shimmering surface that quivered impatiently to leave the earth.

At 5:00 A.M. inflation was completed, ropes were checked for tightness, the gondola had a last-minute test, and a bag of mail for the stamp collectors was lashed on. Anderson and Stevens climbed into the gondola, leaving to the senior pilot, Kepner, the final task of directing the take-off. The soldiers who held on to the many ropes hanging from the balloon released their grip and only a few small ropes attached directly to the gondola now restrained the bag from take-off. After some adjustment with the weight of the gondola and the ballast, Kepner sensed that everything was well and the balloon was buoyant. He gave the order, "Cast off!"

The balloon, "Explorer I," rose rapidly. The aeronauts, who had flown balloons before, were astonished at the seeming eagerness of the bag to rise and found themselves handling a "new beast." Kepner and Anderson, the two pilots, were outside of the gondola adjusting the rigging and supports, while Stevens was on the inside working the hydrogen valve under the direction of Kepner. He pulled the lever several times and considerable gas had to escape before the rate of ascent was slowed down. The gas valve at the top of the balloon was controlled by a pneumatic line from the inside of the capsule. There was an emergency rope line on the outside of the balloon that was available for quick pulling by the aeronauts. However, the pneumatic line worked well, and at around 13,000 to 14,000 feet Anderson and Kepner climbed back into the gondola and closed the hatches.

The air pressure inside the gondola was now the equivalent of an altitude of 15,000 feet. Before the gondola was sealed, Stevens, always the scientist, was anxious to activate a heavy spectographic instrument that had to hang below the balloon. He assisted Kepner in lowering this from the outside, all the time with the balloon rising and the swaying, slippery spherical gondola their only solid substance to rest on.

The 15,000-foot altitude was now past and the balloon swept upward. Tests had shown that the gondola was airtight. This was an important precautionary test and the lack of it had raised problems for Piccard in his flight. The three aeronauts were well equipped with radio transmitters and receivers and were in continuous contact with the ground. The enterprising National Broadcasting Company had supplied them with a special lightweight radio transmitter and they were able to broadcast when they had some free moments, but there were not many of those. They were delighted at the smooth working of all instrumentation. There is little time and scope for the repair of instruments in an undertaking of this type.

They rose to 40,000 feet after some hesitation by the balloon, and Captain Anderson was able to achieve something that had not been done before by other balloonists during stratospheric exploration. By careful juggling of ballast and gas valving he was able to maintain the balloon at around 40,000 feet, where the aeronauts planned to do a series of measurements.

After reading their cosmic-ray instruments and noting that the cosmic-ray intensity had greatly increased from ground level—a result that was not unexpected—they began the ascent once more, after dropping ballast, while the sun now warmed the gas in the bag. "Explorer I" was now approaching the 60,000-foot level and the pilot was planning to establish equilibrium once more at this point in order to take measurements.

The balloon capsule had many new and interesting instruments in it and some new designs. As with the "Century of Progress" gondola, the bottom half was painted black and the upper silver, while from its side protruded a fourteen-foot arm with a large fanlike propeller on it. In spinning this propeller by electric motor the pilots were actually able to rotate the entire balloon, permitting the various instruments to scan different parts of the heavens.

At an altitude of 60,000 feet Stevens was all ready to turn on his instruments again and begin measurements. A noise outside the gondola startled the inhabitants of this little enclosed world. What conceivably would make a banging and clattering noise? Looking through the porthole in the top of the capsule, Kepner saw a heartbreaking situation. The bottom of the balloon had puckered like a prune and there was a large rip in its lower surface. This was serious. If the balloon expanded any more and its bottom filled out, then the rip would surely extend completely the length of the balloon. The sun was inexorably heating the hydrogen so fast that the balloon kept rising. This they wanted to prevent in order to stop the hydrogen from filling out the available bag volume.

The instruments went on clicking and whirring imperturbably. Stevens was even able to obtain samples of air at 60,000 feet in evacuated glass flasks attached to the gondola. They still had time to marvel at the magnificent deep gentian blue of the sky above them with the sun an intensely brilliant clear disc far above them. Their observations of the beauties of nature, however, were tempered by their increasing concern with the growing rip in the bag.

The balloon was now sinking. Anderson had operated the gas valve continuously to allow the descent to occur, but hydrogen was also pouring out of a growing number of rents and the balloon was losing lift and beginning to drop more quickly. The sink rate increased as the aerostat went through the 40,000-foot level and soon reached 20,000 feet. The two pilots, Kepner and Anderson, opened two hatches in readiness for a quick escape if necessary.

Army Major E. L. Hoffman had designed a large eighty-foot parachute, with a special attachment to the gondola, that would be capable of lowering the entire gondola to the ground in case the balloon exploded suddenly. Several times Kepner had had his hands on the lever, ready to release this parachute, but later when a real emergency arose no one was handy to the lever and the parachute was never released.

The bag above them was still spherical and it looked rather pretty with its big open bottom now almost completely shredded. The bag tended to act as a parachute and slowed the rate of descent. The men now dropped various disposable items out of the gondola but left the precious instruments alone, with the hope that these would reach the ground safely. Hundreds of pounds of lead ballast, empty containers, liquid oxygen, and other objects were thrown out.

The 10,000-foot level approached. The balloon continued to plummet down. The men strapped on their parachutes, coupling them to the harnesses that had been worn all through the flight. What should be done now? Ten thousand feet looked like a good altitude for abandoning the ship. Captain Anderson had climbed outside to be ready for a parachute jump and check on balloon conditions to see what, if anything, could be done. The 6000-foot altitude was reached.

The men were actually able to discuss their plight and plan some action. The not unnatural conclusion they arrived at was that it was high time to leave, what with the altimeter reading 6000 feet. With the ground in that area being about 2000 feet above sea level, their real altitude was less than a mile above the earth.

Anderson was fiddling with his parachute, which had come undone and did not seem in the proper condition for jumping. He picked up the parachute, put it under his arm like a suitcase, and made for the porthole. To Captain Stevens' chagrin, Captain Anderson ("Andy") had rested his feet on the open porthole prior to jumping. In Stevens' own words, "Never before had I noticed that his [Andy's] feet were large." Anderson took a mighty leap forward with arms flailing and parachute trailing behind him; it then opened and there he was floating alongside the balloon, which now was also acting as a parachute, with the whole bottom of the balloon having ripped open. A second or two after Anderson's jump there was a mighty "woofing" sound and the straining bag, distended like a giant mushroom from the air pressure on its rush downward, trying to act like a balloon and parachute at once, exploded its top! The top of the fabric disappeared into small shreds and the gondola now became a free-falling object plummeting to earth at tremendous speed. Not a second was to be lost. Stevens had to get out.

The air pressure had built around the gondola on its way down, to a point where egress was impossible by merely climbing through the porthole. Stevens, after several tries, leapt right through the porthole, cleanly, like a dog through a hoop; normally it took some wiggling and straining to get through this porthole. He plunged down and out, tumbling over and over, jerking his parachute cord until that device opened with a tug. He was now falling slowly and apparently safe until a large mass of balloon fabric fell on his parachute. Would it carry him downward to the earth, or slide off? It did slide off and the balloon fragments went on their way. Kepner followed quickly.

As the gondola plummeted downward to the earth, trailed by bits and pieces of floating silk and debris, three white parachutes like three blossoms drifted down, and our worthy aeronauts hit the ground in succession at a much lower speed then they thought might have been the case if they hadn't got out of the balloon in time. The capsule crashed to earth with a loud boom, making a small crater; the spectrograph that had been released earlier by Anderson and Kepner had floated to earth with its unprecedented and valuable data intact. Despite the terrific impact, many instruments were saved and much data was recovered from this flight—that is, those things that were not stolen or picked up by souvenir hunters, who even went so far as to steal Captain Stevens' two suits of underwear, which he had hung on a fence at a nearby farmhouse when he changed to cooler clothing in the hundred-degree heat.

The Army, which had been following the flight by aircraft and surface vehicles, converged on the scene; the tired and relatively unruffled stratosphere explorers returned to their Army headquarters and later visited Washington and the headquarters of the National Geographic Society, which had so generously helped back the flight with money and facilities.

This undertaking—the first to be done on a large scale with many organizations supporting it and with the full support of the U. S. Army—was a milestone in high-altitude exploration, mainly because of the large amount of data that was recovered from the many recording instruments that survived the impact, all of which had worked. The entire expedition, equipment, balloon, gondola, and much of the instrumentation cost less than $60,000, with the funding provided largely by the National Geographic Society and many interested scientists and corporations. For this, by today's values, minute sum, a historic undertaking was tried and, in large measure, succeeded.

The aeronauts, undismayed by their inability to reach their expected ceiling altitude of 72,000 to 75,000 feet, immediately formed plans to try another expedition with a newly designed balloon bag, based on the old one but with greater strength in the top and better support webbing.

On November 11, 1935, the new balloon, now "Explorer II," this time with only Anderson and Stevens,[2] made an uneventful ascent from the Stratobowl to 72,395 feet. Not only was a new high-altitude record set, but new advances were obtained in cosmic and upper-atmospheric data as well as in radio communication. Much was also learned about high-altitude design; Captain Stevens declared soon after the flight that altitudes "up to 95,000 feet" might be obtained with a lighter rubberized silk (instead of cotton) bag. He speculated also on the remarkable "ride" that men would experience were they to cut their gondola loose from their balloon above 70,000 feet. These were prophetic speculations, since a little over twenty years later a remarkable high-altitude parachute jump was accomplished from around 100,000 feet by Captain J. Kittinger, USAF, leaping from an open gondola.

[2] Three men in the small capsule resulted in uncomfortable crowding.

↲↳ *Fifteen*

SPACE LABS

On the morning of August 19, 1957, a remarkable manned balloon flight began from an open iron-mine pit north of Minneapolis. This flight, called Manhigh II, one of the outstanding examples of the brilliant post-World War II era of high-altitude ballooning, was to set an example of unparalleled endurance and altitude.

The pilot, Major (now Lieutenant Colonel) David Simons, USAF, a talented medical scientist and dedicated officer, was to conduct various experiments and at the highest possible altitude obtain readings related to the stratosphere and his personal biological reactions to survival in a small sealed cabin.

Persistent and very thorough, he learned to pilot a balloon and assisted in much of the preparation for his flight. Never had a balloon ascent of this type been more intensively prepared beforehand. Leaving nothing to chance, the Air Force in conjunction with the Winzen Corporation,[1] the builders and designers, did many ground tests, as well

[1] Minneapolis, Minnesota. The president, Otto Winzen, began much of the post-war research and development on polyethylene plastic balloons and their methods of construction and launching.

as flight tests. Simons was poked, pushed, and prodded into chambers, measured, evaluated, and weighed. His responses were doubly, triply, quadruply checked, while at the same time the capsule being built by Winzen was checked for leaks and cracks and general operation. The achievement of Manhigh II was no accident. Manhigh II was also to prove one of the most meticulously observed and carefully analyzed balloon flights in history.

Simons jotted down every reaction from the moment he entered the capsule until the time he landed. He also had the help of a tape recorder on which many of his remarks were preserved and the record produced from this machine helped to complete the story of this flight. This flight was mainly a test of a space capsule and pressure suit and the reaction of an intelligent observer subjected to many of the conditions of near space and isolated from all human contact except by radio link. It was also the first demonstration of ground control of such a system, with Winzen and Colonel John P. Stapp, USAF,[2] and other personnel carefully noting the situation within the capsule and the state of the pilot from telemetry records and making decisions based on those readings. While the pilot had at all times the means to make decisions and even to lower the balloon or raise it, or do what he wished, nevertheless he remained obedient to ground command, realizing that his own judgment might be affected by the pressure within the cabin, or other factors. At one point in the flight this condition was dramatically demonstrated.

The evening before the launching, at 10:43 P.M., the Manhigh II capsule was sealed tight at the Winzen plant in Minneapolis. Simons, ready and eager for his adventure, was inside. The capsule was rather small compared to those used for the Navy's Strato-Lab and other experiments. It is true that it contained only one man, but nevertheless it

---

[2] Colonel Stapp, the senior Air Force aerospace medical officer, was essentially in charge of the aero-medical aspects of the operation.

seemed constrictive, since all he could do was sit on a nylon-webbed seat; no walking movement was possible.

Simons was transported in this tiny capsule like a fish in a can to an open-pit iron mine at Crosby, Minnesota, near Minneapolis. This area had been used before for launching large plastic balloons. The capsule was by no means comfortable, as almost every utterance of Simons shows during his truck ride and later during the flight. The volume was so small that the temperature rose very rapidly inside, not only from the heat of his body and instruments, but also from exterior heat, and it was necessary to connect a cold-air blower to the capsule and also to his suit. During the flight he had a small air cooler that kept blowing through or between the suit and his underwear, and he was alternately sticky hot or coated with icy perspiration. The capsule while on the ground became so hot at one point that it became necessary to put dry ice on its top in order to lower the temperature. Later, this dry ice acted as a nice dehumidifier, since the copious moisture in the cabin's atmosphere was frozen to the roof of the capsule, and thus eliminated from the air.

Near 9:00 A.M. on August 19 the launching was ready to take place, with Simons having been in the capsule most of the night. Rarely is a balloon of such size launched without some incident and there were several at this time; one was particularly noteworthy. The balloon had a band around its lower extremity, much as a child's rubber balloon has a string to seal it off. This band or reefing sleeve had tangled with the balloon and had not come off when it should have. Had it stayed on, the balloon would ultimately have burst, since there was no place for the gas to escape as the bag expanded. A great commotion arose and Simons was understandably worried, since the radio communication told him that the launch was about to begin. He squatted in his little capsule trying to peer out, but the windows became coated with frost in the chilly morning. There seemed no way to get rid of this band and the launching couldn't be attempted.

Everyone was primed for the take-off, not the least David Simons, who had his share of troubles in the capsule, what with the temperature rising and the terrific discomfort of being strapped into his restrictive pressure suit. He was worried about the effect of the truck ride on his instrumentation, since as a doctor and scientist he was most seriously concerned with the functioning of all the equipment. As an indefatigable observer and recorder of his own data, he wanted to leave nothing to chance, and luckily most things worked well, so that this flight became one of the best monitored in history with no phenomenon left untouched by Simons' curiosity.

But to return to the troublesome plastic sleeve. The huge balloon, almost 200 feet high, was restive and "anxious to leave" and the wind was whipping it around to the detriment of the structure. How could anyone reach this band, which was about thirty feet in the air? It would take a remarkable act of Levitation for an individual to reach it. There was no ladder to be found that could reach that high. At long last, after much searching, a short ladder was found in the mine area and with six men to hold it, and the ladder extended to its full length, Mrs. Vera Winzen, chosen for her light weight, herself an enthusiastic "balloonatic," climbed up on the shaky height. A man on such a ladder could not have been held, even by six men. She deftly cut away at the restrictive band and in one swipe severed it. The band was gone, the balloon was now all clear and ready to go. Never let it be said that balloonists are not capable of improvising with their simple but sensitive equipment.

At 9:22 A.M. the balloon, now free of all encumbrances, rose—"Bombs away," as one of the men remarked. It rose majestically and steadily out of the iron-mine pit with practically no surface winds to disturb it. Simons had barely noticed the launch in all the excitement and as he saw the walls of the mine receding from him, he realized he was away. The flight that now began was to last thirty-two hours, with a final touchdown at 5:32 P.M., August 21. The balloon ascended swiftly in the clear warm atmosphere. Simons, while not a professional balloonist, had been trained enough to know how to handle this aerostat, and by judicious valving and control he finally reached 105,000 feet at 1:19 that afternoon.

This flight was noted not only for the large quantity of medical and biophysical data noted by Dr. Simons, and the advance achieved in the operation of manned capsules at high altitudes, but also the unusually detailed remarks of wonderment expressed by the pilot as his balloon floated at unprecedented heights. He was aware, as few aeronauts before him, of the subtle beauty of the great void around him. While he seemed detached and remote from the earth, this void was filled with scenes of rare beauty and color. Talking into his little tape recorder he described the vivid bands of color as "deep indigo," "intense almost black," and looking up at the sky he observed that it was nearly black, while other parts of the sky near the horizon had a color of ocean blue, or pure lapis-lazuli blue at the interface between the dark purple sky above and the white alabaster earthbound masses of fluffy clouds. He even saw beauty in the gossamer balloon, which he could observe through his ceiling porthole and whose shape he photographed. To him it seemed "like a lady holding on to her skirt—it drapes down so gracefully. The ravelled edges wave very, very gently in the breeze."

The heat of the unfiltered sun had warmed the helium in his balloon enough to drive it to the altitude of 105,000 feet. As night came on the situation changed and a typical decrease of buoyancy of the balloon occurred because of night cooling. His altitude decreased, at first alarmingly, then more slowly. During that long vigil in the jet-black emptiness he retained his spirits and even took a little nap while being closely monitored by radio from the ground by his Air Force colleagues and the meticulous and wary Otto Winzen. Despite some fears for the balloon's silk-thin fragile skin in the cold of the night, it survived nicely and as the new day dawned the heat of the glaring sun gave new life to the sluggish cold helium and it rose once more. Simons had suffered many discomforts. During the night he had to struggle in an agonizing way into a thermal protective suit to cover his pressurized high-altitude suit, since he was freezing. This amazing demonstration of contortionism should qualify him for a circus act, since he had no room at all to move around in the capsule and yet he put on a bulky suit which zipped up to the neck.

Early in the morning around 5 A.M., after that long night, a sudden emergency arose—or so it seemed. All that previous day thundershowers with their anvil-topped cloud heads had thrust into the sky far higher than most men had previously believed possible. That night while the balloon was reaching its low level of around 70,000 feet it sank within a couple of thousand feet of the top of that most fearsome of all airman's bogies, the thunderhead. The balloon was still sinking slightly. The question was: would it sink more and be drawn into this thunderhead?

By great good fortune, at around 6:00 A.M. the balloon began to climb slowly again as the heat of the sun warmed the helium. Now, nature, in apparent contriteness for the vicissitudes of the night, repaid Simons by creating enough lift in the helium to push the balloon to a new record of 115,000 feet[3] at about 10:00 A.M. of that second day. Everything thereafter that day was an anticlimax, and after various instructions from the ground and checking

---

[3] This 115,000-foot altitude as well as the 105,000 feet measured the day before were read from an "uncorrected" altimeter which had some error at these extreme altitudes. The actual "corrected" altitude corroborated from ground measurements was 101,516 feet; this was the official altitude—and a record one.

the remaining oxygen and electrical power, the decision was made to descend, with Simons getting instructions from Otto Winzen on the valving of the gas for the descent. This proceeded in orderly fashion and he landed safely that afternoon at 5:32 P.M. He had been aloft higher and longer than any other man in history.

Manhigh II was the culmination of a series of Air Force sponsored unmanned and manned stratosphere balloon flights. Captain Joseph W. Kittinger, Jr., USAF, had distinguished himself by a manned test flight called Manhigh I. This was done on June 2, 1957, and Kittinger remained at a high altitude, almost 90,000 feet, for six and a half hours during a daylight flight, landing his balloon safely eighty miles away from the balloon launch center at Fleming Field, Minnesota.

Kittinger later set another record on August 16, 1960, when he parachuted in a pressure suit from an open gondola which his balloon had lifted to 102,800 feet, above the Tularosa Valley in New Mexico. By this daring feat he at once achieved the double distinction of having attained the highest official altitude in a balloon, to that date, and performed the longest parachute leap.

These flights were part of a larger group of illustrious balloon experiments performed after World War II. The development of thin plastic polyethylene or "mylar" sheets and new methods of heat-sealing these few-thousandths-of-an-inch-thick sheets made possible the production of very large, but very strong and inexpensive, balloons.

From 1947 on, almost a dozen historic manned flights were made by U.S. aeronauts. Each one of them was an outstanding feat of daring and discovery. Some flights were made to study only the cosmic-ray radiation. Others were undertaken to test military equipment. Still others were direct predecessors of manned rocket flights, while several were astrophysical observatories suspended almost twenty miles above the earth to study the planets and the ambient conditions at that altitude.

The U. S. Navy proved to be one of the more altruistic agencies in the country for using the manned plastic balloon as a research tool. The Navy first subsidized the development of the technique of plastic-balloon manufacture. The great story of the manned balloon flights following the last war began in the Office of Naval Research (ONR) during 1946.[4] The upper atmosphere beckoned enticingly to researchers, with its vast untapped fountain of aerodynamic, cosmic-ray, and electrical data that needed to be studied before man could venture into near space in high-altitude aircraft, or later with rockets. Airplanes, rockets, and the old-fashioned rubberized-fabric balloons for high-altitude studies had many limitations that precluded their use for maintaining observers in the stratosphere for extended periods.

Those were exciting days, the late '40s. The upper atmosphere was a new challenging frontier to be conquered and modern research was providing the tools to do so without the excessive expenditure in money and manpower needed for the flights of the pioneers of the middle '30s. The ONR initiated some studies around 1946 and 1947 with the General Mills Corporation in Minneapolis. Under the general name of Helios a study was made of the feasibility of using a large plastic balloon that would make possible a flight to the stratosphere lifting a manned gondola equipped with scientific instruments to an altitude not yet attained, around 100,000 feet, with the ability to stay at altitude about ten hours. The ONR turned to various individuals in the country who had already made contributions, both in aerostatics and high-altitude research.

Unfortunately, lacking research funds to push rapidly the

[4] Commander George Hoover of the ONR was a well-known and respected figure among balloon-research scientists because of his enthusiastic support of new areas of research, especially plastic-balloon investigations.

further development of plastic balloons, the supporters of Helios had to abandon plans for manned flight, temporarily; not enough was known of the behavior of plastic balloons at high altitudes. It was felt that more studies were necessary before a manned capsule could be entrusted to this new but promising tool.

On the other hand, funds were available for unmanned flights, requiring far less equipment than a manned flight, because, for one thing, no pressurized gondola would have to be carried. A spherical gondola, incidentally, was constructed for project Helios. It was to be first used some years later, while in the meantime, many unmanned flights were made under a new project called Skyhook, again supported by ONR. Skyhook provided a vast body of experience for plastic-balloon launching and construction and with that experience obtained, the stage was set for the application of this proven technique to manned flights to the stratosphere.

On November 3, 1949, Charles Moore, then of the General Mills Corporation in Minneapolis, made the first manned flight in a plastic balloon over Minneapolis. However, Moore, who was to participate in other pioneering flights later, then ascended to only a few thousand feet.

Commander Malcolm D. Ross, USN, and Lieutenant Commander Lee Lewis, USN,[5] made a historic flight under ONR support on August 10, 1956. They ascended into the stratosphere with a plastic balloon and in an open gondola. This flight was historic not only because an open gondola was used to a 40,000-foot altitude, but also because a plastic polyethylene balloon using new methods of gondola suspension and new construction techniques was used.

Ross and Lewis set the stage by their relatively low-altitude flight for the much more extensive "Strato-Lab"

[5] Ross and Lewis were key officers in the ONR balloon program. Both made significant contributions to the techniques of upper-atmosphere exploration.

flights, which were to come in regular sequence. These all had the purpose of permitting observers to make scientific measurements of the environment about them, or of studying stars and planets with telescopic aids.

Even in this first 40,000-foot flight Lewis and Ross were able to photograph jet contrails and make other observations of the atmosphere, and they also tested some special cosmic-ray equipment. Lieutenant Commander Lewis was to be a companion of Ross in several of the Strato-Lab flights and together they reached some of the highest altitudes ever attained by man in balloons. Lee Lewis, a cheerful and able man, beloved by all who knew him, spent many of his best years in the Navy as a meteorological and radiosonde project officer for the Bureau of Aeronautics. He had suggested in the late '40s the possibilities of attaching rockets to balloons and launching these rockets from high altitudes. Various scientists, notably Dr. James Van Allen of the University of Iowa, applied this technique later and called the rocket-balloon combination Rockoon. It was cruel irony that Lewis, who had joined the Winzen Corporation, should be killed in a seemingly trifling accident in Minneapolis while testing a balloon-suspension rig indoors in a gymnasium.

While unmanned plastic-balloon flights were now becoming commonplace, contributing also to many of the flying-saucer rumors that swept the world, the Strato-Lab flights were to dominate the high-altitude exploration picture because the interest and glamour of a manned expedition always outweighs that of the unmanned scientific package experiments, even though some of these latter reached altitudes 30,000 to 40,000 feet higher than the best attained by manned flight.

On November 8, 1956, Ross and Lewis, by now as experienced and well-working a team of balloonists as could be had in the United States, set a new polyethylene balloon record of 76,000 feet in the first sealed gondola of Strato-Lab. This Strato-Lab flight was launched from the same sheltered Stratobowl, twelve miles southwest of Rapid City, South Dakota, from which the Army's "Explorer II" balloon had been launched. Almost twenty-one years to the day after that great flight, Ross and Lewis made their assault on the stratosphere in the first large plastic-balloon, high-altitude exploration system. Ross, as always the cautious and methodical experimenter and scientist, trusted the plastic envelope material enough to use it for his high-altitude balloon flight.

As had been the custom since the time of Gray and Piccard, their flight had a scientific purpose for studies in aeromedicine, meteorology and atmospheric physics, astronomy, and other related fields. For the first time in high-altitude exploration, the two men planned some astronomical study with binoculars and special light filters for observation of the sun and stars, auroral particles, and sodium distribution in the upper atmosphere. A great deal of research went into the design of the balloon-suspension system and the gondola. The latter was the one built in 1946 for project Helios.

At 6:19 A.M. on November 8, 1956, they took off from the Stratobowl and made a rapid ascent of 500 feet per minute. At 10,000 feet Lewis closed the two hatches and turned the oxygen on full volume. One of the launch crew had painted an amusing picture of an Indian chief's face on the inside hatch surface. As this was closed our two explorers saw an Indian with his head and chest pierced by arrows and the slogan, "Keep smiling—have faith" and a handwritten "Good-by, good luck."

Their climb was interrupted from time to time by changes in atmospheric temperature, but by dumping sufficient ballast they were able to make an ascent to 76,000 feet, at which point the balloon leveled off. This happened around 9:00 A.M. of that day. The gondola was nicely sunlit and the temperature was comfortable. In this particular case the gondola was painted black below and white above for the exercise of some control over temperature. The sun from above would shine upon the gondola, which with its white top would be relatively cool, whereas at night or afternoon, radiation from the earth would tend to warm the now cooling gondola through the black underside. The gondola was made of aluminum, one-eighth-inch thick, instead of the magnesium tried in earlier U.S. flights. With a balloon of large weight-lifting capacity the small difference in weight increase caused by aluminum over magnesium is insignificant and the aluminum is easier to fabricate.

Ross and Lewis greatly enjoyed the magnificent panorama of sky and horizon around them and looked forward to several hours of useful study and observation as soon as they could tear themselves away from the entrancing view. Lee Lewis was just ready to take a picture of the instrument panel for record purposes when, suddenly, emergency! A long-delayed look at the altimeter needle showed that it was dropping, and dropping rapidly. They were descending! Could their fragile plastic balloon have burst at the great altitude they had reached? After all, plastic was a relatively new material for such a large manned flight. They were apparently in for a very fast and long plunge into the dense atmosphere below. They hoped that soon their cargo parachute, which formed part of the suspension system, would open and float them to earth—probably, however, not without a very severe jolt. They jumped into their seats, strapped themselves in, and hooked the faceplates onto their pressure helmets connected to their high-altitude pressure suits.

They tried to reach Dr. Norman Barr, who was the Navy flight surgeon, monitoring the flight from an airplane. As they were explaining the situation they heard the tail end of Dr. Barr's calm professional voice congratulating them, "Congratulations on a fine flight." Apparently Dr. Barr had not yet heard the latest urgent message and was still jubilant about the previous message, which described the peak altitude and the success of the experiment. Lee Lewis once again described the situation and this time Dr. Barr's quiet voice requested readings of their instruments.

In the meantime the descent rate increased and they felt as if they were in a falling elevator; Ross broadcast an emergency message to all stations on the ground advising them of the situation, while their plunge continued toward the Dakota Badlands. Dr. Barr, who was following the flight in the airplane and now fully aware of the situation, radioed the two men not to parachute into the Badlands, but to stick with the balloon if they possibly could. Barr also cleared the air by a "mayday" signal, reserving the special radio channels for the two plummeting aeronauts.

They were not idle during this plunge and were busy throwing out ballast and releasing everything that was not fastened down in the gondola. This ballast-jettisoning has been an almost monotonous occurrence for many balloonists, and one wonders how, in the days when ballooning was much more popular as a sport, especially in densely populated Europe, many a head was not broken on the ground when instruments, personal effects, and even cooking stoves and entire pieces of gondola were thrown out by desperate aeronauts.

The balloon approached 17,000 feet; the terrain coming up at them did not look inviting. They dropped out everything, including instrument panels, radio, tracer-chemical absorbents, etc. They were descending at the rate of 1000 feet per minute and had gone through the 15,000-foot level, at which point the hatch blew open. They even jettisoned one of the hatch covers as they approached the earth, while Lewis kicked the second cover away from the gondola at about a thirty-foot altitude!

Just before impact they had to make a decision on the timing of releasing the balloon. If too soon, they would fall free like a rock, and if too late, they would bounce up and down like a ball and then, perhaps, fall heavily on the earth.

They were tightly strapped in and waiting for the impact when Ross threw the first of two switches that had to be closed to release the balloon, while Lee closed the second one exactly at the moment of impact, with remarkable timing. CRASH! A bounce and a roll and another bounce and the gondola stood upright back on terra firma four hours and four minutes after take-off.

The balloon had not fallen apart, as they feared, but had yielded enough buoyancy to reduce the falling-rate to about 800 feet per minute near impact time. A final speed of about 400 feet per minute had been hoped for. The descent rate was not great enough to open the parachute. A thick layer of Styrofoam cushioned the bone-jarring touchdown so that neither man received so much as a scratch. Even the balloon was in one piece, not having split or burst. That old stand-by, the gas valve on top of the balloon, had stuck open and let much of the gas out. It was a surprise to them that the entire balloon had not deflated and just whipped itself into shreds on the way down.

Although they were not at their peak altitude very long the flight had yielded very valuable information on plastic-balloon operation, some upper-altitude data, and substantial knowledge was added to the early experiments in space medicine. Dr. Barr, who was the physician in control of the aerospace medical aspects of the flight, was able to collate the data on the men's physiological reactions into reports that were later used for other flights and helped to form a basis for space medical research.

The ubiquitous Malcolm Ross piloted a Strato-Lab V balloon to still another, and then greatest, altitude of 113,700 feet on May 4, 1961. He was accompanied by a scientific observer, Lieutenant Commander Victor A. Prather, Jr., (MC) USN. Their huge balloon had a ten-million-cubic-foot volume, the largest ever used for manned flight. A cage-like unpressurized gondola, weighing about 1800 pounds carried the two men; the major objective of the flight was the testing, under near-space conditions, of pressurized space suits such as those worn by the NASA Mercury astronauts.

The Navy aircraft carrier *Antietam* was used as a launch platform in the Gulf of Mexico. Launching this eighty-story-high balloon system required extraordinary coordination of ground operations and zero or near-zero wind velocity. The Winzen Corporation, builder of the entire system, and the Navy crew provided the launch support, while the carrier, steaming with the light wind, eliminated wind disturbances.

The pilots reached the new world-record balloon altitude at 10:40 A.M., EDT. They observed the wonderful world of sky and sea through the Venetian-like sun-shielding blinds of their gondola and were able to marvel at the breath-taking iridescence of blue horizon and jet-black heavens. As in previous flights, an effective control team of scientists and doctors monitored the flight by telemetry. This carrier-based team was able to detect several small malfunctions in pressure-suit equipment even before Ross and Prather were able to notice any trouble.

After reaching peak altitude Ross decided that dallying there might lead to trouble, since the oxygen supply was dwindling rapidly. He pushed the button which would signal the electric vent valve, in order to release helium so that the descent could begin. He was a very surprised aeronaut when the balloon rose, instead of sinking, after the valve opened! The solar heat was still resulting in a faster rise in lifting capacity than the loss of gas yielded in decreased lift.

However, the altitude gain was small and of short duration. Soon the balloon began its descent, which was agonizingly slow, in Ross's estimation. It was going to be touch-and-go on the oxygen supply; they would have to reach a life-supporting region of the atmosphere, around 15,000 feet, within three hours or so, if they were to survive. By grimly hanging onto the valve-control button for one and a half hours, Ross managed to release enough gas to speed their descent rate so that around 3:00 P.M. it became normal in the denser atmosphere near 15,000 feet.

The gondola gently touched the water at 4:02 P.M. Ross and Prather had added knowledge about manned operation in near-space, with special astronauts' pressure suits.

What grim irony it was, then, that Lieutenant Commander Victor Prather should drown just at the moment of his pickup, by helicopter, from the gondola! For reasons never clearly determined, Prather slipped out of the helicopter lifting harness and disappeared beneath the waves. Like his famous balloonist predecessor, Lieutenant Commander Lee Lewis, Prather lost his life in an "unexpected" accident, not directly during a stratosphere flight. His loss was not in vain; the mission had been accomplished with great success. In the great but perilous coming age of manned space flight many astronauts will live because of the knowledge that Ross, Lewis, and Prather obtained.

Will the age of space finally displace the balloon, man's oldest flying vehicle? With men orbiting hundreds of miles above the earth and planning to land on the moon, will there be a place for a balloon that cannot rise much above twenty-two miles?

The answers are that the giant rockets and the space exploits of the future will overshadow the technical exploits of *any* other technical enterprise in which men engage. However, even if flights to 100,000 feet or so do not look so spectacular any more, there is still a rich harvest of scientific data to be reaped that cannot readily be gathered with rockets costing two or three million dollars per firing.

Plastic balloons, using even better materials than polyethylene or mylar, with lightweight pressurized gondolas can take potential astronauts to a near-space environment for hours or days. Much can be (as has been already) learned about the functioning of space-vehicle components and cabins and the psychological problems of men confined in a closed environment.

The astronomers, keeping a wary but slightly pessimistic eye on the use of rockets for space observatories, are at the moment among the most enthusiastic supporters of balloon systems for the lifting of telescopes to high altitudes. Above 100,000 feet only one per cent or so of the atmosphere remains. Given a stable balloon-gondola platform at such altitudes, the astronomer can see the undistorted splendor of the heavens in their full clarity, with no interfering trace of dust or clouds.

Astronomers, who prefer to personally control their instruments, instead of leaving them to the mercies of remote automatic equipment in rockets, have made several proposals and several flights for astronomical research.

The U. S. Navy has sponsored several open-basket and one closed-gondola flight, carrying men and telescopic equipment. This latter flight was really a small well-equipped balloon-borne astronomical observatory which reached an altitude of 81,000 feet on November 28–29, 1959. Almost as a matter of course Malcolm Ross was the pilot, assisted by Charles Moore[6] of the Arthur D. Little Corporation, Cambridge, Massachusetts. Professor John Strong of Johns Hopkins University, Baltimore, had proposed the experiment, whose main purpose was the detection of water vapor in the atmosphere of Venus. The sixteen-inch-diameter telescope and spectroscope yielded new data on that planet's atmosphere that may show the presence of water vapor there. Such data would be impossible to gather lower down in the atmosphere because of the absorption of the weak Venusian radiation by the earth's own water vapor at low altitudes.

The Navy is also supporting another balloon-observatory project called Stratoscope, managed by Princeton Univer-

[6] The same Moore who made the first plastic-balloon flight in the United States.

sity. Its purpose is to obtain solar data with unmanned balloon systems; much new information about the sun has already been obtained. However, a manned balloon observatory undoubtedly has greater versatility and flexibility when complicated and precise manipulations are required.

With balloons and observatory gondolas now feasible for altitudes up to 100,000–120,000 feet at a small fraction of the cost of a rocket-borne observatory, we will no doubt see several balloon-observatory attempts made during the coming decade, each of them surely adding very significantly to man's understanding of the planets and the universe.

CHRONOLOGY OF
OUTSTANDING
BALLOON FLIGHTS

1783 September 19. First balloon ascent with living creatures (sheep, cock, and duck). Montgolfier balloon at Versailles, France.

1783 November 21. First manned balloon voyage, by Pilatre de Rozier and D'Arlandes, from Paris.

1783 December 1. First flight of a hydrogen balloon with J. A. C. Charles from Paris, and M. N. Robert.

1784 June 4. First ascent of a woman, Mme Thible, in a Montgolfier from Lyon.

1784 September 19. First aerial balloon voyage approaching one hundred miles distance, by the brothers Robert, and Colin-Hulin, from Paris to Beuvry.

1785 January 7. First aerial crossing of the English Channel, by Blanchard and Jeffries in a hydrogen balloon.

1785 June 15. First victims of the air age: Pilatre de Rozier and Romain killed in a balloon near Wimereux, France.

1794 June 2. First military use of a balloon: Coutelle used a captive balloon at the seige of Maubeuge, France.

1849 October 7. First balloon crossing of the Alps, by F. Arban, from Marseille to Stubini, near Turin, Italy.

1859 July 1–2. First aerial balloon voyage over six hundred miles and first transport of airmail, by John Wise and several passengers, from St. Louis Missouri, to Henderson, New York.

1862 September 5. Highest non-fatal balloon ascent without

special breathing equipment, over 29,000 feet, by Glaisher and Coxwell.

1870   September 23 to January 28, 1871. First regular airmail service from besieged Paris, with sixty-six balloon flights.

1897   July 11–14. First exploration expedition by balloon: Andrée, Strindberg, and Fraenkel leave Spitsbergen for the North Pole.

1901   July 31. First balloon ascent above 30,000 feet, by Berson and Süring, from Berlin.

1912   October 27–29. First aerial balloon voyage over one thousand miles: Bienaimé and Rumpelmayer win the Gordon-Bennett cup in free-balloon-flight competition with a journey from Stuttgart, Germany, to Ribnoyé, Russia.

1927   May 4. Captain A. C. Gray reached 42,470 feet over Scott Field, Illinois

1931   May 27. Piccard and Kipfer reach 51,458 feet, leaving from Augsburg, Germany.

1932   August 18. A. Piccard and M. Cosyns reach 53,152 feet near Zurich, Switzerland.

1933   November 20. Lieutenant Commander T. G. W. Settle and Major C. Fordney reach new altitude record of 61,237 feet over Akron, Ohio.

1934   January 30. Russian balloon "Osoaviakhim" reached 73,000 feet but crew perished when gondola fell. Pilots were Fedosienko, Wasienko, and Vsyskin.

1934   July 28. Major W. Kepner and Captains O. A. Anderson and A. Stevens reached 60,613 feet in "Explorer I" near Rapid City, South Dakota.

1935   November 11. Captains Anderson and Stevens reached 72,395 feet in "Explorer II," setting new official world record.

1949   November 3. C. B. Moore of General Mills Corporation made first plastic-balloon flight over Minneapolis, Minnesota.

1956   August 10. Lieutenant Commanders Ross and Lewis reach 40,000 feet in first stratospheric flight in a polyethylene balloon.

1956   November 8. Strata-Lab I balloon with Ross and Lewis reached 76,000 feet from the Stratobowl, Rapid City, South Dakota.

1957 June 2. Captain J. Kittinger, USAF, reached 96,000 feet in Manhigh I, setting new unofficial world altitude record.

1957 August 19 and 20. Major D. Simons, USAF, MC, set official world altitude record of 101,516 feet in Manhigh II.

1957 October 18. Ross and Lewis reach 85,700 feet in Strato-Lab II balloon.

1958 May 6 and 7. Ross and A. Mikesell (Naval Observatory) reach 40,000 feet in open gondola Strato-Lab balloon; Mikesell is first astronomer to observe from the stratosphere.

1958 July 26 and 27. Ross and Lewis reach 82,000 feet in Strato-Lab III from Crosby, Minnesota, with unofficial record of 34.7 hours aloft.

1959 April 22. A. Dollfus flew from Paris, France with a cluster of neoprene weather balloons to 42,000 feet.

1959 November 28 and 29. Ross and C. Moore reach 81,000 feet in Strato-Lab IV in a sealed gondola with a sixteen-inch telescope and spectrograph—the first balloon-observatory flight.

1960 August 16. Captain J. Kittinger bailed out of an open gondola at 102,800 feet from balloon "Excelsior III," setting new balloon altitude record and parachute-descent record.

1961 May 4. Ross and Prather reach 113,700 feet with a 10,000,-000 cubic foot balloon launched from a Navy carrier.

INDEX